HUON OF BORDEAUX

HUON OF BORDEAUX

First Modern English Translation
by
Catherine M. Jones and
William W. Kibler

Italica Press
New York and Bristol
2021

Italica Press Medieval & Renaissance Texts

ITALICA PRESS, INC.
99 Wall Street, Suite 650
New York, New York 10005

Library of Congress Cataloging-in-Publication Data
Names: Jones, Catherine M. (Catherine Mary), 1956- translator. | Kibler, William W., 1942- translator.
Title: Huon of Bordeaux / first modern English translation by Catherine M. Jones and William W. Kibler.
Other titles: Huon de Bordeaux. English
Description: New York : Italica Press, 2021. | Series: Italica press medieval & renaissance texts | Includes bibliographical references. |
  Summary: ""Huon of Bordeaux" is the first modern English translation of the late thirteenth-century Old French epic poem. This "chanson de geste" follows the exploits of a medieval knight wrongly exiled from Charlemagne's court. Includes introduction, notes, bibliography, glossary, and list of characters"-- Provided by publisher.
Identifiers: LCCN 2020055112 (print) | LCCN 2020055113 (ebook) | ISBN 9781599104003 (hardcover) | ISBN 9781599104010 (trade paperback) | ISBN 9781599104027 (kindle edition) | ISBN 9781599104034 (pdf)
Subjects: LCSH: Chansons de geste--Translations into English. | Epic poetry, French--Translations into English.
Classification: LCC PQ1485 .H8 2021 (print) | LCC PQ1485 (ebook) | DDC 841/.1--dc23
LC record available at https://lccn.loc.gov/2020055112
LC ebook record available at https://lccn.loc.gov/2020055113

COVER ILLUSTRATION: Fol. 394r from Bibliothèque municipale de Tours MS 951, *Estoire del saint Graal, Joseph d'Arimathie, Merlin, Suite du Merlin*, 1287–91.

For a Complete List of
Medieval and Renaissance Texts
Visit our Web Site at
www.ItalicaPress.com

CONTENTS

ABOUT THE EDITORS — VI

ACKNOWLEDGEMENTS — VII

INTRODUCTION
  AN AGE OF RENEWAL — IX
  SUMMARY — XII
  TEXT AND INTERTEXT — XV
  RECEPTION — XXI
  MANUSCRIPTS AND EDITIONS — XXII
  NOTE — XXIII

THE BOOK OF HUON OF BORDEAUX
  AND KING AUBERON — 1

APPENDIX
  JONGLEUR'S INTERVENTIONS — 319

MAJOR CHARACTERS — 321

GLOSSARY OF MEDIEVAL TERMS — 323

SELECT BIBLIOGRAPHY
  PRIMARY SOURCES — 325
  SECONDARY LITERATURE — 326
  REFERENCE TOOLS — 328

ABOUT THE EDITORS

Catherine M. Jones is the Josiah Meigs Professor of French and Provençal at the University of Georgia. She is the author of *The Noble Merchant: Problems of Genre and Lineage in Hervis de Mes* (North Carolina Studies in the Romance Languages and Literatures, 1993), *Philippe de Vigneulles and the Art of Prose Translation* (D. S. Brewer, 2008), and *An Introduction to the Chansons de Geste* (University Press of Florida, 2014). She is the co-translator of *An Old French Trilogy: Texts from the William of Orange Cycle* (with William Kibler and Logan Whalen, University Press of Florida, 2020).

William W. Kibler has published *An Introduction to Old French* (Modern Language Association, 1984) as well as a number of editions and translations of medieval French texts, many in collaboration. His translation of the *Arthurian Romances of Chrétien de Troyes* is in Penguin Classics (1991). With François Suard, he published an Old French edition of *Huon de Bordeaux* with a facing-page translation into modern French (Champion, 2003). Recently he completed an edition with Françoise Denis of all the known manuscripts of *Gui de Bourgogne* (Champion, 2019). This is his second translation in collaboration with Catherine Jones, following *An Old French Trilogy: Texts from the William of Orange Cycle* (University Press of Florida, 2020, also with Logan Whalen).

ACKNOWLEDGEMENTS

We are deeply grateful for the contributions of those who assisted us with this translation. Laura Scott served as a research assistant at the beginning of the project and helped lay the groundwork for the introduction. Mary-Alis Kelly and Asmah Hyat read drafts of the manuscript and offered valuable suggestions and corrections. Stacey Casado provided unwavering support and encouragement along the way. It has truly been a pleasure to work with Eileen Gardiner and Ronald Musto, who welcomed and shepherded our project at Italica Press. Finally, we wish to thank our spouses, Nancy Kibler and Richard Neupert, for patiently accompanying us on yet another epic journey.

To our daughters,

Sophie, Mary-Alis, and Charlotte

INTRODUCTION

An Age of Renewal

Huon of Bordeaux is an Old French epic poem from the second half of the thirteenth century. It belongs to a textual tradition known as the *chansons de geste*, a group of approximately 120 works dating from the late eleventh to the fifteenth century, which share a particular lyric and narrative heritage. The label *chansons* ("songs") attests to the poems' original mode of transmission: the earliest works were likely sung by itinerant performers called *jongleurs*. Composed in assonance or rhymed *laisses* (stanzas of varying length), the *chansons de geste* retained a certain lyrical quality long after they ceased to be sung and began to be recited or read aloud. The word *geste* in Old French designates both "great deeds" and "family" or "lineage." The *chansons de geste* thus sing of great exploits accomplished by a hero or his extended family. Core narratives typically revolve around Christian–Muslim conflict, matters of feudal justice, territorial disputes, royal vs. seigneurial power, and lord–vassal relations. Scholars have long celebrated *The Song of Roland* as the exemplar of the genre. This late eleventh-century tale of betrayal and reckless courage is rendered in an allusive, incantatory style infused with the bellicose language and ideology of crusade. In establishing the *Roland* as a model text, however, literary histories have tended to ignore subsequent waves of epic production or to dismiss later epics as corrupt and inauthentic.[1]

In fact, the *chansons de geste* flourished throughout the Middle Ages by adapting in diverse ways to changing audience expectations. The thirteenth century witnessed the proliferation of generic hybrids, epic poems that incorporate narrative material typically associated with

---

1. See Catherine M. Jones, *An Introduction to the Chansons de Geste* (Gainesville: University Press of Florida, 2014), 24. It is important to note that French medieval poets were not operating in a system of rigid, normative generic categories.

IX

romance.[2] A masterpiece of this sub-genre, *Huon of Bordeaux* conjoins a conventional epic conflict with a marvelous quest that allows the hero to construct his chivalric identity through a series of otherworldly adventures. The narrative framework situates the poem in the tradition of "epics of revolt," which pit their heroes against an unjust monarch. Owing to a treacherous plot, Huon incurs the wrath of Charlemagne, who bears little resemblance to the beneficent emperor of the *Song of Roland*. Huon's expiatory mission unfolds as an exotic journey to the East, which occupies approximately sixty percent of the poem. Along the way, the hero comes upon the realm of the fairy king Auberon, who functions as both surrogate father and substitute monarch. In the final segment, the action shifts back to the epic world of Charlemagne's court, where the political conflict finds a utopian solution.[3]

Like other *chansons de geste* of the second and third generations, *Huon of Bordeaux* preserves the structural framework associated with the genre. Composed in assonanced *laisses* and narrated by the emphatic voice of the *jongleur*, the poem participates in a long tradition of heroic storytelling. Audiences accustomed to such tales would have recognized conventional schemas of feudal custom and warfare inherited from a rich oral–formulaic repertory. The judicial duel, for example, is used to determine innocence or guilt and includes a familiar set of stock motifs: hostages are demanded and secured, oaths are sworn in the presence of relics, and the hero pronounces a traditional epic prayer recalling major events from Scripture. Similarly, battle scenes are recounted by means of the time-honored expressions common to all *chansons de geste*:

> But young Huon spurred Blanchandin;
> He struck the first pagan he encountered
> And separated his head from his body.

2.   The tendency culminated in the voluminous works of the fourteenth and fifteenth centuries. See William W. Kibler, "La chanson d'aventures," in *Essor et fortune de la chanson de geste dans l'Europe et l'Orient latin, Actes du IXe congrès international de la Société Rencesvals,* ed. Alberto Limentani (Modena: Mucchi, 1982), 2: 509–15.

3.   See Luke Sunderland, *Rebel Barons: Resisting Royal Power in Medieval Culture* (Oxford: Oxford University Press, 2017), esp. 229–36.

Then he struck a second pagan, slicing him in two,
And with his third blow killed another.
He did not stop until he had slain a dozen.
Turks and pagans fled in all directions. (lines 8072–78)

The ritual slaughter of Muslim adversaries (indiscriminately called "pagans," "Turks," "Slavs," and "Saracens") reiterates the crusading propaganda that permeates the French epic. In the original decasyllabic verse, the various stages of combat are rendered in four-syllable and six-syllable formulas that can easily be adapted to any armed conflict.[4]

Yet *Huon of Bordeaux* also attests to generic innovation on several levels. The *laisses* are quite lengthy, averaging 118 lines (compared to thirteen for *The Song of Roland*). Moreover, the poet employs fewer of the strophic repetitions characteristic of earlier epics.[5] As William W. Kibler and François Suard have written, the text is largely driven by narrative rather than lyric considerations, with the *laisse* functioning as a flexible framework to highlight symmetrical episodes in different parts of the story.[6] In addition to stock motifs, new units of repeatable content have been forged to suit the demands of hybrid source material. The magical objects associated with Auberon, for example, are described in similar terms throughout the poem:

For I tell you truly,
None can drink from this goblet but the virtuous,
Those who are pure, innocent, and free from mortal sin.
As soon as an evildoer touches it,
The goblet loses all of its powers. (lines 3673–77, cf. 6907–9, 10557–60)

4.   On formulaic style in the Old French epic, see Jean Rychner, *La chanson de geste: Essai sur l'art épique des jongleurs,* Publications romanes et françaises 53 (Geveva: Droz, 1955), 126–69; and Jones, *An Introduction,* 16–17.

5.   Such repetitions include series of "parallel" *laisses,* which depict analogous actions performed by different characters, and "similar" *laisses,* which depict the same action from slightly different perspectives. See Rychner, *La chanson de geste,* 68–125; and Jones, *An Introduction,* 12–16.

6.   William W. Kibler and François Suard, ed. and trans., *Huon de Bordeaux. Chanson de geste du XIIIe siècle, publiée d'après le manuscrit Paris BNF fr. 22555* (Paris: Champion, 2003), xxxiii.

Although it is unlikely that the extant version of *Huon* was sung or even recited in full, the narrator's interventions evoke a certain nostalgia for the immediacy and practical conditions of oral performance. In two oft-cited passages near the midpoint of the poem, the narrator–*jongleur* pauses to demand remuneration for his tale:

> Worthy lords, as you can see,
> It is nearly evening, and I am very tired.
> Thus, I pray all of you, out of esteem for me
> And for Auberon and the valiant Huon,
> To return tomorrow after dinner;
> Let us go and have a drink...
>
> Quiet down now, if you please, and listen:
> I shall tell you a song if you wish.
> By the saints created by God,
> I have told and finished my song
> Unless you give me some money.[7]

The playful appeal unites narrator, fictional characters, and audience in an imagined negotiation that reignites narrative interest while calling attention to its own artifice. Like the *laisse* and the repertory of motifs, the narrator's voice is a locus of both continuity and change. A creative synthesis of innovation and tradition, *Huon of Bordeaux* marks an important transition in the history of French epic literature.

7. See Appendix below, 319–20. Many scholars believe that the *chansons de geste* were originally sung over a period of days in sessions (*séances*) of 1000 to 2000 lines. If this was true of early epic, it would certainly not have been possible for a lengthy work such as *Huon of Bordeaux*. Andrew Taylor argues that the epics were most likely sung or recited in fragments. See his "Was there a *Song of Roland*?" *Speculum* 76 (2001): 28–65.

Summary

The venerable Charlemagne, who is nearly two hundred years old,[8] has assembled his barons to formalize his succession. He asks that they crown his son Charlot, despite the boy's flawed character and troubled history. Charlemagne recalls the events recounted in another epic of revolt, *La Chevalerie Ogier de Danemarche*, in which Charlot murdered Ogier's son and precipitated a war between Charlemagne and his illustrious vassal. The barons reluctantly agree to the succession, but Charlot immediately becomes involved in a plot devised by the treacherous Count Amaury to ruin Huon and Gerard, the young sons of the deceased Seguin of Bordeaux. When the brothers are ambushed on their way to Charlemagne's court, Huon kills Charlot in self-defense without knowing his adversary's identity. Falsely accused of murder, Huon must engage in a judicial duel against Amaury, but Charlemagne stipulates that the knight who prevails in the duel will not be considered the victor unless the loser confesses his guilt. When Huon defeats and slays Amaury without extracting a confession, Charlemagne banishes the young hero, but agrees to pardon him under the following conditions: Huon will be sent on a mission to Babylon (Cairo), where he will kill the first Saracen he meets at the table of the emir Gaudisse, kiss the emir's daughter three times, tear out Gaudisse's mustache and four molars, and bring the tokens back to Charlemagne as proof of his achievement.

Thus, begins the period of Huon's adventures. Accompanied by a small group of knights, he first visits his uncle the pope, who absolves him of his role in Charlot's death. After a brief stay in the Holy Land, he travels through strange and marvelous countries on his journey to the Red Sea. Choosing the most direct but the most perilous route, he passes through the forest of the fairy king Auberon, son of Julius Caesar and Morgan la Fée. Auberon, a diminutive creature of great beauty, befriends Huon and bestows upon him

---

8. The two principal manuscripts diverge on the matter of Charlemagne's age. In *M* (Bibliothèque Municipale de Tours 936), he was knighted sixty years before the opening events of the story; see Pierre Ruelle, ed., *Huon de Bordeaux* (Brussels: Presses Universitaires de Bruxelles, 1960), line 56. In *P* (BnF fr. 22555), the version we have adopted for our translation, he was knighted 140 years prior and has been mounting horses for 180 years; see lines 81–83.

two magical gifts: a goblet from which only a virtuous man may drink and a horn that will allow him to summon Auberon from any distance, to be sounded only in the event of grave danger. The impetuous hero soon blows the horn to test its efficacy, incurring the wrath of Auberon. The fairy king pardons Huon but forbids him from stopping in Tormont on his way to the Red Sea. Huon nonetheless proceeds to Tormont, where, attacked by his renegade uncle Dudon, he once again puts the horn to the test. Auberon immediately appears with 100,000 men to assist Huon in vanquishing the Saracen forces. In Dunostre, assisted by a Christian captive named Sebille, the hero penetrates the castle of the giant Arrogant, which is guarded by two fearsome automatons. Huon slays the giant and appropriates a magic hauberk that Arrogant had stolen from Auberon.

The fairy king sends a sea creature named Malabron to transport Huon across the Red Sea. Once in Babylon, the hero accomplishes his mission and accepts the love of the emir's daughter Esclarmonde. Auberon forbids him to consummate the relationship before the couple can be married in Rome, but during their sea voyage, Huon forces himself upon the lady, whereupon they are caught in a violent storm and washed up onto an island. Pirates kidnap Esclarmonde and bring her to the Saracen King Galafre, whom she is forced to marry; however, the king vows to delay conjugal relations for three years. Meanwhile, Huon is rescued by Malabron and enters the service of a wandering minstrel. The hero eventually joins a Saracen army besieging Galafre's kingdom and is reunited with Esclarmonde and his Christian companions.

In Rome, Esclarmonde is baptized, and she and Huon marry. During their return voyage, they fall into a trap prepared by Huon's brother Gerard, who has revealed himself to be a vile traitor. Gerard steals the material evidence of Huon's successful mission (i.e., the emir's mustache and four molars), imprisons him in Bordeaux, and denounces him in Charlemagne's court, claiming that Huon has not fulfilled his promises. Charlemagne submits the case to the judgment of his peers, but the worthy Duke Naimes is Huon's only advocate. Auberon magically appears equipped with his talismans and subjects all those present to the test of the magic goblet. Charlemagne has a secret sin that prevents him from drinking from the vessel, but Huon and Esclarmonde pass the test. Auberon forces Gerard to confess his crimes and has him hanged.

Reconciled with Charlemagne, Huon recovers his fief of Bordeaux. Auberon announces that when he enters heaven in three years, Huon will inherit his kingdom.

TEXT AND INTERTEXT

Huon of Bordeaux draws upon a variety of source material, beginning with the Old French epic of revolt. By recalling the events of *La Chevalerie Ogier de Danemarche* at the beginning of the story, the poet situates the narrative within a well-established framework of conflict between monarchs and powerful barons. Epics of revolt served as a response to increasing royal power, notably during the reigns of Philip Augustus (r. 1180–1223) and Louis IX, "St. Louis" (r. 1226–70). Marguerite Rossi has convincingly argued that *Huon of Bordeaux* is a response to a specific historical event, the trial of Enguerrand de Coucy in 1259.[9] This high-ranking noble, who had ordered the execution of three young Flemish aristocrats for alleged poaching, was incarcerated in the Louvre before his trial and denied the right to a judicial duel. This aroused the wrath of the upper aristocracy, who believed that the king had overstepped his bounds. The trial itself bears many similarities to the events recounted in the first part of *Huon of Bordeaux*, as does the sentence: among Enguerrand's numerous punishments was the requirement of a pilgrimage to the Holy Land (which he managed to avoid by paying a substantial fine).[10] In the poem, it is Duke Naimes who objects to the extraordinary clause requiring that the judicial duel cannot exonerate Huon unless Count Amaury confesses his guilt:

> "Be aware, noble king, that you abuse your power
> And wrong him, by God in majesty!" (lines 1749–50)

When Charlemagne exiles Huon, Naimes warns of dire consequences:

> "When the news spreads through the land
> That you have disgraced a young man in this manner

9.   See Marguerite Rossi, *Huon de Bordeaux et l'évolution du genre épique au XIIIe siècle* (Paris: Champion, 1975), 296–315.
10.   Rossi, *Huon de Bordeaux*, 303–06.

And chased him from his lands,
What will the worthy high barons say?
Your judgments will never again be respected in France."

(lines 2271–75)

Other features of the epic repertory include the stock figure of the Saracen princess, who renounces her religion and her family for love of a Christian knight.[11] More assertive than the conventional romance heroine, the Saracen princess typically initiates the love relationship and serves as a valuable auxiliary. Esclarmonde becomes enamored of Huon as soon as he gives her the obligatory kisses included in Charlemagne's orders. Stealing the jailer's keys, she offers to free Huon and his companions from her father's dungeon in exchange for Huon's love:

"I am the daughter of Emir Gaudisse,
And you kissed me this morning during breakfast;
Your sweet breath has so wounded my heart
That I will love you for as long as I live.
If you agree to do as I desire,
I will arrange for you to be freed." (lines 6038–43)

When Huon demurs, declaring that he cannot love a Saracen, Esclarmonde cuts off his food supply until the starving hero gives in. Once the couple's adventures conclude, she is formally assimilated into Christian society:

The pope had the bells rung for mass,
And they brought the young lady to the church,
Where they baptized her in honor of our Lord.
They did not, however, change her name:
She would always be called Esclarmonde. (lines 9060–64)

11. On the Saracen Princess figure, see Norman Daniel, *Heroes and Saracens: An Interpretation of the Chansons de Geste,* Edinburgh: Edinburgh University Press, 1984), 69–93; Jacqueline de Weever, *Sheba's Daughters: Whitening and Demonizing the Saracen Woman in Medieval French Epic* (New York: Garland, 1998); Sarah Kay, *The Chansons de Geste in the Age of Romance: Political Fictions* (Oxford: Clarendon Press, 1995), 25-48; and Lynn Tarte Ramey, *Christian, Saracen, and Genre in Medieval French Literature* (New York: Routledge, 2001), 39–49.

By virtue of her name and conversion, Esclarmonde recalls the widowed Queen Bramimonde, who embraces Christianity at the end of *The Song of Roland*. Like most Saracen converts, Bramimonde takes a new name at baptism (Juliane). Esclarmonde, however, retains her given name, a luminous word with more obvious French roots (*esclar*, "brighten" + *monde*, "world"), perhaps as a reminder that the Saracen princess is always already destined for conversion. Yet even after her conversion, in speaking to Huon, Esclarmonde casts an outsider's gaze on the flaws in Charlemagne's court:

> "It will be a great pity, my lord, if you die like this,
> For you are a faithful and loyal man.
> In this place, however, as far as I have heard,
> There is not a single virtuous man.
> Even the king, who reigns over them,
> Is corrupt and deceitful, from what I have seen,
> For he has treated you most disloyally.
> But if God permits such a great injustice,
> Allowing you to be hanged and dragged by horses,
> Then I declare that Mohammed is certainly more worthy.
> Be assured that if you die,
> I will never invoke your God,
> But rather I will renounce holy Christianity." (lines 10342–54)

Among the many other allusions to the epic tradition is Auberon's horn, which pointedly recalls Roland's celebrated *oliphant*, the object of a bitter dispute between Roland and his companion Oliver. Having refused to sound his horn early in the battle, Roland summons Charlemagne toward the end, so that the emperor may avenge the fallen rearguard:[12]

> Roland said: "I shall sound the Oliphant
> And Charles, who is going through the pass, will hear it."...

12. The quarrel between Roland and Oliver is itself a matter of dispute among scholars. For a summary of the arguments, see: Catherine M. Jones, "Roland versus Oliver," *Approaches to Teaching the Song of Roland*, ed. William W. Kibler and Leslie Zarker Morgan (New York: Modern Language Association of America, 2006), 201–06.

> Oliver said: "That would be most shameful
> And all your kinsmen would then be blamed.".....
> Count Roland with pain and distress
> Sounds his oliphant in great agony.
> The clear blood gushes forth from his mouth...[13]

Like Roland, Huon faces opposition from a cherished companion (Geriaume), but staunchly defends his decision to call for the sovereign's help:

> "Huon, fair sir, for the love of God,
> Who was nailed to the cross,
> Don't blow the shiny ivory horn:
> I don't see a single wound upon you!"
> On hearing this, Huon was greatly angered:
> "What is this? The devil's to pay!
> Am I to wait until I'm killed?
> I'll blow the horn, no matter what anyone says!"
> He took the shiny white ivory horn,
> Raised it to his lips, and blew it
> So loud and hard
> That bright blood flowed from his mouth. (lines 4514–25)

Subsequently, the two poems diverge. Roland's sounding of the horn leads to his tragic demise, and Charlemagne's return to Roncevaux is full of pathos. Huon, on the other hand, summons forth the fairy king Auberon who arrives on the scene instantly "through magic and the will of God" (line 4540) to provide reinforcements. The contrast illustrates *Huon*'s permeability to the otherworldly interventions more common to romance through folktales. Auberon himself is a composite figure, with antecedents in Celtic and perhaps Germanic folklore.[14] By virtue of his fanciful parentage, he has credentials from the Arthurian world as well as classical antiquity: Julius Caesar lends an aura of military strength, while

13. *The Song of Roland*, trans. Glyn Burgess (London: Penguin, 1990), lines 1702–03, 1705–06, 1761–63.

14. Rossi, *Huon de Bordeaux*, 35–36, 88–90.

Morgan la Fée evokes magical powers from the Celtic-based otherworld of the Arthurian prose romances. Indeed, Auberon's magic goblet, a gift from fairies, has been linked to the Grail for its inexhaustibility and power to distinguish good from evil; a storm conjured by Auberon recalls the tempest of the fountain in Chrétien de Troyes' *Knight of the Lion*.[15] At the same time, the poet takes great care to Christianize the fairy king.[16] The magical powers bestowed on him at birth by fairies include beauty, eternal youth, mind-reading, teleportation, and dominion over animals — but he also knows the secrets of the angels, and when he chooses to leave this world, he will occupy a throne beside God.

Huon's expiatory journey to the East similarly combines motifs from diverse traditions. It begins as a traditional epic pilgrimage, exemplifying the profoundly ambiguous representation of the Orient characteristic of the *chansons de geste*. These works reproduce the ideological subdivisions that medieval Christianity imposed on the East. Poets aligned the Orient on a vertical axis, with places consecrated by Biblical events clearly distinguished from the native lands of Muslim adversaries. Accordingly, Huon's voyage includes a stop in Jerusalem, where he visits the Holy Sepulcher and kisses its relics. Between Jerusalem and the Red Sea, he encounters a transitional space, including the stereotypically horrible countries of Femmenie, where the sun never shines and women cannot bear children, and Coumant, where the red-eyed, large-eared, furry populace feasts on raw meat. Beyond these infernal spaces lies the land of "Faith," where loyalty and faithfulness reign supreme and strangers are welcome to the fruits of the harvest. Huon's entry into Babylon (Cairo) inspires both wonder and terror: awed by the pure gold architecture, he is soon overwhelmed by the thousands upon thousands of "pagans" watching him intently.

The mission itself, however, takes the form of a quest that tests the hero's prowess and character. This structure, common to romances

---

15. Ruelle, *Huon,* 75–76.

16. Jean Subrenat, "Merveilleux chrétien et merveilleux païen dans le prologue d'*Huon de Bordeaux,*" in *Société Rencesvals, Proceedings of the Fifth Conference (Oxford, 1970)*, ed. Geoffrey Robertson-Mellor (Salford: University of Salford, 1977), 177–87; Kibler and Suard, *Huon,* 197, n. 1.

of the period, makes heavy use of source material from the folktale (accomplishing impossible tasks, capturing a treasure) as well as myth (slaying the emir's knight, kissing his daughter).[17] Like the heroes of Chrétien de Troyes's romances, Huon makes a serious error in the course of his quest, in this case a sexual transgression. Once again, his trajectory recalls that of the Knight of the Lion: Before he can achieve true chivalric and moral excellence, Huon — like Yvain — first descends into a pre-civilized state, "running through the meadows / As naked as the day he was born" (lines 7446–47). The initial phase of recovery, i.e., his stint as a wandering "Saracen" minstrel, involves the temporary loss of social status and religious identity, but sets him on the path to redemption and reunion with his beloved.

This complex web of allusions is not meant to suggest that the text is a mere hodgepodge of motifs borrowed from diverse sources. As Luke Sunderland argues, "the bricolage of genres becomes a way of getting over an impasse."[18] The poem purposefully and artfully invents a romance solution to an epic dilemma fraught with political anxieties, involving not only matters of kingship, but also the efficacy of the judicial system.[19] *Huon* is certainly the most entertaining epic of revolt. The seriousness of the subject matter is frequently offset by humorous interludes mocking the hero's impulsiveness and naïveté or exploiting the comic potential of disguise.[20] Thanks to the ingenious combination of political conflict, initiatory quest, and magical intervention, *Huon of Bordeaux* is one of the few *chansons de geste* that has enjoyed virtually uninterrupted popularity up to the present day.

17. William Calin, *A Muse for Heroes: Nine Centuries of the Epic in France* (Toronto: University of Toronto Press, 1983), 57–71.

18. Sunderland, *Rebel Barons*, 236.

19. The poem specifically addresses, for example, the increasing role of intentionality in the determination of guilt or innocence. See Catherine M. Jones, "'Je ne soz queil homme j'oz ocis': Ignorance et innocence dans *Huon de Bordeaux* et *Garin le Lorrain*," in *La faute dans l'épopée médiévale: ambiguïté du jugement,* ed. Bernard Ribémont (Rennes: Presses Universitaires de Rennes, 2012), 123–36.

20. Calin, *A Muse for Heroes,* 71–77.

RECEPTION[21]

Within decades of its appearance, *Huon of Bordeaux* inspired a number of spinoffs, including a prequel titled *The Romance of Auberon* and sequels devoted to Huon's later adventures and those of his descendants: *Esclarmonde, Clarisse and Florent, Yde and Olive, Croissant,* and *The Song of Godin.* In the fifteenth century, the poem was rewritten in rhymed alexandrine verse and also translated into prose. The prose version was first printed in 1513 and reprinted eleven times in the course of the sixteenth century. Adaptations appeared in the popular *Bibliothèque Bleue* series in the seventeenth and eighteenth centuries as well as the *Nouvelle Bibliothèque Bleue* in the nineteenth century. In 1778, the Count of Tressan published a version in the *Bibliothèque universelle des romans.* The story has also been a favorite of children's literature: since 1898, at least twenty reworkings for young people have appeared in France.[22] Given the dramatic structure of the narrative, it is not surprising that *Huon of Bordeaux* has frequently been adapted for the stage.[23] Early French productions include those by the *Confrères de la Passion* in 1557 and Molière's troupe in 1660–61, followed by numerous theatrical versions in the nineteenth and twentieth centuries.

Huon of Bordeaux found favor with audiences outside of France as well. Toward the end of the medieval period, the text was translated into Middle Dutch verse and prose. Of particular note is the 1533 English translation by John Bourchier, Lord Berners, thought to be the inspiration for Shakespeare's Oberon in *A Midsummer Night's Dream.* In the United States, the epic was popularized by the science fiction and

---

21. William W. Kibler, "*Huon de Bordeaux* in Its Manuscripts," in *De Sens Rassis: Essays in Honor of Rupert T. Pickens*, ed Keith Busby et al. (Amsterdam-New York: Rodopi, 2005), 325–37; Caroline Cazanave, *D'Esclarmonde à Croissant: "Huon de Bordeaux," l'épique médiéval et l'esprit de suite* (Besançon: Presses Universitaires de Franche-Comté, 2007), 247–60.

22. Caroline Cazanave, "*Huon de Bordeaux* à la sauce enfantine," in *Grands textes du moyen âge à l'usage des petits*, ed. Caroline Cazanave and Yvon Houssais, (Besançon: Presses Universitaires de Franche-Comté, 2010), 123–61.

23. Caroline Cazanave, "*Huon de Bordeaux* au théâtre: Les Temps Modernes," in *Études médiévales*, ed. Danielle Buschinger (Amiens: Presses du Centre d'études médiévales, Université de Picardie–Jules Verne, 1999), 71–102.

fantasy writer Andre Norton in *Huon of the Horn* (1951), a novel in paperback illustrated by Joe Krush and described as a "classic of heroic fantasy.... Against unbelievable odds, armed with only a few magical gifts and his own supply of courage, Huon's adventure in a world of swordplay, romance and medieval witchcraft will leave Norton fans breathless."[24]

MANUSCRIPTS AND EDITIONS

Huon of Bordeaux has come down to us in three manuscripts: Bibliothèque Municipale de Tours 936 (*M*), edited by Pierre Ruelle in 1960; BnF fr. 22555 (*P*), edited with a facing modern French translation by William W. Kibler and François Suard in 2003; and Turin L-II-14 (*T*), which was partly destroyed in the 1904 fire that ravaged the Turin National Library. A fragment, housed in the Historical Society of Massachusetts, was edited by Keith V. Sinclair in 1979.[25] We chose to base our translation on *P*, following the Kibler–Suard edition: this manuscript is the most complete and considered to be closest to the hypothetical original.[26] While *Huon of Bordeaux* has been very loosely adapted into English (such as the retelling by Andre Norton), there has been no rigorous modern English translation to date. We have attempted to fill this gap by rendering the Old French assonanced decasyllabic verse into line-by-line standard modern English, conveying the meaning of the original text without attempting to preserve or imitate its formal properties. Although we adhere closely to the text of manuscript *P* edited by Kibler and Suard, there are a few instances in which we found the reading in manuscript *M* clearer or more logical; these variants are indicated in the notes.

24. Andre Norton, *Huon of the Horn* (New York: Harcourt Brace, 1951), back cover.

25. Keith V. Sinclair, "Un nouveau manuscrit de la version décasyllabique de *Huon de Bordeaux*," *Le Moyen Âge* 85 (1979): 445–64.

26. Ruelle, *Huon*, 14–15; Kibler and Suard, *Huon*, xxxvii.

NOTE

As we complete this translation in the spring of 2020, protesters around the world are calling into question the value of historical and cultural artifacts that recall and even celebrate past injustices. Indeed, one might legitimately challenge the validity of resurrecting a text that displays the stereotypical medieval intolerance toward non-Western peoples. Throughout the Old French epic, Muslims are depicted as morally, racially, and culturally Other; their alterity serves in part to justify Western hegemony and the notion of "holy war" celebrated in so many *chansons de geste*. Clearly, we can neither champion these values nor exploit their entertainment potential uncritically. We can, however, appreciate medieval narratives as documents of a particular worldview that informs today's racial and religious intolerance. Far from presenting a simplistic view of the clash of civilizations, the *chansons de geste* display a web of contradictions, offering both a glorification and a critique of hatred and violence. It is our hope that *Huon of Bordeaux* will afford readers a glimpse into one troubling but fascinating projection of the medieval imagination.

THE BOOK
OF
HUON OF BORDEAUX
AND
KING AUBERON

1

My lords, now be quiet, in the name of God and his image,
And you will hear a finely crafted song.
It is not about Arthur, nor Aumont the Savage,
Nor Agolant,[1] who inflicted so much harm
On good King Charles, the noble and wise.   5
My lords, this song is about a noble man of great lineage,
Brave in war and exceptionally valiant,
Who endured much suffering across the fearsome sea.
My lords, this song is about the birthright of Huon of Bordeaux,
Son of Seguin, who was wise and courteous   10
And who accomplished many fine deeds in his time,
But Huon accomplished even more through his bravery,
As you will hear before too long,
For Auberon, the little dwarf of the forest,
Helped and supported him through many perilous ordeals.   15
My lords, let us recall that this Auberon of whom I am speaking
Was the son of Julius Caesar, the brave and wise,
And Morgan la Fée, in a union freely chosen.[2]

1.   Arthur is the leader of the knights of the Round Table, first celebrated in France in the twelfth-century romances of Chrétien de Troyes, then in the *Prose Lancelot* of the thirteenth century. Agolant and his son Aumont are the enemies of Charlemagne in *Aspremont*, a late twelfth-century *chanson de geste*. In this poem, a youthful Roland proves his valor by killing Aumont and gaining his *oliphant* (horn) and sword Durendal.

2.   Auberon's rather peculiar lineage is designed to explain the character's combination of chivalric excellence and supernatural traits. In the Middle Ages, Julius Caesar was celebrated as a fierce warrior and brilliant military strategist, while Morgan, King Arthur's half-sister, was associated with magical powers and objects. An invention of the *Huon* poet, the fairy king's origins unite two important textual traditions of the thirteenth century: adaptations of Latin historical works (especially the *Faits des Romains*) and Arthurian romance. See Marguerite Rossi, *Huon de Bordeaux et l'évolution du genre épique au XIIIe siècle* (Paris: Champion, 1975), 334–39, 353–54.

Julius was very powerful and held many possessions.
He conquered many lands through his great bravery.   20
He was lord of Armenia and Hungary,
And all of Austria paid him homage.
He was lord of Constantinople all of his life
And sovereign of many other fine lands.
Morgan, his legitimate wife,   25
Was queen of the fairies in mighty Avalon
And mother of Auberon, who was small of stature,
For he was only three feet tall,
But his body and face were the fairest
To be seen in any land,   30
And he was the most honorable and upright man in the world,
Never guilty of any folly or shameful behavior.
My lords, Auberon lived in a forest
Called Monmur, a dreadful and shadowy place.
He remained hidden there for more than a hundred years.   35
It was there that the clever young Huon of Bordeaux found him,
After Huon had been banished from France[3]
Because of Charles's son Charlot, who sought to harm him.
Charlot was rash and vile,
For he wanted to kill Huon in a forest,   40
But Huon killed him instead, thanks to his valiant courage,
For which he suffered many trials and tribulations,
As you will hear in this fine song.

3.   The royal domain of France in the twelfth century was little more than the area around Paris now known as the Ile de France. Between 1180 and 1285, however, two ambitious, powerful, and long-lived kings, Philip-Augustus (r. 1180–1223) and St. Louis (r. 1226–70), were able to extend royal control over many of the surrounding counties and duchies. Bordeaux and its immediate area passed under the control of the English kings with the marriage of Eleanor of Aquitaine to Henry II in 1154 and did not return to French possession until 1453, at the end of the Hundred Years War. In *Huon of Bordeaux*, there is no allusion to this English occupation, although Huon's family clearly do not consider their duchy to be a part of France.

2

My lords, now listen, may God preserve you,
And you will hear a most worthy song   45
That tells a noble and authoritative story
About Huon of Bordeaux, the noble warrior,
Who held Bordeaux and all the surrounding region,
And about King Auberon, who agreed to help him,
As you will hear if you quiet down.   50
It was Pentecost, a feast day that must be observed.
Charles was in Paris, in his great palace,[4]
Holding court with his vassals: Germans and Bavarians,
Burgundians, Flemish, and Hainuyers,
Lorrainers, Angevins, Bretons, and Berruyers.   55
The court was filled with valiant knights;
More than a thousand princes were assembled there
To pay homage to Charlemagne, their rightful lord.
Eleven peers of the French kingdom were there;
The twelfth was proud-faced Huon of Bordeaux,   60
The subject of the story I am about to begin.
But the sprightly young man was not at court:
At that time, he was on his own land.
More than a hundred knights were seated at the table.
Needless to say, they were richly served.   65
When they were seated at the table for their meal,
They talked about one thing and another.
Some were saying, "Where is brave Huon?

---

4.   The "palace" generally designates the royal residence within a walled castle
or city. In *Huon of Bordeaux* it is most commonly modified by either *plennier*
or *listé*, more rarely by *voltis* or *lusant*. These latter we have translated "vaulted"
and "shining" respectively. The others are a little more problematic. For *palais
plennier* we have generally opted for "great palace" or "great hall," though it also
can imply a large gathering of the king's or noble's men. For *palais listé*, Godefroy
gives "entouré d'une bande ou bordure, peint à bandes," and Hindley et al. give
"palatial floor with marble or mosaic border; decorated with a painted frieze."
Such descriptions are obviously too lengthy to serve as a translation, so we have
opted each time for "splendid palace."

He is one of the twelve peers. It is disturbing
That he is not among us here at court.   70
If Charles knew this, he might be angry."
"You're right," said a foul slanderer,
"After the meal, I'll go and inform Charles."
My lords, this is what he did, you can be sure of it,
And he upset Charles and angered him,   75
As you will hear if you will kindly quiet down.
When they had all eaten their fill,
The servants and squires removed the tables.
The king then spoke to the valiant knights:
"My lords," said Charles, "be silent and listen to me!   80
I am old and frail, and my hair has gone white.
I have been mounting horses for a hundred eighty years,
And it has been a hundred forty years since I was knighted.
My body trembles beneath my soft ermine clothing,
And I can no longer travel or ride a horse.   85
I beg you, in the name of righteous God,
Choose a king, I beseech you,
Who can rule over the lands of France."
"Lord," said Naimes, "in the name of God in heaven,
Please give up this idea!   90
Go to the archbishopric of Reims,
Or to Saint-Omer or Orleans,
Or remain here at your palace in Paris,
And have yourself cared for in comfort.
We will help you govern your land   95
And protect your country and fiefdom.
Even if you spent forty years in bed,
You would still be feared and respected.
Be at peace and hold on to your land."
"Naimes," said Charles, "you plead in vain,   100
For in the name of the One who judges all,
I will never again place this crown
Of pure gold upon my head.
Rather, I beseech you, in the name of righteous God,

Choose a king who will rule over my land."   105
"Lord," said Naimes, "this saddens me;
Nonetheless, since it is your wish,
Please help us to decide
Whom we should choose as king to govern the realm."
"Barons," said Charles, "in the name of God, whom could you choose   110
If not the son of my wife?
I am speaking of my son Charlot, whom I love and hold dear,
Even though he is worthless.
When I fathered him, so help me God,
I was a hundred years old, I tell you truly.   115
It was by the command of the One who judges all,
Our Lord, delivered by St. Michael the angel,
That I lay with my noble wife,
And I did so freely and willingly,
But I fathered a poor heir   120
Named Charlot, and I am outraged
When he refuses to help or assist me.
He greatly prefers vile traitors
To honest men, which wounds my heart.
In France he caused a true calamity: 125
He incited a war with Ogier the Dane[5]
By killing his son Baudouinet with a chessboard.
This was Ogier's son, and he loved him dearly.
Many valiant knights died as a result.
Naimes's son was slaughtered —   130
Young Richier, so worthy of esteem —
And Ogier killed more than ten thousand men.
Many knights died because of this conflict.
To Lombardy at the court of the powerful king Desier
Ogier fled when he could not prevail   135
Against me, and I then had him banished.
He had to flee to Castelfort
Without a palfrey or a packhorse,

5.   Lines 126–216 summarize portions of a previous epic of revolt, *La Chevalerie
Ogier*, which serves as both source and analog for *Huon of Bordeaux.*

Accompanied by one lone squire.
I followed him, briskly spurring my horse,   140
And then I besieged him from all sides,
Accompanied by many a valiant knight.
I sustained the siege for seven years with many noble princes,
But I could never capture him, which infuriated me.
The duke suffered great hardships,   145
But in the end, after he had fought so hard,
He was forced to leave his fine castle
And flee with his squire one evening,
Following a deserted path.
The next day, at dawn,   150
I had his great palace attacked,
But when I seized it, Ogier was nowhere to be found.
As you can imagine, I was furious.
I returned to Paris, my rightful fief.
Archbishop Turpin, my dear friend,   155
Was returning to the archbishopric of Reims
When he found Duke Ogier asleep in a meadow
With his squire.
Turpin captured him, had him tied up,
And kept him there, sending a messenger   160
To inform me by sealed letter
That he had captured Ogier, who had done me such harm.
When I learned this, I was overjoyed.
I wanted him killed and cut to pieces,
However, his powerful family urged me so strongly to reconsider   165
That I had him imprisoned in Porte de Mars.
The worthy archbishop
Made sure that Ogier had everything he needed:
He had plenty of food and drink.
Two years after the events I have just related to you,   170
I was in Laon, in my great palace,
When Saracens and pagans arrived
To ravage and destroy my land.
They brought with them the evil pagan Brehier,

A huge giant measuring nineteen feet tall.   175
I sent for my worthy barons
With sealed letters,
And forty thousand answered my call.
I sent my army to face the giant,
Who was coming daily, shouting at me   180
To arm twenty knights.
If they could defeat him by the sword,
He would leave my land in peace.
I had forty knights armed and fitted with hauberks,
And I sent them to attack the giant,   185
But they couldn't harm him one bit.
He killed all but ten of them.
After that, I had no knight brave enough
To dare engage him in mounted battle.
Then my principal councillors advised me   190
That if I didn't release Ogier,
That devil would never be vanquished.
I sent for Ogier and had him unshackled.
When he saw me, he fell at my feet.
I raised him up willingly and with pleasure,   195
And I told him most affectionately
That if he agreed to fight Brehier,
I would return to him his entire fief,
But only if he conquered the giant by the sword.
But Ogier absolutely refused to do this   200
Unless my son were handed over to him first.
My valiant knights were so insistent
That I gave him my son, albeit with great anger and sorrow.
I had him taken to the hill of Renne.
Then the valiant duke Ogier seized him   205
By the hair, his sword unsheathed.
He would have killed him, you can be sure of it,
When the holy angel came down from the sky
And blocked the valiant knight's blow.
Seeing this, Ogier was joyful and happy.   210

He ran to embrace my son
And returned him to me in my great palace.
When I saw him, I was joyful and happy,
But, in the name of the One who judges all,
It would have been better for me if he had cut my son to pieces,   215
For he isn't worth a penny."[6]
Just as Charles finished speaking, Charlot arrived
With a very fine sparrowhawk on his wrist.
He came up to the palace.
He was young and quite handsome, believe me,   220
Not yet twenty-two years old.
"Barons," said Charles, "here is a handsome knight.
It greatly distresses me that he is of no help to me
And that he neglects his land and his heritage.
Nonetheless, I ask you in the name of God,   225
And urge you to make him king.
He is the rightful heir to France."
 "Sire," said Naimes, "in the name of God, ask him
If he wants to receive the land and the fief."
Charles replied, "As you wish."   230
He summoned Charlot before the knights, saying:
"My son, come forward at once
And receive your land and inheritance.
By God, you will have as noble a fief
As paradise, the realm righteously governed   235
By the Lord our God who rules all things.
If any man under the arc of the heavens
Were to take from you even the smallest portion,

6.   Here, and over thirty additional times in our poem, the poet uses the word *denier*, the most insignificant medieval French coin, to indicate something of little or no value. We have generally translated this (as here) by the English "penny," or by some expression like "worthless," "not a bit," etc. If minted in Paris, the coin was often called a *paresis*, or "Parisian penny," (lines 694, 727) and was equally "worthless." Of much more value was a *livre*, or "pound," containing about 12 ounces of silver (lines 445, 450, 474, and 4962). A *mark* of silver was eight ounces (lines 1681, 1945, 5550, 6699, 7846, and 8938).

You could easily strike him down and kill him.
In every single region, borderland, and stronghold   240
Where God is served and glorified,
You are feared and dreaded.
My son, have nothing to do with cowardly traitors;
Get to know the most honorable men,
For from honorable men come all good things.   245
Honor and hold dear the clergy,
And remember to go to holy church;
Give willingly of your possessions to the poor."
"Sire," said the young man, "I will do as you wish."
Just as he said this,   250
An evil traitor stood up.
He was from Rivier, and his name was Amaury.[7]
He hurried over to Charles,
Eager to stir up a conflict
That would bring great harm to sweet France.   255
He said to the king, "Your words are wrongheaded,
And your actions as well, God help me!
For you are giving your son the governance
Of a land where you possess not a single penny,
And where you are neither loved nor esteemed.   260
I know a land situated not far from here,
Where he would be torn limb from limb
If he even attempted to act in your name."
"Good God, where is that?" asked proud-faced Charles.
Amaury replied, "I will tell you: 265
I mean Bordeaux, which is not far from here.
The duke has been dead for a good seven years.
He left two worthless sons,
Two rotten scoundrels, Gerard and Huon,
Who can't be bothered to serve or honor you.   270
Now then, emperor, do the right thing!

7.   Although he hails from the town of Rivier, Amaury is henceforth named
Amaury of Viemez, probably to associate him more closely with Gerard's other
traitorous companion, Gibouart of Viemez, later in our poem.

Entrust me with forty knights,
And I will also take members of my great lineage.
We will make the journey to Bordeaux immediately.
I will easily take those two troublemakers   275
And bring them here to your great palace.
You can then have them hanged and put to death."
The king replied, "Very well, I will allow it."
"Sire," said Naimes, "upon my soul, this is a terrible idea!
One should never give traitors a position of power,   280
Nor heed their advice.
You should know that the two boys are young;
They live far away and have a large territory to govern.
They have neglected their duties from lack of experience.
Duke Seguin served you willingly.   285
He had great affection for you and held you dear."
"He was right," said proud-faced Charles,
"To serve me gladly and willingly.
The benefits he gained were considerable.[8]
Three days each year he served at my table: 290
On Easter, when all must take communion;
At Pentecost, the solemn feast day;
And on Christmas, the revered holy day.
But it was not mere crumbs of white bread
He received for this service.   295
Rather, he carried away large cups of pure gold,
Fine table linens, and steel knives,
And golden goblets and splendid silver.
He could well brag and boast
That for the three days he served at my table,   300
He was richer by three thousand pounds.

8.   At lines 290, 295, and 487 Old French uses the word *rellief*, which we have translated "benefits," to refer to objects, properties, or favors that a vassal earns from his lord for service at his court, and specifically at his table. Some of the possible benefits are enumerated in the lines that follow. The word is related to *relever*, which in an expression like *relever nous terre* (line 667) means "do homage for our lands."

Now let me tell you what he gave me in return for his fief:
Whenever I sent for him by sealed letter,
He came to help and assist me
By bringing ten thousand knights   305
To accompany me on journeys or expeditions.
I didn't have to contribute a penny,
Other than oats for the horses at night, after meals."
"Sire," said Naimes, "in the name of righteous God,
I implore you, if you care for me at all,   310
Send for the two noble heirs.
If they come, treat them honorably;
If they do not, then you can destroy them."
"Certainly," said Charles, "I will gladly do this.
I will send two noble messengers to summon them."   315
"Sire," said Naimes, "a hundred thanks.
These two young men are my cousins, you know."
"Truly," said Charles, "this makes them dearer to me."
When Amaury heard this,
He became truly outraged,   320
But the king called Agorant and Gautier,
Saying, "My lords, now hurry, do not delay.
Saddle your swift horses
And ride all the way to Bordeaux.
Tell the proud-faced duchess on my behalf   325
To send me her sons.
If they do not come, I will destroy them."
And they replied, "We will do as you please."

3

"Sire," said Naimes, "in the name of God the Redeemer,
What messengers will you send to the young men?"   330
"Naimes," replied Charles, "Gautier and Agorant."
"They are truly brave and valiant," said the duke.
"Barons," said Charles, "come forward.
Saddle your smooth-gaited palfreys,

And bring along as much gold and silver   335
As you need and desire.
Ride all the way to Bordeaux,
And tell the duchess on my behalf
To send me both of the young men;
And if they do not come, so help me God,   340
I will inflict great harm and suffering upon them."
And they replied, "We will do exactly as you wish."
They saddled their smooth-gaited palfreys
And took as much gold and silver as they desired.
They mounted their horses without delay   345
And set off straight for Bordeaux.
When Amaury learned that the young men had been summoned,
He was filled with rage and sorrow.
He swore to almighty God
That if Huon and young Gerard came to court,   350
They would be slain, no matter who might protest.
The messengers rode on without delay,
Hurrying their horses all the way to Bordeaux.
There they dismounted from their smooth-gaited palfreys
And went up to the gleaming palace.   355
They found the lady there with her two sons
And greeted her properly and courteously.

4

The two messengers pressed on,
Riding all the way to Bordeaux without delay.
On a Tuesday, as I heard it told,   360
Just as people were leaving church,
Both messengers entered the city.
They hurried to the palace,
Where they dismounted from their swift horses.
They went up to the great hall   365
And found the lady seated at her meal.
Beside her sat proud-faced Huon;

Gerard, his younger brother, was feeding a sparrowhawk,
Gorging the bird with the wing of a plover.
Behold the worthy messengers!   370
They spoke forcefully, for they were quite eloquent:
"May the Lord God — who judges all,
Who created land, sea, and skies,
Flowering meadows and fields of wheat,
Fish in the sea, of great benefit to all,   375
And who suffered on the cross —
Keep and protect the proud-faced duchess,
Along with her children and all her knights!
We speak in the name of Charles, who rules France."
Hearing this, the lady rose quickly   380
And ran to kiss them both.
"My lords," she said, "in the name of God, welcome!
How are my lord, the proud-faced Charles,
And gray-haired Duke Naimes,
And all the barons and knights?"   385
"My lady, they are quite well," replied the messengers.
"The king bids you to send him your sons.
Charlemagne is very angry
That they do not deign to appear in court
To serve him in his great palace.   390
If they do not come, so help me God,
He will have them destroyed and killed,
For traitors have gained such favor at court
That your sons will lose their land and their fief."
Hearing this, the lady thought she would lose her mind.   395
"My sons," she said, "you have delayed too long!
Unless God, who was raised on the cross, attends to it,
You have lost your entire inheritance."
"My lady," said Huon, "you were very wrong
Not to inform us of this matter.   400
By this judgment, we have lost our fief."
The messengers replied, "Don't worry,
For Duke Naimes intervened so forcefully

That you are completely reconciled with the king."
"I thank God for that," said the lady.   405
"Proud-faced Duke Naimes is a very good man.
He has never given poor advice.
Duke Seguin — may God have mercy on his soul! —
Was very fond of him,
For the two noble warriors were quite close."   410
The lady then spoke to both messengers,
Saying, "My lords, if you please,
I would like you to stay here for the night.
I will make sure that you are comfortable and well fed,
And in the morning, once it is light,   415
You can return to court."
The messengers said, "That is out of the question.
We cannot stay the night,
For we must return right away with our message.
Tell us, then, without delay,   420
What will we tell our rightful lord?"
"My lords," said Huon, "so help me God,
You may tell Charles, the proud-faced emperor,
That we will go to France and pay him court.
We will do so gladly and willingly.   425
Serving the king, we will fall at his feet
And kiss his cordovan leather shoes.
We give thanks to glorious God on this day
That Charles has remembered two undeserving young men!"
The lady summoned proud-faced Huon   430
And the worthy young Gerard.
"My sons," she said, "you will go to court,
But not outfitted like wretched peasants.
Bring as many as thirty packhorses
Laden with my riches.   435
Get to know the most honorable men,
For from honorable men come all good things.
My sons, have nothing to do with vile flatterers.
Remember to go to holy church

And honor and hold dear the clergy.   440
Give willingly of your possessions to the poor.
As for these noble messengers,
Exchange their palfreys for good chargers,
Replace their cloaks with fine embroidered mantles,
And let each receive a hundred pounds."   445
"My lady," said Huon, "gladly and willingly."
Thus did he have the messengers equipped:
He exchanged their palfreys for good chargers,
Replaced their cloaks with fine embroidered mantles,
And gave to each a hundred pounds.   450
The messengers left in excellent spirits.
They hurried their horses all the way to Paris.
Dismounting before the carved stairway,
They went up to the great hall.
Seeing them, King Charles said: 455
"My lords, in the name of God, welcome!
Tell me, for the sake of righteous God,
Did you go to Bordeaux?
What did the worthy lady say?
Will Seguin's sons come to court?"   460
And they replied, "Yes, most willingly.
They send through us their greetings and affection,
And we can assure you, in the name of righteous God,
That since the hour Christ was baptized
And tortured on the cross for all sinners,   465
No one has ever beheld men so valiant,
So courtly, or so hospitable.
They wish us to inform you that they will come to court.
They will serve you gladly and willingly
And kiss your cordovan leather shoes.   470
We assure you that they treated us most honorably:
In place of the palfreys, we returned on good chargers,
And instead of our cloaks, we wear fine embroidered mantles.
We were each given a hundred pounds."
"Thanks be to God!" said Charles.   475

"Whoever honors my noble messengers
Would do the same for me if I were there.
Amaury, you scoundrel, leave my palace at once!
No good ever came to me from your lineage.
If I had believed you, by righteous God, 480
I would have killed and destroyed them.
However, by God who judges all,
If Huon comes to Paris to attend court,
He will be the standard-bearer of France
And Gerard will be my chamberlain. 485
Their income will increase by two thousand pounds,
And in France they will have the benefits from my table
Just like their father, who loved and cherished me."
Hearing this, Amaury thought he would lose his mind.
He now planned to stir up a conflict 490
That would cause great suffering in sweet France.
He stormed out of the great hall at once
And returned home in a fury,
Where he began to devise a course of action.
One evening, after eating, he went to see Charlot 495
In his lodgings, where he could usually be found.
As soon as he saw him, he fell at his feet.
Charlot raised him up and asked,
"My friend, what's wrong? Don't hide it from me."
Amaury replied, "I will gladly tell you: 500
I am so upset that I am about to lose my mind,
Because your land and your fiefs are being taken away from you."
Charlot said, "How could that be, by God in heaven?"
Amaury replied, "I will tell you how:
Those two troublemakers are coming to court. 505
They will be so good at cajoling and flattery
That no one will be able to speak in court
Without going through them. So help me God,
They will take a quarter of France away from you."
Amaury, the murderous traitor, said: 510
"Ah, my lord Charlot, help me get revenge!

Their father Seguin once caused me great harm:
He took a castle from me with help from Ogier.
Don't fail me, by St. Richier.
You are my close cousin   515
On your mother's side, and so you should help me,
As I will help you, if you ever need me.
Don't fail me, son of a noble mother!"
"What can I do?" asked proud-faced Charlot.
Amaury replied, "I will tell you: 520
I will bring along my fierce family,
And you will bring forty knights.
We'll all be armed and wearing hauberks.
Near Paris, in a leafy woods,
We will lay ambush in a thicket.   525
When those scoundrels ride by,
We'll attack and cut off their heads;
No one will know who killed them."
And Charlot replied, "Agreed!"
The vile traitors made their preparations: 530
They put on their hauberks and laced their helmets,
Girded their swords on the left-hand side,
And then mounted their swift steeds.
They hung quartered shields around their necks
And grasped stout, sharp spears in their fists.   535
God! Why was proud-faced Charles unaware of all this?
He would have had them all put to death!
May God protect Huon and Gerard the warrior,
For without his help, they are finished.
The traitors — may God bring them misfortune —   540
Numbered one hundred, all ready to fight.
They waited till nightfall,
Not daring to travel by daylight,
For they greatly dreaded fierce Charlemagne.
When night came and all was quiet,   545
The perfidious scoundrels left the city.
They lowered their lances and shields

And rode swiftly to the thicket,
Which they entered with their green-gold helmets fastened.[9]
Now we shall take leave of these villainous traitors —   550
May God, who was raised on the cross, confound them!
I shall tell you next about Huon the warrior.
He made the necessary preparations for his journey
And summoned his barons and noble knights,
Who came gladly and willingly.   555
He took ten of them along, to serve as his councillors.

5

Worthy Huon was ready to depart.
He summoned his barons from far and wide.
From Gironville he summoned Guiret,
An honest provost who merited his affection,   560
Because his father Seguin held him dear,
And he had guarded their land for a full thirty years.
So mighty Huon
Ordered him to watch over his land:
Guiret was to defend it loyally   565
Until Huon returned from France.
He replied that he was most willing to do so.
Young Huon did not delay
And made splendid preparations for his voyage:
He had thirty packhorses laden   570
With good silver and pure gold,

---

9. The formula "green-gold helmet" (*vert heaume*) appears in many *chansons de geste* and has been the subject of much debate. Some historians believe that *vert* designates green paint, while others interpret *vert* as an adjective designating brilliance. May Plouzeau has argued that the formula refers to the greenish cast of superior metal. In our poem, *vert helme* appears alone five times, associated with *gemez* (gemmed, bejeweled) three times, and once with *luisant* ("shiny"). Most common in *Huon* is *helme gemez* (12 occurrences). See May Plouzeau, "*Vert heaume*: Approches d'un syntagme," in *Les Couleurs au Moyen Age* (Aix-en-Provence: Centre Universitaire d'études et de recherches médiévales d'Aix, Université de Provence, 1988), 589–650.

With good cups and gilded goblets,
With expensive cloth of silk and taffeta.
He brought along hunting dogs and greyhounds,
And he had with him a great number   575
Of molted goshawks, falcons, and sparrowhawks.
With him came ten knights,
His closest and most trusted advisers,
Who had counseled him all his life.
He brought squires to ready his lodgings   580
And stableboys to look after his horses.
Then he and Gerard and their mighty companions
Asked for leave and set off.
Their noble mother came up to them
And began to address them with gentle words: 585
"My lords," she said, "in God's name,
Don't leave until I've spoken with you."
She wept bitterly. No one could console her.
Oh God, if only she had known the great misfortune
That was to befall her young son: 590
She would not live to see Huon again!

6

Eager to be off, Huon turned away,
He and Gerard and all the knights.
The noble woman came up to them;
She began to kiss them tenderly   595
And then went to speak to them:
"My children," she said, "you are going to the royal court.
I beg of you, in the name of righteous God,
That you not listen to evil advisors,
But to the most honorable men you encounter.   600
Remember to go to holy church,
Honor and hold dear the clergy,
And give willingly of what you have to the poor.
Be noble and generous providers,

And you will be loved and esteemed the more."   605
"My lady," said Huon, "we will do what pleases you."
With these words they asked for leave,
And the duchess rushed to embrace them.
As they left, she began to weep.
Oh God, if only she had known the deadly danger   610
That was to befall the young prince!
Had she known it, she would have suffered:
She was not to see Huon again in her lifetime.
They set off at once
Along the high road toward Paris.   615
The assemblage of packhorses was impressive.
May God, who judges all, be with them!
They had no idea what grief and suffering
The traitors, hidden in the leafy woods, had prepared for them.

7

The sad orphans were now heading to court.   620
The youths' entourage was impressive.
Huon spoke to his young brother Gerard:
"Gerard, as the ever-truthful God is my witness,
We are going to the court in Paris
To see and visit the best king   625
Who ever dwelled in the land of France.
We should be happy to associate with such a man,
So sing now, my brother, and cheer up!"
"And what should I sing, miserable me?" replied Gerard.
"I have dreamt a dream that has stunned me: 630
Last night in my bed I dreamt
That three leopards attacked me
And tore my heart from my breast.
You escaped, but I was overwhelmed.[10]

10. The prophetic dream to announce a coming event, usually a disaster, is a frequent motif in Old French epic poetry. Most famous are Charlemagne's prophetic dreams in the *Song of Roland* anticipating the coming disaster at Roncevaux. The enemy king Marganice is represented by a leopard (laisse 57).

For God's sake, let's return to Bordeaux,   635
To our mother who raised us so tenderly."
"May it not please God," replied Huon,
"That I ever see Bordeaux's walls again
Before I have beheld Charles of Saint-Denis!
Don't worry, Gerard, my dear friend,   640
But let's ride on, for God in paradise.
May He who died on the cross watch over us!"
And so, the sad youths continued their journey:
The poor orphans rode onward
Until they caught sight of the abbot of Cluny,   645
Who was accompanied by eighty monks.
Huon spoke to his brother Gerard:
"Brother," he said, "listen to me:
Do you see those monks from Cluny before us?
Let us offer them our company,   650
Because our mother often told us
That it is good to seek the company of good men."
"What you propose is good," replied the young man.
So, the two noble brothers rode on
Until they caught up with the abbot of Cluny   655
Who, when he saw them, turned toward Huon
And spoke reassuringly to them:
"Noble youth," said the good abbot,
"From what land or what country do you come?
Who is the father who begot you?"   660
"My lord," said Huon, "for God in paradise,
We are from the city of Bordeaux.
Our father was the brave Duke Seguin,
But our father died some seven years ago.
You see here my brother, who is with me;   665
We are headed to France, to the king of Saint-Denis,
To do homage for our lands and country,
For the emperor has summoned us by letter.
Our hearts tremble, and our bodies are weak,
For we are afraid of being betrayed."   670

"Young men," the abbot replied, "you are my cousins:
Your father Seguin was my first cousin.
So help me God, you are most welcome!
Now don't be frightened in the least,
But ride along with me.   675
I will always speak up for you.
I will give you the keys to my treasure boxes,
The marten pelts, the ermine furs,
All the wealth of Saint-Peter's of Cluny.
Take from it, brothers, as much as you wish."   680
"My lord," said Huon, "in God's name, we thank you profusely!"
Then the noble princes continued onward;
The worthy youths, along with the abbot,
Who was accompanied by eighty of his monks,
Rode in the direction of the city of Paris.   685
Suddenly the ambushers came out of the thicket.
Amaury was the first to see them
And easily recognized noble Huon
Along with his brother, princely Gerard.
Amaury called to Charlot, as you will hear: 690
"Look, lord Charlot," said Amaury,
"Here come Seguin's two sons.
If you don't kill them at once,
Then you're not worth a Parisian penny!"
The land is yours and should come to you,   695
But first you must slay them."
"Right!" replied Charlot, "I'm going to kill them!"
The traitor sprang from the thicket
And separated from his companions.
His shield suspended from his shoulder, his helmet laced,   700
His sword with its gilded hilt at his side,
A lance in his fist with a gonfanon attached,
He spurred his horse and rode forward.
"Let him go, men," said Amaury,
"And may he meet his end today!   705
May God grant that Charlot be killed:

France will have no heir, and I will rule the land!
Before the year is out, I'll have killed Charlemagne."
Charlot rode timidly forward.
The abbot of Cluny was the first to see him.   710
He called to Huon and said:
"Fair nephew, listen to me:
I see a hundred helmets shining in this thicket,
And I see one coming provocatively toward us,
His shield suspended from his shoulder, his helmet laced,   715
A lance in his fist, and a burnished sword belted on.
For the love of God who died upon the cross,
If you have wronged or stolen
From anyone at all in this world,
Go forward and offer compensation: 720
For every penny taken I'll repay a golden mark."
"My lord," said Huon, "may God reward you for this;
You speak nobly, and I thank you five hundred times!
But, as God who died upon the cross is my witness,
I do not know anyone in all of Christianity,   725
So help me God, who has reason to hate me
Nor from whom I've taken so much as a Parisian penny.
Nevertheless, dear brother Gerard,
Go see, in the name of God in paradise,
What that knight, who approaches so provocatively, wants." 730
"My lord," his brother replied, "I will do as you wish."
He spurred his horse, went ahead of the others,
Rode swiftly on toward Charlot,
And shouted out to him as politely as possible:
"Noble knight, welcome to you!   735
Are you a watchman? Are you guarding this land?
If we owe any payment, by God in paradise,
You will have it most willingly."
"Where are you from?" proud Charlot replied.
Gerard said, "You will hear at once: 740
I am from the city of Bordeaux
And am son of the brave Duke Seguin.

Here you see my brother who is with me,
A very bold and hardy knight.
We are traveling to the court in Paris   745
To see and visit King Charlemagne.
If we have wronged or stolen
From anyone at all,
We will make amends at the court in Paris
According to the judgments of the princes and marquis."   750
Then Charlot said, "You have wasted your breath.
I wasn't searching for anyone, by St. Denis,
Other than yourselves, thanks be to God!
Since I've found you, I'm quite pleased:
You are deep in debt, by God,   755
Because your father stole three of my castles.
Since I cannot recover anything from him,
You are a good substitute, I think,
Because, by the One who died on the cross,
You are about to die yourselves.   760
Prepare yourselves, for I am about to strike you!"
Gerard heard all this, and his blood surged,
Nonetheless he replied politely to Charlot:
"Oh, noble knight, have mercy for God's sake.
You are armed, and I am defenseless.   765
You have a hauberk and a burnished sword.
I am unarmed in a sable tunic,
With no sword or burnished spear
With which to defend myself against you.
Ah, gallant gentleman, what would you gain   770
By having slaughtered and killed me?
For the love of God, have mercy on me.
Look over there, it's my older brother.
We are going to see the king of Saint-Denis,
Who has sent for us by sealed letters.   775
If we have wronged you in any way,
We will make it right in the court in Paris
According to the judgment of the barons of the land."

Charlot replied, "By St. Denis,
That's nothing to me, I swear by my friends,   780
Because, by almighty God, I'll not eat again
As long as you are alive.
Prepare yourselves, for I am about to strike you.
You are going to die a painful death!"
Hearing this, all Gerard's blood surged.   785
"My lord," said the young man, "this troubles me indeed."
Young Gerard tried to turn his horse
For he was eager to rejoin Huon,
But proud-faced Charlot pressed him
So closely that he could not get turned   790
To make it back to Huon.
Charlot spurred his mighty warhorse
And charged rapidly toward Gerard
With his lance lowered and shield before him.
He struck Gerard, ripping open   795
His fine clothing from Bordeaux, his ermine cloak
And then his linen undergarment.
He thrust his unbending spear through his body
Until a good foot of it came out
The other side of his chest.   800
He did not kill him, because God did not will it,
But nonetheless he had so wounded him
That he was knocked from his horse to the ground.
The young man, wracked by pain, fainted.
When the abbot of Saint-Peter's of Cluny saw this,   805
You can be sure that his heart was heavy.
Weeping, he said to Huon:
"Good cousin, your brother is dead."
"My lord," replied Huon, "I am deeply sorry.
Woe is me! What an evil encounter this was!   810
Alas, dear mother, you raised him so tenderly.
If you knew what has befallen us,
I know for sure your heart would be broken.
Holy Mary, what will become of me?

Heavenly queen, mother of Jesus Christ, 815
May it please you to counsel me!
Lord abbot of Cluny, for the love of God
Will you help me to uphold my rights?
Because, by almighty God,
I will go see what sort of man killed him, 820
And I will kill him, or he will kill me."
"Fair nephew," said the abbot, "you are wasting your breath,
For we are holy and blessed priests
And must not even be present where someone is killed.
Do your best, because I have failed you here." 825
"Alas," Huon said, "what a useless relative!
And you, the ten knights I've brought with me
From the city of Bordeaux, will you help me?"
And they replied, "Yes, we would die for you!"
"My lords," said Huon, "may God reward you for this." 830
Angry and irate, he turned away.
He and his ten men left the abbot behind.
When the abbot saw this, he was moved to pity;
He began to shed tears tenderly
And prayed to God in paradise 835
To protect Huon from being killed,
To see that both he and his men were safe.
The abbot and his monks rode ahead
So they could watch the cruel battle
To see if Huon and his men would escape with their lives. 840
Huon spurred his worthy steed
And came to where his brother lay in the clearing.
Seeing him, he said:
"Dear brother, in the name of God in paradise,
Tell me if you think you'll live." 845
"I don't know, my lord," his brother answered,
"So help me God, I am prepared for death.
Look to yourself, for I am finished.
In the name of God in paradise, you must flee,
For I see a hundred helmets shining in this thicket." 850

When Huon heard this, he was overcome with grief.
"Dear brother," he said, "you are wasting your breath.
May it never please God, who died upon the cross,
For me to run away when you are lying here,
Nor for me ever to see the great city of Bordeaux again.   855
I will learn what sort of a man killed you,
And I will kill him, or he will kill me."
Then he spurred his Arabian steed
Without waiting even a second for his men.
Grieving, he rode after Charlot,   860
Who was returning to the leafy thicket.
When Charlot saw that Huon was in pursuit,
He rode calmly along
As the traitor Amaury watched.
You could hear Huon shouting loudly after him: 865
"Vassal," he said, "where were you born?"
And Charlot replied, "You will soon hear:
In Germany, the son of Duke Thierry."
Huon thought he was telling the truth,
Because he was not wearing his own armor.   870
The low-born scoundrel was sporting another's arms,
Which was why Huon could not recognize him.
Listen now to what Huon said to him:
"Upon my word, may God damn you,
And may your life be a tale of misfortune!   875
Why did you kill my younger brother?"
And Charlot replied, "As God is my friend,
Because your father stole three of my castles,
And I cannot recover anything from him,
So I killed your brother, and I will kill you too!"   880
"It is in God's hands," Huon said to him,
"But, if it pleases God, I will slay you first!"
Charlot said, "I defy you to the death.
On guard, because I am about to strike you!"
Then he spurred his good and valiant steed,   885
Lowered his lance, held his shield before him,

And charged full speed at Huon.
It was unfortunate that Seguin's noble son
Was not wearing his white hauberk on his back,
But fortunate that he was carrying his burnished sword.	890
Now hear what the young gentleman did:
He seized his heavy scarlet cloak
And wrapped it around his arm,
Then drew the sword with which Seguin had knighted him.
He dug his golden spurs into his horse	895
And raced madly toward Charlot, while he —
May God damn him! — charged toward Huon.
The worthy youths attacked one another.
Charlot struck proud-faced Huon
On the arm around which he had wrapped his cloak,	900
Ripping off the ermine lining
And then the Beauvais cloth.
He thrust his Poitevin spear right between
Huon's ribs and his white linen undergarment,
But God prevented him from being wounded.	905
As Charlot passed by on his worthy steed,
Huon struck him so powerfully
On the top of his helmet where the carbuncle shone[11]
That it could not offer the least protection:
Neither the white coif over his head	910
Nor the hauberk, which was shining with interlaced mail,
Could protect him or keep him
From being sliced open down to his chest.
Huon broke his neck and knocked him from his horse;
Charlot fell dead on the ground upon his back.	915
The traitor Amaury observed this from the thicket.
You can be certain that he was very pleased.
He said to his men, "Now I'm overjoyed!
Charlot is dead, may God be blessed.
France has no heir, and I will rule the land.	920

11. A carbuncle is a bright red precious stone, often identified as a garnet, placed
on top of a helmet. It was thought to have magical, protective properties.

Before the year is out, I'll have killed Charlemagne!"
Meanwhile Huon seized the Arabian steed
That was running loose after he had killed Charlot.
He quickly grabbed it by the reins,
Led it to Gerard, and said: 925
"My brother, in the name of God in paradise,
Are you still able to ride a horse?"
"I'm not sure," the young man replied,
"But bandage up my wound, I beg you."
"By my head, I'll do so!" said Huon.   930
He dismounted from his Arabian steed
And took his burnished sword in hand.
He cut off a piece of his own tunic
And carefully bandaged his brother's wound.
Then he helped the young man to his feet.   935
All ten of his knights approached
To be of any assistance they could.
They grasped Gerard by his sides
And lifted him up upon his worthy steed.
Once up, he nearly fell from his saddle   940
And fainted three times from the pain he was feeling.
When he came to, he called to Huon:
"My brother," he said, "listen to me:
To where will we flee? By the ever-truthful God,
Let's return to the city of Bordeaux,   945
To our mother who raised us so tenderly.
I'm so frightened that my blood is boiling,
Because we have slain a man here.
We don't know what sort of people are his friends,
And in these woods, I see a hundred helmets shining.   950
By the God of paradise, I'm quite surprised
That they haven't come out of the bushes.
Otherwise they'd have attacked and killed us!
But I'm very sure, by St. Denis,
That treachery has brought them here.   955
By God, let's return to the city of Bordeaux,

To our mother who raised us so tenderly."
"May it not please God," replied Huon,
"That I ever see Bordeaux's walls again
Before I have beheld the king of Saint-Denis!   960
If I find Charles, the proud-faced king,
I will accuse him of treason in your name,
Because he tried to have us killed in his safe conduct."
Gerard replied, "My lord, let it be as you please."
Then they spurred on their worthy steeds   965
And set forth directly for Paris.
The men in hiding called to Amaury:
"What will we do, mighty and noble count?
Charlot, the noble youth, is dead.
Are we just going to allow these evil men,   970
Who killed him before our eyes, to ride away?"
"Listen to me," replied Amaury,
"Let these poor orphans go.
We will follow them to the court in Paris,
And when we reach the vaulted palace   975
And present ourselves to the mighty king,
I will lay his son's body down before him.
When you agree with everything I say,
I will reward you, as God is my witness,
So generously that you will never be poor."   980
And they replied, "Let it be as you wish."
With this, they left their hiding place
And came straight to Charlot, still lying in the clearing,
Sliced open down to his chest.
The traitor Amaury was in the lead;   985
Together with his men he seized Charlot's body
And placed it upon a curved shield.
Amaury mounted his worthy steed
And placed the noble youth before him —
May he be damned by God in paradise!   990
They then set off after Huon.
May God watch over Huon and Gerard,

For if not, they have come to the end of their days.
The two young men were riding along
In the company of their men, grieving with heads bowed.	995
The sad orphans rode and rode
Until they overtook the abbot of Cluny.
When the abbot saw them, he stopped
And called pleasantly to Huon:
"What have you done, good cousin?" he asked.	1000
"My lord," said Huon, "we have killed a man."
"Young men," said the abbot, "this is truly upsetting.
Ride along in my company.
I will always speak up for you."
"My lord," replied Huon, "may God reward you for this."	1005
At this moment proud-faced Huon looked
And saw the hauberks and shining helmets
Of the traitors that were pursuing them.
Count Amaury was in the lead,
Keeping his distance at a gentle pace.	1010
When Huon saw him, his blood surged.
He called to the abbot as you will hear:
"My lord, what is to become of me?
I am being pursued by the same evil traitors
Who attacked me in the leafy woods."	1015
"Fair nephew," the abbot replied, "don't be afraid.
Ride on and may God be with you,
Because it seems to me, they are making no effort
To overtake you. They don't appear to be in a hurry."
So they spurred their good valuable horses	1020
And rode swiftly toward Paris.
Without slowing down, the noble youths
And the abbot of Cluny and his monks
Entered the beautiful city of Paris.
They did not slow down until they reached the palace	1025
Where they dismounted before its marble steps
And strode up into the vaulted palace.
Huon walked to the right of his brother Gerard,

While the noble abbot supported him on the left.
When they entered the room with the marquis,   1030
The good and noble Huon spoke out:
"May the Lord, who died on the cross
And whose side was pierced by Longinus,
Save and watch over gray-haired Duke Naimes
And the exalted men and all the marquis   1035
Whom I see sitting here with him,
And may He condemn Charles of Saint-Denis
As a traitor and a wicked king,
Who sent for us by his sealed letters.
We came here in order to serve him,   1040
But he sought to have us killed while in his safe conduct."
"Vassal," said Charlemagne, "be careful what you say!
In all my life I've never countenanced treason,
So watch out, for God in paradise,
Because by the noble St. Denis   1045
And by the beard that reaches my chest,
If you cannot back up your words
I'll have you put to a painful death."
"My lord," said Huon, "you are the one I mean:
Watch out, king, and may God damn you!"   1050
He took hold of his brother whom the abbot was supporting;
He removed his sable cloak
And then the ermine lining;
Next he unbandaged the young man's wound,
Which opened and began to bleed.   1055
The youth fainted from the pain.
Charles saw all this and began to grieve.
"Upon my word," he said, "this boy is about to die!
Whoever did this to him had little love for me.
Holy Mary, what is to become of me?   1060
In foreign lands they will recount
That in my old age, when I was about to die,
I had this young child murdered!
But, by almighty God above,

I knew nothing of this and am sorely grieved.   1065
Had I known, this would never have happened!
And I swear by the beard that reaches my chest
And by my faith in Jesus Christ
And by the noble St. Denis,
That if there is any man from Reims to Paris —   1070
However high born or however much my friend —
Who is guilty of this and I can catch him,
I will make him suffer a terrible death.
Upon the body of St. Fremin, he will regret this ambush!"
Charles called for a skilled doctor   1075
And had him examine the boy's wound.
"See if he can be healed," Charles said,
And the doctor replied, "As you wish."
Then he examined the wound carefully
And told the king, "Don't worry so much,   1080
This wound won't keep him from drinking wine:
I'll have him healed within a month."
Hearing this, Charles was much relieved.
They laid Gerard upon a bed
And Charlemagne said to Huon: 1085
"Listen to what I have to say, my friend:
Go over and sit on those benches
And drink from my cup of wine."
"My lord," Huon replied, "may God reward you for this!
For the love of God, noble emperor,   1090
Listen to me, both you and your marquis.
Why hide it? I killed the man
Who struck my brother in the side.
I don't know where he was born,
But I do know that he is being brought here now.   1095
No matter whom I killed with my burnished steel sword,
I submit to the laws of this land
As judged by the peers and marquis."
"Huon," said Charles, "don't worry,
No man alive will do you any harm."   1100

8

Now quiet down, my lords, by almighty God,
And you will hear a song filled with terrible deeds:
How Amaury, the vile scoundrel,
Came to Paris on his swift steed,
And the fierce and heavy sorrow that ensued.   1105
Young Huon stood upright in front of Charles
In the gleaming palace.
He stepped forward to address the king.
"Righteous emperor," said noble Huon,
"May God help me, I have something to say: 1110
You summoned me by a sealed letter,
And I came to serve you,
For I have nothing but the greatest affection for you.
My brother and I were riding along,
Accompanied by ten valiant knights   1115
And the noble abbot with all his monks.
My guard was down, and I suspected nothing,
When suddenly I was attacked in a leafy thicket,
Where I don't know how many knights were lying in wait.
I think there were a good hundred,   1120
With dark shields and gleaming helmets.
One of them came forward,
Clad in a white hauberk, his helmet laced,
His shield suspended from his shoulder, and a sharp blade in his fist.
The noble abbot spotted him first   1125
And immediately pointed him out to me.
He then made me a most courteous offer,
Saying that if I knew anyone alive
From whom I might have wrongly
Taken even a penny, he would repay it: 1130
He was prepared to replace it with a besant.[12]
I sent my brother ahead

12.   The offer is indeed generous, as the *besant* was a gold coin from Byzantium
worth considerably more than a *denier*.

To find out what this man wanted.
He rode up quickly
And spoke to him civilly and courteously,   1135
But I don't know exactly what they said.
I never heard a word of it, so help me God.
I saw the knight draw back,
And I thought he was returning
To the thicket, so help me God,   1140
But he turned around swiftly
And struck my valiant brother
Right in his side with his sharp, unbending spear.
You can see the wound clearly, right here.
I saw my brother fall from his horse,   1145
And when I saw him, my heart filled with sorrow.
Tearfully, I asked the abbot
If he and his noble monks could help me,
But he replied quite frankly
That their task was to say mass,   1150
And thus, they could be of no help whatsoever.
When I heard this, my heart filled with sorrow.
I called upon the ten knights
I'd brought from Bordeaux,
Asking them to help me,   1155
And they said, by almighty God,
That they would help me even if they lost their limbs.
I rode forward, angry and sorrowful;
My men followed close behind,
But I was ahead of them by about seventy-five yards.[13]   1160
I came up to my brother, who lay bleeding in the meadow;
He kept fainting from the excruciating pain.
Weeping, I asked him
If he had any hope of recovery,

13. Medieval distances are measured in leagues and "acres" (*arpents*), as we today
use miles and "football fields." A league is equal to about three miles, while an
arpent is a unit of land area approximately equal to an acre. As a unit of length,
it is equal to one side of a square forming an *arpent*, or about seventy-five yards.

And he replied that he didn't know. 1165
I left him lying there in the grass
And spurred my horse toward the knight,
Who was going back to the thicket,
Riding confidently and looking quite smug.
I followed him at a gallop 1170
And shouted at the top of my lungs:
'Why have you killed my valiant brother?'
He replied that he'd do the same to me,
Wounding me in the side, as he had done to my brother.
I asked him who he was and from what family, 1175
And he said he was from mighty Germany.
He also claimed that my father, when he was alive,
Seized three well-situated castles from him
And that he has never been justly compensated for them.
That was why he was challenging me. 1180
I then became frightened,
For he wore a hauberk and a shiny green-gold helmet,
While I had only my sharp sword.
I removed the mantle that was around my neck
And wrapped it around my arm. 1185
He spurred his horse toward me
And struck me with his sharp spear,
Ripping my mantle to shreds.
By the grace of God the Redeemer,
He did me no harm whatsoever. 1190
As he rode by, I dealt him such a fierce blow
On the top of his green-gold helmet
That it sliced through right to his chest.
I took his horse and rode back
To get my brother and raise him onto the swift steed. 1195
I then hurried to rejoin the abbot,
Who had been watching and waiting for me.
He saw everything I am telling you now.
The men in the thicket remained still
Until I had put a good league between us. 1200

I then looked and saw
That they were advancing softly and slowly.
One of them was out in front,
Carrying the bloody corpse."
"Truly," said Naimes, "I have no doubt   1205
That these men are all vile traitors."
"Sire," said Huon, "in the name of God the Redeemer,
There is no point in belaboring the matter:
I killed that knight in self-defense,
As witnessed by the abbot, here present,   1210
And all his monks, whom I call upon as guarantors,
For I know quite well that they are bringing the body here,
And I don't know where the knight is from or who his people are.
I came to ask you for protection:
Handle my case fairly, in the name of God the Redeemer.   1215
I am one of your peers, as you well know.
Whoever it was that I killed with my sharp sword,
I leave the matter to the judgment
Of the French, the Bavarians, and the Germans."
"Huon," said Charles, "sit down on that bench   1220
And drink some white wine from my cup,
For, by the One who spilled his blood for mankind,
However valiant the knight who ambushed you,
I will make him suffer for it.
If I get hold of him, so help me God,   1225
I'll see to it that he dies a horrible death!
I'll have him burned, hanged, or strung up to sway in the wind.
By the faith I owe St. Amand,
Even if you killed one of my own children,
Such as my son Charlot, whom I love so dearly,   1230
You would have no cause to fear
Unless you were guilty of treason."
"Sire," said Huon, "I thank you a thousand times over."
The king called Gadin and Guinemant:
"Go and find my son Charlot.   1235
He will keep company with these two noble young men."

And they replied, "Just as you command."
They went into the city and looked everywhere,
But believe me, their search was in vain,
For at that very moment, Amaury was bringing the bloody corpse,   1240
Stretched out on a gleaming shield
In front of him.
Just as Charles and Huon were speaking,
Amaury was riding into Paris.
He entered the city with his companions,   1245
Bringing Charlot's lifeless body.
They were weeping and sobbing in a show of profound grief,
Wringing their hands and tearing out their hair.
When the townspeople recognized Charlot,
You may be sure they were overcome with grief.   1250
Ladies, squires, and servants wept,
Lamenting the loss of Charlot the warrior.
Amaury and his men rode on,
Making their way swiftly to the palace.
There the wretched traitors dismounted.   1255
Charles heard his son's name
And said to Naimes, "I hear people grieving and lamenting."

9

White-haired Charles listened carefully
And heard the hue and cry.
He spoke to Naimes, saying softly,   1260
"Naimes, I heard my son's name.
I think he is the one Huon killed.
For God's sake, go and see!"
"Certainly," replied Naimes.
He leapt to his feet and obeyed without hesitation,   1265
Hurrying down the marble staircase.
He arrived at the landing where Amaury stood
And saw Charlot lying on the shield,
Dripping with blood, his body split all the way to his chest.

Seeing this, Naimes began to tremble all over.   1270
He fainted three times on top of the prince.
When he came to, they took the body
And carried it into the vaulted palace.
All of the lords were lamenting.
Behold Amaury, the vile scoundrel!   1275
He was holding one side of the curved shield
And Naimes the other.
Amaury was shouting:
"Righteous emperor, here is your son,
Young Charlot, whom you loved so dearly!"   1280
When Charles heard this, all his blood surged.
Seeing his son dead and mutilated,
He fainted on the body five or six times.
When he came to, he exclaimed:
"Blessed Mary, what a horrible gift!"   1285
"Sire," said Naimes, "in the name of heavenly God,
Do what is expected of your noble rank:
Ask that scoundrel Amaury,
For God's sake, who killed your son."
"I hereby ask him," said Charlemagne.   1290
Amaury declared, "You will hear it now:
The young man I see sitting over there,
Drinking your wine from a cup,
He is the one who killed your son, so help me God."
When Charles heard this, all his blood surged.   1295
He looked at noble young Huon.
Seeing a knife lying on a table,
He seized it with both hands
And was about to stab Huon in the chest
When Duke Naimes snatched the knife, exclaiming: 1300
"Sire, have you lost your senses?
This morning you guaranteed this young man's safety,
And now you want to stab him with your knife?
For God's sake, that would be murder!"

10

There was great sorrow in the gleaming palace.   1305
Ladies, squires, and servants wept bitterly.
All were lamenting the loss of Charlot the warrior.
King Charles was brokenhearted.
He fainted repeatedly on his son's body.
Duke Naimes said to him: 1310
"Lord, in the name of almighty God,
Conduct yourself as befitting a sensible man:
Do not be carried away by grief,
For this is how a child would behave."
"Naimes," said Charles, "it is heartbreaking   1315
To see my beloved son dead!"
"Charles," replied Naimes, "by St. Vincent,
When the brave and valiant Ogier
Fought against you and all your people,
He killed my son, whom I loved dearly   1320
And who served as your brave and valiant messenger.
Did I carry on like this, grieving and lamenting?
Not at all, by God! I consoled myself.
Ah, emperor, by almighty God,
Put aside your immoderate grief.   1325
Since he is dead, grieving is of no use.
Instead, for God's sake,
Ask Lord Amaury who killed your son."
"I hereby ask him," said noble Charles.
Amaury replied, "You will hear it now: 1330
The young man seated on that bench,
Whom I see drinking your white wine from your cup,
So help me God, he is the one who killed your son!"
When Charles heard this, his blood boiled.
He gave Huon a furious look   1335
And clenched his teeth in anger.
Seeing a knife on the table,
He grabbed it quickly

And was about to stab Huon in the side
When Naimes snatched the knife from his fist.   1340
"Sire," said Naimes, "have you lost your senses?
What are you trying to do, by St. Amand?
When Huon came to this shining palace,
In the presence of all the French you assured him
That he had nothing to fear from a living soul.   1345
If you stabbed him with that sharp knife,
It would be murder, I assure you,
And you would bring shame and disgrace upon yourself."
"Naimes," said Charles, "it is heartbreaking
To see my beloved son dead like this!"   1350
When Huon heard Charles speaking in this manner
And saw his ferocious countenance,
You may be sure that he was quite alarmed.
When he realized that the man he had killed with his sword
Was Charlemagne's son, he was terrified,   1355
And with good reason.
Nonetheless, he maintained an agreeable expression
As he rose to his feet
And moved away from noble Charlemagne,
Addressing him in a suitable manner: 1360
"Righteous emperor," said valiant Huon,
"Don't threaten me with that knife.
I recognize, God help me,
That I killed the man I see lying there.
However, by the One who spilled his blood,   1365
I didn't know he was your son.
Had I known, by St. Amand,
That it was your son I killed with my sword,
Do you think I would be so foolish
As to come to your court looking for protection?   1370
Certainly not, by God the Redeemer!
I would have fled to Bocidant
Rather than come to your court looking for protection.
I do not deny that I killed this man,

But I did so in self-defense. 1375
Do not threaten me, sire!
Why would you burn towns and castles
And send poor people to their death?
As you can see, I am here in your shining palace:
Whomever I killed with my sharp sword, 1380
I submit to judgment by the French.
I will make reparations to you, valiant emperor,
As judged appropriate by Bavarians and Germans."
The French declared, "What he says is fitting:
If Amaury has anything to say about your son, 1385
Let him do so immediately."

11

Charles looked at white-haired Naimes
And said, "Give me counsel, Lord Naimes.
What do you have to say about my son's murder?"
"Sire," said Naimes, "I am deeply saddened by it. 1390
For the love of God, who never lied,
Ask that scoundrel Amaury
Why your son, whom I see lying there,
Went into the woods wearing a hauberk.
Blessed Mary, what was he looking for?" 1395
"I will tell you," replied Amaury,
"And if I am lying, may God destroy me:
Last evening, at twilight,
Your son Charlot came looking for me at my lodgings
And asked me to go hunting with him. 1400
I did so, but by God, what a mistake!
I feared Thierry of Ardennes:
That is why we wore our hauberks.
In that wooded area not far from Paris,
We went to hunt together, he and I, 1405
And we flew our goshawks over the moor.
We lost a bird late in the day, at dusk.

This morning, at daybreak,
We happened upon Gerard and Huon.
Huon, the elder brother, had captured the bird.   1410
When your son Charlot asked him for it,
The traitor flatly refused.
They argued so vehemently that Charlot struck Gerard.
When Huon saw this, he drew his burnished sword
And sliced Charlot all the way down to his chest.   1415
He then turned around and fled right in front of me,
Along with his brother, both on their worthy steeds.
To my dismay, I was unable to catch up with them.
He killed your son knowingly and deliberately,
And if he claims that I have lied,   1420
Here is my pledge: I swear to you
That I will make him confess out loud
That everything I told you here is true."
"Blessed Mary," said the abbot of Cluny,
"No one has ever heard such a monstrous lie!   1425
I am prepared to swear, along with eighty monks,
That everything this scoundrel said is a lie."
"That is certainly persuasive testimony," said Charles.
"What is your response, Count Amaury?"
"Sire," he said, "I swear to God,   1430
The abbot may say whatever he likes,
For I do not seek to contradict him in your presence.
He is a man of high standing with noble allies,
An ordained holy priest.
But, by the One who was hung on the cross,   1435
I will make Huon confess aloud
That everything I told you here is true."
When the abbot heard this, he was incensed.
Turning his eyes toward Huon, he said:
"Huon, what are you doing? Fair cousin,   1440
Offer your pledge, for you are in the right.
If you are defeated or severely injured,
And God consents to the injustice,

If ever I am able to return to Cluny,
I will beat St. Peter's statue   1445
Until I make all the gold fall off his head!"
"My lord," said Huon, "do not get so angry.
I will do as you please."
Young Huon came before Charles
And spoke to him graciously, saying: 1450
"Sire, please listen to me.
Here is my pledge: I swear to you
That everything this scoundrel has said is a lie.
I will make him swear out loud
That when I came into Paris   1455
I didn't know whom I had killed.
I didn't know it was your son."
"You must provide hostages," said proud-faced Charles.[14]
"Sire," replied Huon, "Just as you please.
My brother Gerard is over there.   1460
I have no other hostage in this vaulted palace,
For I see no cousins or relatives
Of mine here in this vaulted palace."
"You have me," said the abbot of Cluny.
"Out of friendship,[15] I will vouch for you as well.   1465
If you are defeated or severely injured,
And God consents to the injustice,
May Charles, the king of Saint-Denis, be shamed
If he does not hang me before nightfall,
Along with my eighty monks!"   1470
"Abbot," exclaimed Charles, "you are wrong, by holy Christ!

14. The *judicium Dei*, or judicial combat, inherited from Germanic custom, was used to resolve conflicts and determine the innocence or guilt of those accused of a crime. Both parties offered hostages as security. In principle, the outcome was assured by divine intervention, justifying the righteous and condemning the guilty. The practice had already begun to decline by the twelfth century but continued to be a standard motif in the epic repertory.

15. Old French *amour* designates social as well as personal bonds. The abbot acts out of affection for Huon, and also out of family loyalty.

May it never please God, who hung on the cross,
That I do you any harm in my lifetime.
Please leave the arrangements to us.
Provide hostages, Amaury."   1475
"Sire, I offer you Rainfroy and Heudri, here present:
One is my uncle, the other my cousin."
"And I accept them," said proud-faced Charles,
"Under the following conditions:
If you are defeated or severely injured,   1480
I will have them dragged behind packhorses."[16]
Hearing this, Rainfroy replied to Charles:
"Cursed be anyone who agrees to such conditions!"
"And what do you propose?" asked Charlemagne.
"In God's name, sire, the risk of losing our lands."   1485
The emperor replied, "As you wish.
But remember, by the One who was raised on the cross,
If Amaury is defeated or severely injured,
You will no longer hold even a foot of your land.
Instead, you will be driven out and banished!"   1490

12

The pledges were given
And the hostages turned over to Charles.
They were bound hand and foot with solid shackles,
And you may be sure that the king had them closely guarded.
Charles summoned the two combatants: 1495
"Barons, stand up at once
And go without delay to the field of honor.

16. Rainfroy responds so angrily here because Charlemagne proposes to have
the loser's hostages dragged behind *roncins*, or packhorses, which would be much
more degrading even than being dragged behind riding horses (*chevaux*), as the
formula states elsewhere in our poem. A defeated knight would rather lose his
lands than lose face. Medieval texts distinguish between packhorses (*roncins*,
sommiers), saddle horses or palfreys (*palefrois*) for general riding, and horses to
be ridden in combat (*destriers*, *chevaux de garde*, or simply *chevaux*). These latter
are more valuable, better fed, and better cared for.

By the One who suffered on the cross,
Before my son is put in the ground,
The loser will be dragged to the gallows and hanged."   1500
Charles called to bearded Duke Naimes:
"Naimes, listen to me carefully:
You will take a hundred armed knights,
And you yourself should be fully prepared.
Go to the field of honor in the midst of those meadows   1505
And take these two knights with you.
Please guard the area with great care
To prevent any sort of treachery or wrongdoing.
Under no circumstances should there be
Any talk of treachery."   1510
"Sire," said Naimes, "it will be as you command."
The good duke armed himself,
Putting on his hauberk and fastening his helmet.
He girded his gold-pommeled sword
And quickly mounted his horse, Morel.   1515
He had a hundred knights armed to accompany him.
They too mounted their horses, which were saddled and ready.
King Charles issued a proclamation:
"If anyone should be so bold or foolhardy —
However high his rank, however powerful his family —   1520
As to harm the combatants in word or in deed,
He will be hanged or dragged by horses."
The barons proceeded to the church
To attend the mass celebrated by the lord abbot.

13

Toward the church went the noble barons.   1525
Now, listen to what Huon did:
He had a large barrel
Filled with Parisian coins
And ordered them to be distributed to the poor,
Who cried out in clear, resounding voices: 1530

"May the One who was raised on the cross protect you
And grant you a joyful return!"
The abbot of Cluny celebrated mass.
When the service was over,
Huon prostrated himself on one side of the altar   1535
And Amaury on the other.
All around them blazed tall candles
Arranged in the form of a cross on the paving stones.
Amaury's candles would not stand upright
But fell to the ground with all the barons watching.   1540
Huon's, however, stood tall.
The Frenchmen said, "That knight should be glad.
By God, he will be victorious on the battlefield!"
Huon prostrated himself before the altar in the form of a cross
And prayed to God in heaven: 1545
"God, you who have never lied,[17]
Just as it is true that you were born
In Bethlehem, as it is recorded in Holy Scripture,
Without a single woman present to receive you
Except a fair-faced lady   1550
Named St. Anastasia, I believe,
Who had no hands, as is well known.
She received you, God, with the stumps of her hands.
As soon as she held you, you performed a miracle:
Suddenly she had hands with long, slender fingers.   1555
Then, Lord, the three kings came to see you.
Cruel Herod was infuriated
When he heard about you.
He sent his soldiers throughout the land

---

17.   The prayer that follows is known as an "epic credo." In this traditional motif,
the hero facing great danger invokes sacred history to affirm the validity of his cause
and ask for God's protection. After recounting a series of episodes from the New
Testament and popular religious legend, Huon will swear by these truths to pray
for victory against the deceitful Amaury. Many epic credos include references to the
Old Testament as well. Other epic credos in the poem are pronounced by the abbot
of Saint-Denis at lines 1981–2088 and Huon at lines 2879–98 and 5246–84.

To decapitate all the two-and-a-half-year-old children,   1560
Using burnished swords,
For he believed this was the way to kill you,
But you were able to escape his clutches.
You traveled about for thirty-two years
With your worthy apostles.   1565
One of them hated you from the very beginning:
His name was Judas, and he was a lying traitor.
He sold you, Lord, to the Jews.
You were hung on the cross,
Where you suffered and died, as we all know.   1570
Longinus pierced you with a lance.
Your death was not to punish you, but to benefit us,
That you might save us from the devil's grip.
You were placed in the sepulcher,
And on the third day, you rose from the dead.   1575
You descended into hell
To liberate the righteous.
On a special Thursday,
Called the Feast of the Ascension,
You ascended into heaven.   1580
Deprived of you, your apostles
Were downcast and forlorn,
But on Pentecost, you came to comfort them.
When you kissed them, they were joyful
And so inspired that they suddenly knew   1585
The languages of all countries.
Just as everything I have said is true,
And I fervently believe it,
Please protect me, true and heavenly God,
From defeat, and let me vanquish   1590
That scoundrel Amaury,
For truly, dear King of heaven,
That scoundrel Amaury has wrongly accused me."
Then proud-faced Huon stood up
And made the sign of the cross.   1595

The worthy young man
Kissed the altar and left an offering.
The scoundrel Amaury did the same.
The wine was brought into the church,
And courtly Huon had his meal,   1600
As did the scoundrel Amaury.
When the two noblemen had eaten their fill,
They both left the church:
First courtly Huon,
Who often prayed to the King of heaven,   1605
And then the scoundrel Amaury,
Who did not bow before the altar or the crucifix.
They were brought to the vaulted palace.
The noble abbot stayed close to Huon,
As did white-haired Duke Naimes,   1610
And the powerful men clad in armor.
On the other side was Amaury,
Accompanied by Rainfroy and Heudri
As well as thirty-six traitors.
When the barons reached the palace,   1615
The king spoke to them, saying:
"Barons, put on your armor.
What are you waiting for, by St. Denis?
Proceed to the field of honor, by God in heaven!
By the One who was hung on the cross,   1620
Before my son is put in the ground,
Whoever is defeated will be dragged around Paris.
May the true God allow me to see which man is right,
And may the perjurer be destroyed on this day."
"May God grant your wish!" said the noble barons.   1625
They put on their armor and equipped themselves well.
Worthy Huon prepared for battle:
He laced up his boots, white as lilies,
And attached his spurs.
He then put on the hauberk that Seguin had given him   1630
And girded his gold-pommeled sword.

Amaury equipped himself as well.
When the two barons were armed,
The relics were brought before them.
Whoever perjured himself would not survive the battle.   1635
"Who will take the oath first?" asked the barons.
"The accusers," said white-haired Naimes.
"Then I will take my oath, sire," said Amaury.
The relics were placed on a carpet,
And Amaury knelt down.   1640
In a loud voice, he spoke the words you are about to hear:
"Listen to me, my lords!
I hereby swear upon the relics you see before you
And upon all the other saints in heaven —
May they cause me no harm on this day! —   1645
That when Huon of Bordeaux
Killed proud-faced Charlot, he knew perfectly well
That he was the son of Charles of Saint-Denis.
He knowingly killed Charles's son
And then fled to Paris to cover up his crime.   1650
Thus, I swear by God in heaven,
And upon the relics here before me,
That I will make him confess aloud
Before this evening, when we meet in battle,
That he killed the young man treacherously.   1655
It is only just that he be put to death!"
He tried to kiss and venerate the relics,
But his breath failed him, and he nearly fell.
He could not approach them for all the gold in Paris.
The wretch tottered and nearly fell over backwards.   1660
"He is the liar," said the barons.
Courtly Huon came forward
And seized the traitor by his fist,
Pushing him aside as one would a liar.
He knelt before the relics   1665
And said loudly, so that all could hear:
"Listen to me, my lords," said Huon,

"I hereby swear upon the relics before me,
And upon all of God's saints —
May no harm come to me on this day! —   1670
That everything this scoundrel has said is a lie.
I do not deny that I killed Charlot,
But by the One who was hung on the cross,
When I entered the city of Paris
I did not know whom I had killed,   1675
Nor did I know who his father was:
I didn't know that he was Charlemagne's son."
"Surely," said the abbot, "he has told the truth!"
Huon stood up to venerate the relics
And kissed them before all the assembled barons.   1680
Afterward he made an offering of four marks,
Which the cleric accepted gladly.
The French said, "That man should take heart,
For he will surely win the battle."
The sun indicated that the time had come,   1685
So proud-faced Charlemagne called out:
"Now to the field of honor without delay,
And I pray God, the King of heaven,
That whoever is defeated on this day will be destroyed!"
"May God grant your wish!" said the barons.   1690
Huon's horse was brought to him,
And he mounted. May God help him!
The abbot of Cluny held his stirrups,
Despite Huon's protests.
They kissed each other as they took leave.   1695
God, how the abbot wept!
"My lord," said Huon, "in the name of God, pray for me!"
"I will do so without fail," said the abbot.
"May the One who was hung on the cross guide you!
Just as surely as I know that you are innocent   1700
Of everything Amaury has accused you of,
May God protect you from all harm!"
Noble Huon took his leave,

And the good abbot did not forget him:
He went into the church, in front of the crucifix,   1705
And prostrated himself at the altar, his body forming a cross.
He prayed that Huon would come to no harm.
Huon and Count Amaury
Made their way to the field of honor,
Led by white-haired Duke Naimes.   1710
When the two knights arrived,
They were both struck with fear.
Mighty King Charles and his princes
Took their places at the battlements,
With Rainfroy and Heudri beside them.   1715
On the other side was young Gerard.
The hostages' feet were bound by metal shackles.
They too were at the battlements
To watch and observe the duel.
God! How Charles prayed for Amaury   1720
And cursed courtly Huon!
The two knights were in the flowery meadow.
White-haired Duke Naimes summoned them:
"My lords," he said, "In the name of God in heaven,
Proceed to the field of honor, for it is almost noon."   1725

14

"My lords," said Naimes, "listen to me:
The king has gone up to the battlements,
Surrounded on all sides by his barons.
Everyone is watching us. For God in majesty
And in the name of St. Honoré, enter the field."   1730
They replied, "Just as you wish!"
They headed for the gate at once,
And as they were about to enter the field,
The emperor began to shout:
"My lords, have them turn back.   1735
I wish to speak to them a little more."

So they had them brought back
To stand once more before the king.
"My lords," said Charlemagne, "listen carefully to what I say:
I tell you, as God is my Savior,   1740
I would like to go beyond the law here.[18]
Huon," he continued, "pay special attention
Because, by the One who suffered upon the cross,
If you kill Sir Amaury
And he does not confess, you will lose your lands   1745
And will never again hold as much as a foot of them."
"My lord," replied Huon, "you may do as you wish."
"Truly," said Naimes, "I've never heard anything like this!
Be aware, noble king, that you abuse your power
And wrong him, by God in majesty!"   1750
"Indeed," said Charles, "I have made up my mind.
I will not do otherwise, no matter who objects!"
Then he spoke to Amaury of Viemez.

15

"Listen to me, Amaury," said Charlemagne.
"As God is my friend, I say the same to you: 1755
If you defeat Huon in the field of honor
And he does not confess, so help me God,
You will never again hold a single foot of your lands
As long as I am alive."
"Sire," said Naimes, "by all the saints of God,   1760
You wrong these noble barons,

18. Charlemagne here adds a condition to the judicial combat that is arbitrary and unique. The outcome of the combat itself was believed to indicate unmistakably who was in the right. Charlemagne, however, goes "beyond the law" (or rules) of the combat by adding a non-normative condition: that even if Huon defeats Amaury, the king will not accept the outcome unless Amaury actually confesses his sinful action before he is slain. This abuse of power is clearly indicated by Naimes's reaction in lines 1748–50. The poet has already foreshadowed who is in the right by Amaury's candles falling (lines 1539–40) and his inability to approach or kiss the holy relics after swearing his false oath (lines 1657ff).

For we've often seen two champions die
Before either could speak or confess his wrong."
"I don't care," said Charlemagne,
"So help me God, there is no other way.   1765
Make haste now, for God in paradise,
Because I'm eager for the fight to be over."
Then the noble knights led them back to the field.
They donned their armor and made ready to fight.
Huon, the worthy youth, put on his armor: 1770
He hung a shield of dark blue from his neck
Then laced on his helmet with its carbuncle.
A knight from his own lands
Handed him a good spear of burnished iron
To which a gonfanon was attached.   1775
Huon, who was exceptionally noble, seized it,
Then turned and took his leave
Of the barons who accompanied him.
Wicked Amaury did likewise
And entered the field once he was fully armed.   1780
As soon as he was there, the evil traitor
Spurred on his swift and worthy steed
And executed a flashy French turn.[19]
Amaury was tall and strong, thick of chest,
And a brave and hardy knight.   1785
Had he not also been a dishonest, traitorous liar,
Courtly Huon would not have stood a chance,
But he did not believe in God any more than in a mangy dog.
Next proud-faced Huon entered the field,
Quietly and without show, though unafraid.   1790
He called often upon the God of paradise.
The young man was handsome in body and face.
There was no more handsome youth in any land.

19.   A "French turn" is an equestrian maneuver by which a knight abruptly wheels
his horse around in order to charge swiftly back into combat. It is mentioned also
at lines 6707 and 8059 in our poem, as well as in other French *chansons de geste*.

16

Now both barons have entered the field of honor.
On one side was Amaury of Viemez: 1795
He was tall and strong and beautifully armed.
He was much taller than Huon.
He measured a good foot taller, I believe,
And was over fifty years old.
Huon was a young knight,   1800
Not yet twenty-two years of age.
Across the field he remained completely silent,
His head bowed beneath his helmet,
Although he was not afraid:
He was upset and angry   1805
And called out repeatedly to God in majesty.
Then Duke Naimes shouted:
"Barons, what are you waiting for?
The sun is favorable.
Begin the battle, in the name of St. Honoré,   1810
And I pray to God, the King of majesty,
To let us see and behold the truth.
May the perjurer be shamed this day
And be dragged from the field and hanged."
All the barons responded, "May God's will be done!"   1815
With that, the two barons took the field
About seventy-five yards one from the other, I believe.
Huon spurred his swift steed
And rushed headlong toward Amaury,
Who charged fearlessly toward Huon.   1820
Their unbending lances struck
Their gold-banded shields,
Splitting them open beneath the pointed bosses,
But their hauberks were so tightly woven
That not a single link was severed.   1825
Nonetheless, their chests, their bodies,
Their strong-banded shields,

The breasts of their swift steeds,
And their green-gold helmets clashed together
So mightily that bright blood poured from their nostrils   1830
And their eyes were so shaken
That the pain made them both shed tears.
Their saddle girths failed, their saddle bows split,
And both men were thrown to the ground
Over the rumps of their horses   1835
So roughly and so violently
That the tops of their helmets dug into the earth
While their heels stretched toward the heavens.
The French exclaimed, "What a joust!
By Holy Mary, mother of mercy,   1840
How could Huon withstand such a blow?
It's a great wonder that it didn't kill him."
All the barons rose to their feet.
Huon's horse saw Amaury's across the field
And rushed swiftly toward it.   1845
Mad Amaury's horse
Began to whinny deafeningly,
But Huon's steed was the more powerful.
With its front hooves it started to paw the ground
And with its rear hooves it began to lash out.   1850
It struck Amaury's horse such a blow
Right on the forehead
That its brains spilled forth
And its two eyes popped out.
The horse was finished   1855
And fell down dead upon the field.
Seeing this, Amaury's blood began to boil.
He had not suffered so much since the day he was born.
The French exclaimed, "What a blow!
God has shown us a great miracle.   1860
Young Huon can be very happy
Since this combat will be won by him."
Without hesitating, Amaury

Rushed toward Huon's horse,
Which had returned to the field   1865
And was awaiting its master.
Amaury was holding his steely sword,
Which he had drawn from his scabbard.
Angrily he approached Huon's horse,
Thinking to strike it with his steely sword,   1870
But the horse had never seen him before
And did not recognize him, so it backed away.
Then it raised a rear hoof
And gave Amaury such a powerful kick
Upon the hauberk he was wearing   1875
That it shattered two of his ribs.
He fainted to the ground from the pain,
But stood up again as quickly as possible,
For he was very afraid of young Huon.
The French exclaimed, "He missed his prey this time!   1880
He would have done better to stay home."
And when Huon saw his opponent so overwhelmed,
He felt happier than he ever had.
Holding in his hand the good steely sword
With which he had slain Charlot in the leafy woods,   1885
Huon hastened toward the traitorous Amaury.
He tried to strike the top of Amaury's helmet,
But the traitor raised his shield on high,
And Huon gave it such a whack
That the shield was split in two.   1890
The blow fell onto Amaury's helmet,
Sending its jeweled and flowered decorations flying.
But the green-gold helmet was so well tempered
That it did not do a penny's worth of harm.
Seeing this, Huon was shocked.   1895
And Amaury was so sorely wounded
That he thought he would go crazy!
He raised the sword he was holding
And went bravely after Huon.

Huon feared the blow he saw coming, 1900
Because he feared Amaury more than anyone,
Since he was tall and strong and muscular.
Huon took his gold-banded shield
And held it up before his face;
The traitor struck such a fearsome whack 1905
Upon Huon's shield — may God strike him dead! —
That a piece of it fell to the ground,
And the blow struck young Huon's green-gold helmet,
Knocking off its precious stones
And denting it somewhat, 1910
But it did not harm his white coif.
Seeing this, Huon called out to Jesus:
"Oh, dear God, through your holy goodness
Protect my body from all harm,
And protect me and my honor, if it be your will." 1915
With these words the youth regained his confidence:
He grasped his sword by its gilded grip,
Lifted his shield, and strode forward.
He gave Amaury a powerful blow,
Striking him so hard upon his shield 1920
That it did not do him a penny's worth of good.
The blow ricocheted onto his helmet,
Sending jeweled and flowered decorations flying
And coming to rest upon his coif.
Its steel was smooth and its iron tempered, 1925
And his hauberk was so strong and tightly linked
That it did not do a penny's worth of harm.
His good sword glanced off to the right
Onto Amaury's shoulder, then downward,
Striking him a deep gash to the ribs. 1930
The good sword ripped the hauberk,
Destroyed the lining, and cut open his body;
Its wound went a good hand's breadth deep into living flesh.
But the scoundrel had cowered in fear of Huon's blow:
Had the engraved sword struck him squarely, 1935

It would most certainly have killed him.
Then Huon yelled to him in a strong voice:
"Lying traitor, I've struck you now!
I see your blood flowing over the grass.
By God, when I am finished with you,   1940
You'll never again do harm to a highborn man."
Amaury replied, "Stop your bragging!
By God, you won't get away from me again.
I'm going to strike you so hard, believe me,
That you'd rather die than have a thousand gold marks!"   1945
With these words he lifted his shield to his shoulder
And came toward Huon with his sword in hand.
He struck him upon the top of his helmet,
Sending jeweled and flowered decorations flying.
His helmet split open to its metal lining.   1950
The sword struck the coif of his white and gilded hauberk
And the bassinet below was shattered.
God prevented the blow from wounding his head.
The sword glanced off to the right.
Had it not, his days would have ended.   1955
The blows rained down viciously,
Cutting open one side of Huon's hauberk
And striking him upon the hip.
His armor was of very little protection —
Worth hardly more than a piece of white bread —   1960
And a large piece of his flesh was sliced off.
By the grace of God, the wound was not deep!
Nonetheless Amaury had struck so well
That Huon's spur was slashed off.
Amaury's good sword dug into the ground,   1965
And he pulled it back out mightily.
Huon was so sharply stunned
That he began to stagger from the pain.
He could not keep from falling to his knees
And nearly fell flat upon the ground.   1970
A squire had stopped there.

When he saw how badly Huon was suffering,
He rushed to find the lord abbot,
Who was in the abbey church before the altar.
He called to him in a loud voice: 1975
"My lord abbot, please pray for Huon
In the name of the God of majesty,
For he is nearly at death's door."
Upon hearing this, the abbot was irate.
He prayed to God, the King of majesty: 1980
"True God, in your holy goodness
You created Adam and likewise Eve,
Dear King of glory, to populate your earth.
You gave all paradise to them
Except for a single fruit that was forbidden. 1985
Eve ate of it, by the workings of the devil,
And then she had Adam eat it as well.
When he saw that he'd been deceived,
He wanted to kill himself at once,
But you would not allow him to: 1990
You made them come onto this earth.
When they had left the garden, they had to work:
Adam had to plow, and Eve to weave.
The earth was damned for five thousand fourteen years.
No cleric, no matter how learned, 1995
Nor any holy person, no matter how pious,
Was spared from going straight to hell,
For hell was unlocked and open,
While paradise was locked and closed.
But you did not wish to suffer or permit this, 2000
So you entered the Virgin's womb,
And she carried you for nine months.
You were born on the holy day of Christmas,
When the star shone brightly,
And the three kings came from their lands 2005
To seek you out and visit you.
They brought you, dear King, gifts of

Myrrh, gold, and incense to honor you.
Wicked Herod was extremely angry
And sought to destroy and kill you.   2010
But, my Lord, you were able to save yourself
And were quickly delivered from his hands.
You went immediately into Egypt,
And the traitor's anger was immense.
He had all the children seized   2015
And had all those under two years of age slain,
Thinking thus to capture and kill you.
Yet he was powerless, my Lord, to harm you.
You wandered the earth for thirty-two years,
Preaching and proclaiming your faith   2020
Alongside your praiseworthy apostles.
One among them was unable to love you:
His name was Judas, a most evil man.
He betrayed you for money;
For just thirty pennies, he sold you.   2025
No treasure was ever purchased for so little!
While you were staying in the house of Simon,
Mary Magdalene came to visit you
And to kneel at your feet.
She wept so profusely that your feet were washed,   2030
Then she wiped and dried them with her hair.
There you were captured and taken prisoner,
Attached and tied to the stake,
Beaten and whipped with canes.
Afterwards you were untied from the stake   2035
And taken away and nailed to the cross.
Wicked Longinus speared you in the side,
And your blood flowed down the spear.
He had been blind since birth.
When he felt upon his hands the blood   2040
From your body, he did a wise thing:
He immediately rubbed his eyes with it,
And you, dear Lord, restored his sight.

As soon as he beheld you, he asked for mercy,
And you immediately pardoned him   2045
All the sins he had ever committed.
On Golgotha your bright blood flowed out,
And the stones, unable to resist it, broke open.
In the ancient temple
Founded and built by Solomon,   2050
There was such grief, it is well attested,
That the veil split open for all to see,
Birds ceased their flight,
And fish stopped swimming.
There was a distinguished baron in the vicinity,   2055
Named Joseph, a man of good fortune,
Who had served in Pilate's house for seven years.
He offered to give up everything
If you were removed from the cross.
Pilate readily accepted his offer   2060
And you, my Lord, were immediately taken down.
Nicodemus came at once
And piously pulled out the nails.
Then, my Lord, you were placed in the sepulcher
And rose from the dead on the third day.   2065
You descended straightway into hell
And released all those who were your friends,
For you had thrown open its doors.
Whoever had served you was saved.
Then, my Lord, you ascended into heaven   2070
On a holy day that must be observed:
Ascension Day, I have heard it called.
All of your apostles were frightened,
But before long, you came to visit them:
On Pentecost, the learned clerics say,   2075
You came to them, dear King, on wings of fire,
In order to enlighten them with the Holy Spirit.
True God," said the abbot, "through your holy goodness,
As truly as all this is the truth,

Just as I have told and related here   2080
And believe it faithfully,
If ever I have done anything pleasing to you
Since the hour I entered holy orders —
Keeping vigil at night and fasting all day long,
Wearing a hair shirt and singing many masses —   2085
Deign this day to keep young Huon
From being maimed or killed,
And let him be able to vanquish the traitor."

17

Abbot Lietris finished his prayer:
"Dear God," said he, "who never lies,   2090
Help Huon, that worthy young man
If ever I have done anything to please you.
Since the hour, my Lord, that I entered religious orders
More than forty years ago,
I have never done anything wrong if I could avoid it, 2095
That I have not made up to you.
Whatever I have done good since the day I was born —
Fasting by day, wearing a hair shirt,
All the good deeds I have done up to this day —
May they all be rewarded now, precious Lord.   2100
I renounce even my share of paradise,
If you protect worthy Huon from death.
May he not be slain this day,
And may Amaury be defeated by him."
With these words the abbot leapt to his feet,   2105
Kissed the altar, and returned to the field of combat.
Huon was standing upon the flowered ground,
Wounded seriously and in a bad way:
He was barely able to stand,
But the strength of God in paradise   2110
And the prayers of Abbot Lietris
So restored Huon's strength

That he no longer felt any pain or hurt.
He saw Amaury standing across the field
And approached him, holding his shield before him   2115
And with his burnished sword drawn.
The worthy youth raised it on high
As if he intended to strike him
Upon the helmet with its shining carbuncle.
And the traitor, seeing the blow descending,   2120
Raised his shield against it.
Huon, who was a skilled sword fighter,
Paid this no mind, but instead altered his aim
And struck Amaury with such force
To his forearm below the shield   2125
That both shield and fist fell to the ground.
When the traitor felt this incredible blow,
He yelled so loudly that they heard him in Paris.
Seeing this, Huon rejoiced
And began to shout to Amaury: 2130
"Traitor, thief, now I've struck you!
So help me God, when I've finished with you
You will never again betray anyone!"
"Ah, sir Huon," said Amaury,
"For the love of God, have mercy on me!   2135
I was seeking my own death today, so help me God,
Because it was I who led Charlot into the flowery woods
Where he was slaughtered and killed.
Had you not defeated me here upon this field,
King Charles would have been killed within the year.   2140
I would have made him die a painful death,
But I see that now I am in a bad way."
Ah, dear Lord who never lies,
Why did Charlemagne or Duke Naimes,
Or any other noble, not hear these words?   2145
But only young Huon heard them.
Then evil Amaury spoke to him again:
"Oh, noble youth, what do you have in mind for me?

Please have consideration for me, and mercy!
If it pleases you, I'll turn myself over to King Charles.   2150
Noble men will intercede for me,
Along with my relatives and my friends,
And along with their prayers,
I myself will give so much silver and pure gold
That the emperor will have mercy on me.   2155
I will become the porter at his vaulted palace,
For I never wish to possess land,
Since by your sword you have done me great harm.
Take my sword, sir, come and receive it."
Huon replied, "As you wish it."   2160
He came forward to receive it,
For he believed that Amaury was speaking the truth.
As the worthy young man stretched forth his hand
The traitor struck him such a blow to his arm
That three hundred links of his hauberk were smashed.   2165
He nearly lost his arm,
But God almighty protected him.
Upon seeing this, all Huon's blood surged,
And he shouted with a mighty voice:
"Traitor, thief!" roared Huon,   2170
"You cannot hide your wickedness,
But, by Our Lord who was crucified,
You will receive no mercy or reprieve!"
He strode forward with his burnished sword drawn
And struck such a mighty blow above   2175
Amaury's shoulder, below his flowered helmet,
That it sent his head tumbling onto the grass.
Huon has killed him, but Amaury did not confess.[20]
There is no tongue or heart that can tell you
The great torment that Huon would suffer,   2180

20. The text states clearly that "Amaury did not confess," but only a few lines
earlier he did confess, though only to Huon (lines 2136ff). Apparently, a public
confession was required to satisfy Charlemagne's special condition (see above,
note to line 1741).

Nor the great evil that Charles would do him.
The worthy youth strode forward
And took wicked Amaury's head.
He returned to his horse immediately
And leapt up at once into the saddle. 2185
When he saw Naimes, he said proudly:
"Accompany me to Paris, my lord!"
"You will suffer no evil, unless I do as well!" said Naimes.
"My lord," said Huon, "may God reward you for this."
Then the knights set off together 2190
And conducted Huon to the king of Saint-Denis,
Leaving Amaury dead on the field.
Huon came before Charlemagne.
Seeing him, the king's blood surged,
And young Huon proudly addressed him: 2195
"My lord, listen to what I have to say:
Here is the traitor Amaury's head.
I have acquitted myself in combat.
Give me back now my land and my country."
"Huon," replied Charles, "you will not have it like this." 2200
The king addressed white-haired Duke Naimes:
"Duke Naimes," he asked, "did the dead man confess?"
"My lord, he did not, so help me God.
Courtly Huon rushed him so quickly
That Amaury didn't have time to speak or confess." 2205
"Huon," said Charles, "God has consented to a wrong.
I know courtly Amaury well,
And if he had committed the treason,
So help me God, he would have confessed everything.
I see clearly that God has consented to a wrong. 2210
I banish you from sweet France forever.
Do not ever return to the city of Bordeaux
Because, by God who was nailed upon the cross,
If ever I catch you or capture you,
I will have you die a painful death." 2215
"My lord," replied Huon, "God will watch over me.

Righteous emperor, as God is my witness,
Have I not acquitted myself before you?
In the name of righteous God, do not wrong me,
But grant me my lands, I pray you."   2220
"Huon," said Charles, "you are wasting your breath,
Because, by the faith I owe Jesus Christ,
Never for as long as I live
Will you possess a single foot of your lands."
"My lord," said Huon, "I am deeply grieved.   2225
My lord barons, as God is my witness,
Beg the king to have mercy upon me.
I am a peer of our country France,
And should be your friend and companion."
Then white-haired Naimes arose   2230
And the eleven peers all stood up.
They fell to their knees before the king,
And all intervened for young Huon.
"Barons," said Charles, "by St. Denis,
You can kneel there until Judgment Day,   2235
But I will have no mercy or pity upon him.
So, for God's sake, get away from me."
When the barons heard this they were all dismayed;
They arose and went to take their seats.
But Duke Naimes began to cry out: 2240
"What! Emperor, have you gone mad?
Why are you rejecting your share of paradise?
It is written in both the Old and New Testaments:
Whoever disinherits the orphan or rightful heir
Loses God's favor, you can be sure of it!"   2245
"Naimes," replied Charles, "listen to me:
When they entered the field of honor,
I told them, in the presence of all the barons,
That if the one who was defeated and killed
Did not openly admit to the murder,   2250
Whoever defeated and killed him
Would not possess a single foot of his lands.

I know courtly Amaury well enough to say
That if he had plotted this treason,
He would have owned up to it, so help me God.   2255
By the faith I owe to Jesus Christ,
The worthy high barons are pleading in vain,
Because as long as I am alive
He will never possess a single foot of his lands.
Instead, he will be exiled and chased from them."   2260
"My lord," said Huon, "by holy Christ, you are wrong!
Ah, emperor, most noble and powerful,
Again, I beg you: have mercy on me."
But the king responded, "Enough, miserable wretch!
I hate even having you in my sight.   2265
Leave my court! Get away from me!
I can never again love or cherish you."
"Truly, my lord, I am deeply grieved."
"My lord," said Naimes, "for God's sake, again I urge you,
Think this over, as the ever-truthful God is my witness.   2270
When the news spreads through the land
That you have disgraced a young man in this manner
And chased him from his lands,
What will the worthy high barons say?
Your judgments will never again be respected in France.   2275
Everyone, great and humble, will say
That you've grown senile in your old age.
Again, I beg you, noble emperor,
To grant succor and mercy to him."
"Naimes," replied Charles, "by the saints of God,   2280
I pray and beg of you: let it be!
Even if all the people living in this world
Had come here before me,
And every one of them had begged me for Huon,
Still I would not have done differently."   2285
"My lord," said Naimes, "I am deeply grieved."

18

"My lords," said Charles, "you are very wrong
To press Huon's case so strongly
And to demand that I restore his land and his possessions.
By Holy Mary, think carefully!   2290
Springtime will bring Easter,
When the rightful heir of Bordeaux
Must serve me at my table.
How could I possibly look upon the scoundrel
Who murdered my son?"   2295
"Sire," said Huon, "since you hate me so,
You should be pleased that I live so far from Paris, your city.
Please, return my land to me,
And I will relinquish the fief of your household,
Provided that you give it to my brother Gerard."   2300
The king replied, "You are wasting your breath!
By the One who suffered on the cross,
For as long as I live, I assure you,
You will never hold a square foot of your land."
"Sire, this is outrageous," said Huon.   2305
Naimes now became furious.
He called out to the king, asking:
"Sire, for the love of God,
Will you not reconsider?"
"I will not," replied Charles, "may God save my soul!"   2310
"By God," said Naimes, "this grieves me bitterly."
The duke then addressed all the peers in the royal household:
"My lords," he said, "arise!
Let us take leave of Charles, for he has grown senile.
Never in my life have I seen anyone treated as unjustly   2315
As young Huon has been treated today.
We should not remain at court any longer.
So help me God, I have no intention of staying.
No man can be judged fairly here.
We can expect the same treatment as Huon.   2320

If we found ourselves in the same situation,
We too would be disinherited,
For Charles would never have mercy on us,
Since he disinherited one of our peers
Without judging him equitably."   2325
They stood up and left the court,
And Naimes accompanied them.
King Charles remained,
Attended only by young knights.
When he saw the peers leaving, he was quite distraught.   2330
"Alas! Now I am ill treated," he said.
"My son is dead, to my great despair,
And I will lose my court as well,
If those who just left really do abandon me.
I will have to bend to their will."   2335
King Charles began to weep
And went in person to summon back the peers.
He called out to them, saying:
"My lords, in the name of God, please come back,
And I will do as you wish,   2340
For I see that you are firm in your resolve.
Even if I had sworn fifty times to the contrary,
I would defer to your wishes."
When the barons heard him, they turned back
And reentered the palace.   2345
Fair young Huon came up to Charles
And fell to his knees in front of all the barons.
The king spoke to him, saying:
"Huon, listen carefully:
Do you wish to make peace with me?"   2350
"Sire, yes, so help me God," said Huon.
"There is no torment, ordeal,
Or hardship that I would not endure
If it be your will;
There is no country, borderland, or kingdom   2355

From here to the Dry Tree,[21] or as far as one can go,
To which I would not travel in order to regain your friendship.
I would even go to speak with the devil in hell
If I could have your friendship back again."
"By my faith," said Charles, "your fate will be much worse   2360
Than going to speak with the devil in hell.
By God, if you wish to make peace with me,
You will be going to a place
Where I have already sent fifteen messengers,
Not one of whom has ever returned.   2365
This place is across the Red Sea,
In the splendid city of Babylon.[22]
That is where you must carry my message
And go to speak to King Gaudisse.
If you can accomplish what I ask of you   2370
And manage to return here,
You will recover your land and your possessions."
"Sire," said Huon, "please explain yourself,
And, so help me God, I will do
As you command to the best of my ability."   2375
"Huon, listen carefully," said Charles,
"You must go to Babylon
And convey a message to King Gaudisse.
First of all, you must agree and pledge,

21. The epic formula "from here to (exotic place name)" was often used to
designate a considerable distance. According to legend, the Dry Tree was located
near Hebron and dried up at the time of Christ's death. Marco Polo situated it in
a vast wasteland in Persia.

22. In Old French epic poetry, "Babylon" designates Cairo, in Egypt along the
Nile. After visiting his uncle the pope in Rome, Huon will cross the Mediterranean
Sea to Jerusalem in the Holy Land. From there it would only be a short voyage
overland to Cairo. However, in our poem, he must undergo a treacherous voyage
through mysterious lands and then traverse the Red Sea before reaching his
destination. This may reflect the poet's lack of knowledge of Middle Eastern
geography but is more likely a symbolic voyage in which the hero must overcome
impossible odds and obtain the magical, spiritual aid of a good fairy — a sort of
guardian angel — in the persons of Auberon and Malabron.

By raising your bare hand,   2380
That you will cross the Red Sea alone,
Accompanied by no Christian man.
If Saracens assist you in crossing, however,
You will not be breaking your pledge to me.
Huon, when you reach the other side   2385
And arrive in that fine city,
You must pledge and swear
Not to enter the palace
Until the emir is seated for his evening meal.
Then you will go up to the palace,   2390
Clad in your hauberk, with your gem-studded helmet laced
And your sword drawn.
There you must lop off the head
Of the first person you see eating there,
No matter how noble he is or how powerful his lineage.   2395
After that, you will have one final task:
The emir Gaudisse has a worthy daughter
Named Esclarmonde.
You must swear and pledge
To kiss her three times in front of the entire court.   2400
Only then will you give my message
To the emir in the presence of all his barons.
You will ask the emir on my behalf
To send me a thousand molted sparrowhawks,
A thousand bears, a thousand hunting dogs leashed together,   2405
A thousand young men,
A thousand beautiful maidens,
The white hairs of his mustache,
And four molars pulled from his mouth."
The French exclaimed, "You are trying to kill Huon!"   2410
"By my faith," said Charles, "that is true.
If he cannot bring back King Gaudisse's four teeth
And white mustache,
Proving to my entire court
That he personally pulled them from his mouth,   2415

May he never return to the kingdom of France,
For I will have him hanged from the gallows."
"Sire," said Huon, "do you wish to add anything else?"
"No," replied Charles, "so help me God."
"Sire, let your will be known,   2420
And I will do everything in my power
To adhere to your wishes."
"Huon, there is one more thing," said Charles.
"If God grants you a safe return
From your journey across the sea,   2425
Do not stop in Bordeaux
Or Gironville on the Gironde
Before speaking with me personally.
I say this to you in all honesty:
If I find that you have disobeyed, so help me God,   2430
I will have you dragged by horses and hanged
Without any formal judgment.
For all of this, you must provide worthy hostages."
"Sire," said Huon, "it will be just as you wish,
But allow me to be accompanied   2435
By the knights I brought here with me
Until I reach the Holy Sepulcher."
Charles replied, "They may ride all the way to the Red Sea,
If they love you enough to go that far,
But they must remain on this side."   2440
"Sire," said Huon, "may God bless you for this!"
Huon then prepared for his voyage
And had his knights lavishly equipped.
He could not return to Bordeaux
To see his mother, who had raised him tenderly.   2445
He would never see her again.
The king then placed Huon's entire fief
In the care of Gerard,
Stipulating that he maintain the land loyally
Until such time as valiant Huon returned   2450
From his journey across the Red Sea.

Among those in attendance that day was a sturdy knight,
Cousin to young Huon.
He was a powerful man with considerable lands
Named Guichard.   2455
He left the court with Huon out of friendship.
Huon took his leave without delay,
Taking eleven knights with him;
He was the twelfth, may God save him!
Huon brought with him an abundance of gold and silver   2460
Given to him by Duke Naimes.
He set off in the direction of Rome,
Accompanied by the barons of France.
His brother Gerard and bearded Naimes
Remained with him for two full days   2465
Before leaving him on the third day.
God! How Duke Naimes embraced Huon!
How sad they were to part company!
God! How Huon wept bitter tears
And kissed his brother as they parted!   2470
Alas, Gerard would prove to be as loyal
As Judas who betrayed our Lord,
For since the birth of Jesus Christ,
No one has ever heard of a brother
So evil and so treacherous.   2475
He was just like Cain, the madman,
Who killed his brother out of spite.
Gerard would do the same, as you will hear.
In the end he betrayed Huon
Because of the vast lands he coveted.   2480
As they parted, however, both of them wept.
Huon asked his brother to send greetings to his mother
And to be vigilant in protecting the land.
Gerard replied, "My lord, just as you wish."
Gerard went directly to Bordeaux,   2485
Found his mother, and greeted her.
He then told her the entire story

Of what had happened to Huon:
How he had killed Charlot in the woods,
Fought a duel at court, 2490
And killed Amaury of Viemez.
How Charles had confiscated his land,
And how Huon had been ordered to go to Babylon
Across the Red Sea to find King Gaudisse.
Hearing this, the lady began to weep. 2495
She was so overcome with grief that none could console her.
Sorrow caused her to fall ill,
And she kept to her bed for two full years,
Pining for young Huon.
She languished so long that it pleased God 2500
To take her from this world.
Gerard then took possession of all their lands.
He went directly to France to claim his fief
And pay homage to valiant Charlemagne.
He also intended to become a peer of France 2505
To replace Huon, who was far away.
However, Duke Naimes intervened:
Never would he consent to this request.
Gerard returned to his lands
And promptly decided to marry. 2510
He chose the daughter of an evil traitor,
A duke named Gibouart,
Who possessed Sicily, an important land.
For his part, young Gerard proved to be full of cruelty:
He took money and goods in great abundance 2515
From the rich inhabitants of Bordeaux
And the noblemen he was supposed to protect.
He disinherited orphans
And reduced widows' income.
The people of Bordeaux cursed him mightily 2520
And longed for young Huon.
I shall leave Gerard aside for now
And return to sing of him later.

I shall tell you instead about brave Huon,
Who was making his way to Rome.   2525
I cannot tell you the details of his journey,
But he rode and traveled
Until he came to Rome one evening.
That night he lodged at an inn
Where he was honorably and richly served.   2530
The next day at sunrise
Young Huon arose.
He and his men equipped themselves richly
And went directly to St. Peter's Church,
Where the pope was having mass sung.   2535
Huon and his men heard mass,
And when it was over,
And the pope had left the church,
Huon went to meet him,
Greeting him in this way: 2540
"My lord, may God the Savior of all things
Grant you joy and good health!"
"Young man," replied the pope, "may God increase your virtue!
Where do you come from?"
"My lord," said Huon,   2545
"I am from Bordeaux;
I am the son of fair Seguin, may God have pity on his soul!
He died more than seven years ago."
When the pope heard Huon say that
He was the son of fair Seguin,   2550
He immediately ran to embrace him.
"Fair nephew," he exclaimed, "welcome!
For the love of God, where are you going?"
"My lord, I will tell you everything,
But first I wish to speak to you   2555
In private, just the two of us."
"As you wish," replied the pope.
They drew to one side beside a pillar.
Standing next to the pope,

Young Huon made his confession. 2560
When he had finished,
He said, "My lord, in the name of God, listen to me,
And I will tell you my story
If you wish to hear it.
I was in Bordeaux not long ago, 2565
When the king of France summoned me by letter
To come to court to render homage for my fief.
Outside of Paris, in a thicket,
Amaury of Viemez was lying in ambush,
Accompanied by Charlot, Charlemagne's son. 2570
My brother and I were riding side by side.
When we were about to go through the woods,
Bright-faced Charlot leapt out
Directly in front of us, fully armed.
I sent my brother to speak with him, 2575
But before I knew it, as God is my witness,
I saw my brother lying in the meadow.
I rushed forward with my sword drawn.
What can I say? God help me,
I killed Charlot, son of Charlemagne, 2580
But I had no idea who his father was.
I immediately went to court for protection,
But Charlot's body was carried in just behind me.
I was accused of treason on the spot
And challenged to a judicial duel 2585
By Amaury of Viemez.
I vanquished him in single combat,
But Charlemagne took away my inheritance
Because Amaury did not confess to his crime.
Now I must go to Babylon 2590
And carry a message to King Gaudisse.
I beseech you, grant me absolution for my sins."
"Now listen to me, Huon," said the pope.
"I will not grant you absolution
Until all hatred has been lifted from your heart. 2595

You must immediately forgive
Bearded Charles and all those who denounced you
And bear no further grudge against them,
Or I will never absolve you
Or give you penance."   2600
"My lord," said Huon, "for God in majesty,
I forgive them with all my heart."
"You are noble and wise," said the pope.
"Now I will tell you what you have earned:
You will leave my presence fully absolved,   2605
Just as bright-faced Mary Magdalene
Left our Lord
After washing his feet with her tears.
By my faith, you will do no penance
For any of the acts to which you have just confessed."   2610
"My lord," said Huon, "may God reward you."
The pope continued, "Fair nephew, listen carefully:
You will go straight to Brindisi,[23]
Where you will find Garin of Saint-Omer.
He is your cousin and mine as well.   2615
I will give you a letter of reference
That you will present to him on my behalf.
Greet him for me a hundred times over.
I know that when he recognizes you,
He will welcome you joyfully."   2620
The pope sent for his chaplain immediately
And had him write a letter
Explaining that this handsome young man
Named Huon
Was the son of fair Seguin.   2625
"And ask him in all loyalty
To treat this young man
As he would treat me, if I were to visit him.
Ask him to help Huon cross the sea."

23. Brindisi is a port city in far southern Italy on the heel of the "boot," a regular
departure point for vessels sailing to the Holy Land in the Middle Ages.

The chaplain dutifully wrote the message.   2630
When he had finished,
He had the letter carefully sealed.
"Huon," said the pope, "take this letter
Directly to Garin with my greetings.
He is a mariner and guards the port.   2635
He will help you prepare for your journey across the sea.
You are welcome to take of my possessions.
I offer them to you willingly."
"My lord," said Huon, "may God reward you.
We will now take our leave. We commend you to Jesus."   2640
The pope replied, "Fair nephew, not yet!
You will stay with me until tomorrow,
And then you can leave in the morning."
Huon exclaimed, "You are wasting your breath!
We cannot remain here any longer,   2645
For I am anxious to deliver my message.
May the true God grant me
A safe return,
So that I can make peace with King Charles."
"Go with God," said the pope.   2650
"My dear nephew, hold fast to your loyalty."
"Indeed I will, my lord," said Huon.
Not wishing to speak any longer, Huon departed;
Now he took his leave
And started off for Brindisi with his men.   2655

19

Huon departed without delay.
He often longed for his home and his former life
And cried bitter tears,
But his knights consoled him, saying:
"My lord, in the name of heavenly God,   2660
You lament and weep too much.
Put aside your grief, in the name of the Blessed Virgin."

"My lords, in the name of our true Father," said Huon,
"I am so distraught that I am about to faint,
For I have been banished from my lands   2665
And forced to seek risky adventure."
There was a prince there from Nivelle;
He spoke firmly to Huon, saying:
"My lord, by God in heaven,
I once lost Nivelle.   2670
My lord the duke banished me from my land
Because I had beheaded a nobleman.
It all turned out well, however:
The duke died, and his heirs brought me back
Thanks to my friends' intervention.   2675
They returned my land and my status to me.
Fair lord, the same thing may well happen to you.
You are a highborn man from a very noble lineage.
You will certainly recover everything you have lost.
Do not despair, noble young man,   2680
But pray to God, who governs the entire world,
And to St. James, whom the pilgrims seek,[24]
To guide you safely against the infidels.
Have faith in the Virgin
Whom Jesus Christ chose as his mother and servant: 2685
Anyone she wishes to help cannot be vanquished."

20

Huon set off, lamenting all the way.
As deep sighs poured forth from his heart,
Bitter tears fell from his beautiful eyes
And streamed down his face.   2690
He missed his mother
And his brother Gerard, whom he loved deeply,

24. St. James the Apostle's shrine at Santiago de Compostela in Galicia (NW
Spain) was the most frequented pilgrimage route in the Middle Ages. Two other
longer and more difficult pilgrimage routes were to Rome and to the Holy Land.

As well as his friends, whom he remembered fondly.
He often called upon God
And the Virgin, in whom He was made flesh.   2695
When his men saw him weeping,
You may be sure it caused them much sadness.
Every one of them was grief-stricken.
One of his companions, however, sought to comfort him,
Saying, "My lord, listen to me.   2700
You are wrong to lament so, by God the Creator!
Never has such a high-ranking nobleman displayed so much sorrow.
I think you are acting childishly.
How can you possibly comfort us?
Put aside your sorrow and weep no more."   2705
"My lord, as you please," said Huon.
They rode along, quickening their pace.
Huon spurred his horse so insistently
That he arrived in Brindisi at sunset.
He went directly to the port,   2710
Where he found Garin the mariner.
Huon greeted him courteously, saying:
"My lord, may God who created everything
Preserve you from all evil!"

21

Huon went directly to Brindisi with his men,   2715
All of them mounted on fine horses.
They found the mariner seated in a large chair
Fitted with two cushions.
Above him hung a silken cloth
To protect him from the sun.   2720
When Huon saw him, he dismounted,
For he thought this man was the lord of the land.
He greeted him in the name of God in heaven, saying:
"May the One who was nailed to the cross protect you!"
"You are wrong, my lord," said Garin,   2725

"To dismount from your fine horse.
I am not the lord of the land.
I am a mariner and that is how I make my living."

22

As fair Huon stood before Garin,
The mariner observed him closely   2730
And began to sigh from deep within his heart.
Keeping his eyes upon Huon, he said:
"Noble young man, for God's sake, listen to me.
In the name of our Lord, who suffered on the cross,
I am filled with sorrow when I look upon you,   2735
Because of a nobleman whom I loved dearly,
Named Seguin of Bordeaux.
Even if I were torn limb from limb,
I could not stop myself from weeping.
My lord, you resemble him a great deal.   2740
But tell me, for God in majesty,
Where do you come from?"
"Indeed, I will tell you at once," said Huon.
"I was born in Bordeaux,
And I am the son of that very Seguin."   2745
When he heard this, Garin rejoiced.
He held onto Huon's legs
And kissed his shoes more than twenty times.
When he stood up again, he began to weep, saying:
"My dear young lord, you are most welcome here!"   2750
Huon exclaimed, "May God bring you great honor!
My lord, what is your name?"
"I am called Garin," he replied.
"My lord, listen to me, in the name of God," said Huon.
"I bring you greetings and affection   2755
From the pope in Rome."
He took the pope's missive and gave it to Garin, saying:
"My lord, please read this."

Garin broke the seal
And read the letter, for he knew how to read.   2760
He understood its contents perfectly:
Huon was his cousin and relative,
And also cousin to the pope;
He was the son of Seguin of Bordeaux.
Huon was obliged to cross the sea,   2765
And Garin was to help him,
Treating the young man as though
He were the pope himself.
Once Garin had read all this,
He cried out in a loud voice: 2770
"Huon, fair lord, welcome!
Now tell me where you must go.
For the love of God, who brought you here?
How is your father, bright-faced Seguin?"
"My lord, he has been dead for over seven years."   2775
"Alas! May God have mercy on him,
For I loved him very much, by God,
And he showed me great goodness and generosity.
Does he have other children?"
"He has one other son, my lord," said Huon.   2780
"I have a younger brother named Gerard.
He is a very handsome young man."
"Ah!" said Garin, "Noble young man, tell me truly,
What brings you to this faraway land?"
"By my faith, you will hear the whole story," said Huon.   2785
"Not long ago, proud King Charles
Summoned me by a letter bearing his seal.
I went to court to pay homage for my fief.
My brother and I set off for court,
But Amaury of Viemez, an evil traitor,   2790
Was waiting in ambush.
Charlot, son of Charlemagne, was with him,
And he attacked us in a narrow pass.
God help me, I killed Charlot,

Then I went to Paris, 2795
For I didn't know whom I had killed.
After I arrived, Charlot's body was brought in,
And I was accused of treason
By Amaury of Viemez.
I vanquished him on the field of honor, 2800
But then Charles confiscated my inheritance
And insisted I go to Babylon
Across the Red Sea to find King Gaudisse.
But I don't know how to get to Babylon."
"Ah!" said Garin, "fair nephew, have no fear, 2805
For I have four barges, four large ships,
And three cargo boats that travel the seas.
No matter how early I get up in the morning,
I make ten pounds by lunchtime
In legitimate revenue, every single day. 2810
I also have a beautiful wife
And beautiful children,
But I will give up my wife, my children,
And everything I own, fair nephew, out of friendship for you.
I will accompany you in the spirit of holy charity. 2815
I will endure with you both good times and bad,
And I will guide you faithfully."
"My lord," said Huon, "may God reward you!"
"Fair nephew, listen to me," said Garin.
"You must come home with me 2820
And spend the night there.
In the morning, when the sun is up,
We will go across the sea to the Holy Sepulcher."
Huon replied, "I will do as you wish."
That night, the young man stayed in Garin's house 2825
With his companions. They were treated most honorably
And were given everything they could possibly wish.
After the meal, when the tablecloths had been removed
And the beds prepared, they laid their heads to rest.
The next morning, they rose early. 2830

Garin called his bright-faced wife
And his children, saying:
"My lady, listen to me, in the name of God:
I must leave with Huon.
He is my cousin, and he deserves my support and affection.   2835
Truly, I must accompany Huon.
Take good care of your children, my lady,
Until my return."
Hearing this, the lady began to weep.
Garin said to her, "Do not lament so,   2840
For you will have me back soon, God willing."
They then had a ship prepared.
They supplied it with great quantities of ship's-biscuits,
Bread, meat, old wine, and claret,[25]
As well as plenty of fresh water.   2845
Next, they loaded the swift horses
And brought along an abundance of gold and silver.
They also prepared a smaller boat,
Solid and well constructed,
That would allow them to dock in cities and towns.   2850
When everything had been carefully prepared,
Garin went to kiss his wife
And embrace his children.

25.   Red wines in our text are often, as here, referred to as *viez et clarez*, "old and clear" (7x). They are sometimes just *vin cler*, or "clear wine" (6x). But on six occasions (lines 5712, 7021, 8120, 8764, 10000, and 10012), the poet appears to make a distinction between *vin* ("wine") and *clarez*: for example, "*Se je boy vin, si buvez le clarey*" (line 8120) or "*Por boivre vin et por boivre clarey*" (line 10000). The term "claret" to distinguish Bordeaux wines from other French reds goes back only to the traders of the eighteenth century. Claret as a heated red wine poured over a bag of spices, or "spiced wine," is not attested until the late Middle Ages, well after *Huon*. In modern French, *clairet* is a "*vin rouge léger, peu coloré*" (light red wine, light in color, *Petit Robert*). Since our text on three occasions specifically mentions "white wine" (lines 1221, 1332, and 6190), we have opted to indicate this distinction as being between a deeper-colored "red wine" and "claret," which we presume was a lighter-colored, but still a "red" wine. (https://www.winespectator.com/articles/why-are-bordeaux-wines-called-claret-46560, consulted 5/2/2020.)

He would never see them again.
When they separated, they all shed many tears.   2855
The thirteen knights boarded the vessel.
They brought neither servants nor squires,
Except for two youths to steer the ship.
They commended themselves to God,
Lifted anchor, and set out to sea.   2860
God blessed them with good winds.
Indeed, the old saying is true:
Whoever is helped by God will never know misfortune.
Within two weeks, they had crossed the sea.
When they reached land, they mounted their horses,   2865
Loaded all their baggage,
And started out for the Holy Sepulcher.
They rode and traveled
Until they arrived in Jerusalem on a Tuesday.
They did not stop until they reached the Holy Sepulcher.   2870
There they dismounted from their swift horses
And went to see and observe
The place where the Lord God was buried.
They kissed the lance,
The nails, and the shroud,   2875
And then the altar where God was presented
And where He himself said mass.
Young Huon prostrated himself, saying:
"True God, by your holy goodness,
You were born in Bethlehem   2880
And then brought to this temple,
Where you were presented on this very altar.
St. Simeon, blinded by illness,
Took you in his arms.
As soon as he held you, he saw the light of day.   2885
He then understood and knew beyond all doubt
That it was God who had been presented to him.
You spent thirty-two years preaching,

But then wicked Judas, who hated you,
Sold you for a few coins. 2890
Lord, you were handed over to the Jews,
Nailed to the cross,
And pierced with the lance.
Just as I believe that all of this is true,
Guide me safely, Lord, 2895
And allow me to deliver my message,
So that I might return
To make peace with King Charles."
Huon stood up and kissed the altar.
He left his offering and stepped back. 2900
His companions did the same.
Huon then addressed his men, saying:
"My lords, you may now return
To King Charles and greet him on my behalf."
"You are wasting your breath!" they cried. 2905
"We will accompany you to the Red Sea,
No matter what hardships may befall us."
"My lords," said Huon, "may God reward you!"
Garin called the sailors
Whom he had brought to steer the ship. 2910
"You may return to my wife," he said,
"And bring her my greetings.
Tell her that I am well
And that I am leaving with valiant Huon."
They replied, "Just as you command." 2915
They turned back and entered the ship
And then set sail straight for Brindisi.
Huon mounted his horse
And rode out with his men
Straight toward the Red Sea. 2920
May Jesus guide and protect them!

Huon passed through many a savage land:[26]
He crossed Femenie,
A desolate place where the sun does not shine,
Women cannot bear children,   2925
Roosters don't crow, and dogs don't bark.
He did not stay long in this country.
Next they came to the land of the Cumans,
Where the people eat no wheat
But devour raw meat like mad dogs.   2930
They sleep outside, exposed to the elements.
They have neither clothing, nor breeches, nor shoes.
Their eyes are as red as hot coals,
And they are hairier than dogs or wild boars.
Their ears are large enough to cover their bodies.   2935
Young Huon was frightened by them,
But he needn't have been, for they did him no harm.
He left that land as quickly as he could
And passed through the land of Faithfulness,
Where faith and loyalty were so ingrained   2940
That delicate cakes were baked in silken cloth.
There, it was easy to discern who was guilty of wrongdoing.
Whoever arrived in the country first at harvest time
Could take as much wheat as he wanted
Without anyone interfering.   2945
Young Huon did not remain long in this land,

26. Medieval Europeans had very little and very imperfect knowledge of the lands
of Africa and the East, as well as of the Muslim religion. Travelers to the region,
such as Marco Polo in the thirteenth century, returned with many fabulous and
improbable tales of the lands they had visited, which were repeated and elaborated
upon in popular works like *The Travels of John Mandeville* (14th c.). In spite of
frequent political, commercial, and literary interactions between Christians and
Muslims in Europe after the rapid conquest of Spain and Sicily in the eighth
and ninth centuries, accurate knowledge of Islam was almost non-existent, and
practices attributed to them were often parodies of Christian beliefs. Many of the
French *chansons de geste* were predicated on a hatred of the Muslim Other, as a
result of which Islamic peoples and culture were demonized, with no attempt to
understand or appreciate them.

But passed through it quickly.
They had soon eaten all the food they had brought.
For two weeks they traveled
Without finding enough bread, wine, or wheat   2950
To satisfy a servant-boy.
"God," said Huon, "what a dreadful country this is!
There is no nourishment to be found here.
Alas! King Charles, you have greatly wronged me.
May God forgive you for what you have done."   2955
Young Huon began to weep,
But his men comforted him.
After riding and traveling a great distance,
They came to a thicket, where they found a man
Whom I will now describe to you: 2960
He was over a hundred years old and quite frail.
His long beard flowed all the way down to his belt,
As white as flowers in a meadow,
And carefully braided.
He was holding a pickax and seemed very tired,   2965
For he was working hard to repair faulty passageways.
Huon noticed him and began to observe him closely.

23

Young Huon looked attentively
And with amazement at the penitent,
Then he turned to his men and said: 2970
"My lords, for God the Redeemer,
Look at this man: his hair is iron gray.
I don't know whether he believes in God,
But nonetheless I'll speak with him."
Huon walked toward him   2975
And greeted him in the name of almighty God:
"My friend, may the God who shed his blood
Watch over your body and your soul!"
When the man heard this, he threw down his tool,

Came running toward Huon,   2980
Seized him at once by his leg,
Kissed him more than twenty times in a row,
And cried out to him in a loud voice:
"Young man, sir, may God, who was born
Of the Virgin in Bethlehem, be with you!   2985
I have lived in these woods over thirty years
And have never before seen a Christian.
Where are you from, and what are you seeking?
In the name of the Lord who shed his blood,
I am greatly saddened to see you!   2990
It seems to me that my heart is breaking
Because of a noble man who looks so much like you:
He is named Seguin, from the great city of Bordeaux."
"In the name of God almighty," said Huon,
"Did you know the good duke?"   2995
"Truly I did know him," replied the man.
"My lord," said Huon, "don't hide it from me:
What land are you from and what sort of people?"
The good man said, "You are wasting your breath!
First tell me what you are doing here?"   3000
"You have spoken properly, indeed," said Huon,
By St. Amand, I will tell you."
Huon and his men dismounted at once,
Tied their horses to a tree,
Then sat down upon the green grass.   3005
Huon sat next to the penitent
And told him everything,
Just as he had promised:
"My lord," he said, "do you want to hear my story?"
The good man replied, "Yes, for almighty God."   3010
"In faith," said the young man, "you will hear it at once.
I was born in the great city of Bordeaux,
Son of brave Seguin,
Of whom you just spoke at the beginning."
Hearing this, the good man sighed deeply,   3015

But he did not utter a single word,
Because he was waiting for Huon to continue.
"My lord," said Huon, "in the name of all-powerful God,
My father is deceased, which grieves my heart.
We were left as two orphans,   3020
But we did not go immediately to court
To pay homage for our inheritance.
We did not go, indeed, for over seven years
And would have legally lost our lands
Had it not been for gray-haired Duke Naimes."   3025
"My God," said Geriaume, "is he still alive,
The good nobleman? May Jesus help him!
I knew him as a very young man.
We were companions in our youth."
"Now listen, sir," said noble Huon.   3030
"The emperor who rules all France
Sent for me by a letter bearing his seal.
My men and I went to court
Along with my brave-bodied brother.
South of Paris, in a greening thicket,   3035
Evil traitors were watching for us.
Among them was Charlot, the son of noble Charlemagne.
We were traveling to court under safe conduct,
With no fear of any man alive,
But before we knew it,   3040
The wicked cowards were upon us!
The king's son was their leader.
I didn't recognize him, so help me God,
So I sent my brave brother ahead
To see what he wanted.   3045
I hadn't gone far
When I saw my brother wounded in his side
And lying on the grassy ground.
When I saw him, my heart grieved.
I drew my sword and rode forward.   3050
Why make it a long story?

I killed Charlot with my steely blade
And then fled toward Paris,
Because I didn't know where to go for safety.
The traitors came behind me with the corpse —   3055
May God destroy them!
A certain Amaury, a cowardly traitor,
Accused me of treason
And challenged me to battle before the French.
I defeated him and killed him on the field,   3060
And that is why I have fled the country.
The king banished me to suffering and grief.
I am traveling to Babylon with a heavy heart
To see King Gaudisse, an evil ungodly king.
There I will deliver my message.   3065
Now I have told you everything."

24

"My lord," said Huon, "as God is my witness,
I have now told you about my troubles,
And everything I've said is the truth.
Now I would like to know, if you agree,   3070
Where you are from, from what kingdom,
And who brought you here."
Geriaume said, "My brother, you will learn it.
I was born in Gironville, to tell the truth.
Do you know the noble provost Guiret?"   3075
"Yes," replied Huon, "for the love of God,
When I quit my city of Bordeaux,
I left him to watch over my vast lands."
Geriaume said, "He is my blood brother!"
"My lord," the youth responded,   3080
"For God in majesty, tell me your name."
The good man said, "You are about to know it:
My given name is Geriaume,
And I cannot hide that I'm your relative."

"Geriaume, my lord," said valiant Huon,   3085
"I saw my father weeping for you many a day.
For the love of God, who brought you here?"
And Geriaume replied, "In faith, you'll soon know.
Like you, I have been disinherited.
When I was young and just knighted,   3090
I killed a knight, so help me God,
At a tourney to which I'd gone.
I was offered peace and reconciliation
On condition that I go overseas to the Holy Sepulcher.
I crossed the sea and came to this place,   3095
Making my pilgrimage as I had promised.
When I intended to return,
I came upon Saracens and Slavs,
Who captured and imprisoned me.
I spent five miserable years in prison.   3100
The emir, whose duty it was to guard me,
Had a daughter who fell in love with me.
She got me out of prison.
What more can I tell you, for God in majesty?
I have lived more than thirty years in pagan lands.   3105
I was married twice, I tell you truly,
And I can speak the Saracen tongue quite well.
There is no borderland, country, or kingdom
As far as the Dry Tree or the ends of the earth,
So help me God, where I've not been.   3110
I lived a long time among the pagans
But was finally able to escape them
By the grace of the God of majesty.
Then I came to these leafy woods
And have dwelt here, indeed, for a good thirty years.   3115
I've tasted very little bread since then
But have eaten many roots
And the wild fruits I've found in the woods.
I've worn a hair shirt next to my skin
With a hauberk over it   3120

To atone for my weighty sins.
Armed with my good deeds,
I will gladly accompany you.
I wish to help you and your father
As I have helped myself, bearing my tribulations,   3125
Because your father raised me tenderly.
I will be a good guide for you,
For I have often been to Babylon
And know the emir Gaudisse well.
With you I will endure both the good and the bad.   3130
And I tell you in all honesty
That there are two routes by which I can lead you,
For I have taken them both.
One of the ways is so frightening
That no man can escape it alive,   3135
And I tell you — it's the truth and no lie! —
That if anyone could make it through
He would reach the Red Sea in two weeks.
If you wanted to take the other route,
You would wander about for a year,   3140
But you would find good lodgings
And good cities, castles, and towns."
"By my faith," said Huon, "may God strike me down
If ever I'm so cowardly and crazy
As to spend a whole year   3145
Doing what I could do in two weeks!
But tell me now, gentle Geriaume,
How dangerous is it to take the shorter route?"
Geriaume said, "My lord, you'll soon hear:
There is a forest to pass through, to be sure,   3150
Which is huge, as God is my Savior.
The deep woods is sixty leagues wide,
And in it there dwells a hunchbacked dwarf
Not more than three feet tall,
But more beautiful than the summer sun.   3155
His name is Auberon.

No man, once he enters the woods
And speaks with him, can ever escape him;
And once he has lived with him,
He will never leave again as long as he lives.   3160
And I assure you in all loyalty
That Auberon has such powers
That when you start to cross through the woods,
Before you have gone twelve leagues,
You will see him trotting up toward you.   3165
He is as beautiful as Jesus could make him.
When you see him stop in front of you,
He will speak of the God of majesty
In a way that would inspire anyone.
If you don't wish to address him politely,   3170
He will make such a terrible commotion
That you will be frightened to the core,
For he will call down rain and wind,
Spark lightening, and rip up trees,
And then after all that   3175
He will cause such a river to flow before you
That a large ship could sail upon it.
It would look just like a branch of the sea.
But I tell you — and it's the truth —
That everything you see is just a mirage.   3180
You can cross the water in bare feet
Without getting your shoes or leggings damp!
So I tell you, and you'd be a fool not to believe me,
If you don't speak to him, he cannot harm you,
But if you do, you will lose everything!"   3185
"In faith," said Huon, "there's no more to be said."
Without further ado, they all remounted.
They gave Geriaume a good horse
That they had brought with them.
I do not wish to tell you about their travels,   3190
But they rode so long and hard
That they entered into Auberon's forest.

They found a pleasant spot beneath an oak,
And young Huon stopped there.
"In faith," he said, "I can't go any farther.   3195
As God is my Savior, I'm so hungry
That I can no longer ride or travel.
Let's dismount. I want to rest,
My heart is failing me, and I'm nearly famished!"
So they all got off their powerful horses,   3200
Then removed their harnesses and reins,
So they could graze on the grass in the meadows below.
Huon sat down and began to weep:
"My God," the youth said, "there's no bread or wheat.
Holy Mary, please rescue me!   3205
I haven't eaten enough in the last three days
To make a good dinner!"
Geriaume said, "Don't you know how to fast?
Eat all of these roots you want,
I've lived on them for over thirty years!"   3210
"In faith," said Huon, "I've never tried them.
So help me God, I wouldn't know where to start!"
While they were conversing in this manner,
The little man came through the leafy woods.
He looked just as you will hear me tell: 3215
He was as beautiful as the summer sun
And was dressed in a silken cloth
Decorated with thirty bands of pure gold.
His sides were bound with silken threads,
And he was carrying a bow for hunting.   3220
Its bowstring was of natural silk,
And its arrow was of pure gold.
God has not made a beast so ferocious
That Auberon would fail to hit it
If he took aim and truly wanted to kill it.   3225
From his neck hung a pure ivory horn
Bound together with bands of gold.
It was made by fairies on an island in the sea.

One of the fairies had given it the gift
To heal anyone who heard it sound: 3230
If he were ill, he would regain health,
No matter how serious the sickness.
The second fairy gave it a greater gift:
Whoever possessed the horn — it's the truth —
If he were hungry would find food aplenty,   3235
And if he were thirsty, enough to drink.
The third fairy gave an even greater gift:
Anyone, no matter how weak he felt,
If he heard the blaring of the horn,
He would break into song at the sound!   3240
The fourth fairy wished to do even better
And gave a gift that you will hear about:
Anyone who possessed the horn,
If he blew into it and sounded it
In any borderland or country or kingdom   3245
From the Dry Tree to the Red Sea,
Auberon would hear it in his citadel of Monmur.
The little man began to sound his horn,
And the fourteen men began to dance.
"My God," said Huon, "who is coming to visit us?   3250
I no longer feel weak or hungry!"
Geriaume said, "It's the hunchbacked dwarf.
Soon you will see him trotting up toward you.
I forbid you, my lord, to speak to him,
Unless you wish to remain here with him."   3255
Huon replied, "No! So help me God!"
Behold now the tiny hunchback,
Who began shouting in a high voice:
"You fourteen men who are traversing my forest,
So help me God, you are most welcome!   3260
I beg you by the God of majesty,
By the sacred oil, chrism, and salt of baptism,
By all that God has created and made,
I beg of you to answer me."

But the fourteen men turned and fled.   3265
The little man's heart filled with anger.
He raised a finger and tapped his horn with it.
A storm and a tempest struck.
No creature under heaven could fail
To be frightened to feel the rain and the wind,   3270
To see the trees shaken and uprooted.
They had not gone even half a league
When they saw a river so wide
That a ship could sail upon it.
"Upon my word," said Huon, "we are trapped.   3275
Holy Mary, what a proven fool I am
For having entered these deep woods.
It is clear to me that I cannot escape!"
"There is no cause to be afraid," said Geriaume,
"The wicked hunchbacked dwarf did all this!"   3280

25

Young Huon was very upset.
He said to his men, "Dismount at once.
So help me God, we are condemned to death!
Holy Mary, how deceived I was
When I entered this deep forest."   3285
They looked across the water
And saw four towers with crenelated battlements,
And each was topped with a large bell tower.
But you could not have gone a bow shot's distance
Before the towers and the water disappeared.   3290
"Upon my word," said Huon, "I was frightened for nothing.
Now I no longer see the water or the towers."
Old white-haired Geriaume said:
"The wicked angry dwarf did all this!
But he can't harm us anymore, you have to know.   3295
However, by the One who was raised upon the cross,
I promise you, and you can be sure of it,

He will be coming back in a hurry.
I beg you, in the name of righteous God,
Do not be afraid of him now.   3300
Ride on, don't be afraid,
And no matter what he says to you,
I beg you, dear sir, not to reply to him!"
"Indeed," said Huon, "you are wasting your breath.
I would rather he be flayed alive!"   3305
Then they remounted their rapid steeds
And rode on their way without delay.
They went five leagues as rapidly as possible,
But the barons were very frightened.
Huon, the noble warrior, spoke up   3310
And said to his men:
"Upon my word, barons, Jesus has helped us
Since we are so far from this dwarf.
May God damn him for having called out to me,
Because I've never been so scared   3315
Since the day I was baptized, so help me God!"

26

Our barons did not delay,
But rather mounted their horses,
For they were terribly frightened.
They rode straight toward the sea,   3320
Speaking all the while of the wonders they had seen.
"By my faith," said Huon, "God has comforted me
Now that we've escaped the dwarf."
Geriaume heard him and exclaimed:
"My lord, as God is my Savior,   3325
Soon you will see the devil return.
Before long you'll see him trot up to you!"
While they were talking in this way,
Just as they were about to cross a small bridge,
The little man leapt in front of them.   3330

Seeing him, Huon was frightened.
"My God," said the youth, "the devil has returned!"
When he heard this, Auberon proudly said:
"Young man, you are not telling the truth,
Because, in the name of the One who suffered on the cross,   3335
I am neither an enemy nor a devil.
Instead, I assure you, as God is my Savior,
I am a man like any other mortal,
And I believe in the crucified Christ.
Once again, I beg you in God's name,   3340
By all that God has created and made,
By the sacred oil, the chrism of baptism, and salt,
And by the power given me by Jesus,
I beg of you to answer me."
"Let us run, by God!" said valiant Geriaume.   3345
"He will get us in trouble with everyone alive!"
All fourteen turned at once
And spurred their horses mightily.
They repeatedly looked back,
For it seemed to them that the dwarf   3350
Was at their heels and about to shame and harm them,
Given all the wonders he had worked.
The tiny man remained all alone.
He was terribly upset and angry.
He took hold of his pure white ivory horn,   3355
Raised it to his lips and sounded it.
The riders could no longer advance
And had to sing to the horn's music.
Auberon was incensed.
"By my faith," said he, "they are utter fools   3360
To think they can escape me in this way!
But, in the name of the One who suffered on the cross,
Since they don't want to answer me
When I call to them in the name of Jesus,
I will make them pay dearly for it!"   3365
Then he took up his pure white ivory horn

And struck his bow with it three times.
Then in anger he shouted:
"All my men, come speak with me.
I wish it in the name of all-knowing God!"   3370
Following these words, he saw
Some four hundred men clad in full armor
Come riding toward him,
Asking, "Good sir, what's the matter?"
Auberon replied, "Lords, I'll tell you at once,   3375
Even though, as God is my Savior,
It makes me sad to have to say it:
Since they do not wish to heed my advice,
They will have to pay dearly for it.
Now I'll tell you. I'll no longer hide it: 3380
Fourteen young men are passing through my woods,
And even when I call upon them in Jesus's name,
They refuse to speak to me.
Go after them and kill them!"
A wise knight stepped forward and said: 3385
"My lord, for God's sake, show some mercy!"
"There is no way I can," replied valiant Auberon,
"For they are so evil that they refuse to speak to me!"
Gloriant, a fairy knight, spoke next:
"Sir Auberon, please, you must not!   3390
Don't have them slaughtered or killed,
And I'll tell you what to do:
If it please you, go after them
And greet them one more time.
If they do not answer to your pleasure,   3395
Cursed be anyone who'd show them mercy,
So then we'll dismember and slay them!
But I tell you, as God is my Savior,
When they see you returning so quickly,
They'll be scared to death.   3400
Now do as I advise you:
Go after them and call them once again.

And, if it pleases you, reassure them."
Said Auberon, "I will do as you wish."
Our barons were riding calmly along.   3405
Huon called over to Geriaume:
"My lord, as God is my Savior,
We have ridden some twelve leagues
And are now safe from the dwarf,
But I must tell you in all truth   3410
That I have never seen a more beautiful man.
My God, how beautiful he is to look at!
And, I swear it's the truth:
How wonderfully he speaks of God!
Even if it were the devil Beelzebub himself   3415
Who spoke so marvelously about the God of majesty,
Still I would have to answer him as he wishes.
So, in the name of the One who was crucified,
If he returns, I will go to greet him.
How could such a child do me any harm?   3420
It appears to me, by holy charity,
That he's not more than three years old."
And Geriaume replied, "By our Lord,
This small child, who spoke to you
And whom you've called an infant,   3425
Was born before Jesus Christ was born!"
"I don't care, by God," replied Huon,
"And I assure you — don't be angry at me for it —
That if he returns, I wish to speak to him."
As they were talking in this way,   3430
They had ridden over fifteen leagues,
When Auberon called out to them:
"My lords," he said, "have you thought about it?
Once more I wish to greet you in Jesus's name.
By his strength, by his power,   3435
By all that He has formed and created,
And by the power given me by Jesus,
I beg you to answer me.

So help me God, you were proven fools
To think you could pass through my forest   3440
Without first speaking to me.
But I say to you, as God is my Savior,
That an ox could no more get to heaven
Than could you escape me, by my head,
Unless it were through my will and desire.   3445
Ah, my lord Huon, I know your name well
And where you are headed:
To give your message to King Gaudisse.
And I know everything that has happened to you:
You killed Charlot, Charlemagne's son,   3450
Then slayed Amaury in single combat.
Because of this, Charles disinherited you,
And you must carry your message
To Gaudisse beyond the Red Sea.
But I tell you as your loyal friend   3455
That you cannot get there without my help.
Speak to me, Huon, and I will serve you.
I will help you relay your message
And will help you kill the emir.
I will have him cast dead at your feet.   3460
And I will help you, as God is my Savior,
To pull out the hairs of his white mustache
And the four molars from his mouth
That you must carry back to Charlemagne.
And I will escort you safely back to France   3465
Unless your great folly destroys you!
I am fully aware that you would have spoken to me
Were it not for this old fool, Geriaume.
Speak to me, Huon, and I will serve you even more.
You haven't eaten enough in the last three days   3470
To make a good dinner.
I will give you plenty to eat,
As much meat as you could ask for,
And all the drink that you could want.

As soon as you have eaten your fill,   3475
You may take leave of me at once.
There is no reason to be afraid.
I will let you go immediately."
"My lord," said Huon, "I am glad to see you!"
"May God do you honor," said Auberon.   3480
"Huon, dear friend, now that you have greeted me,
By the One who suffered on the cross,
No greeting will be more richly rewarded
Than the one you have given!"
"My lord," said Huon, "say what it is that you want.   3485
I really wonder why you are pursuing me!"
"Huon, you will hear it now," said Auberon.
"Because of your great trust,
I love you more than I've ever loved anyone.
You don't know what kind of a man you've found,   3490
But you will if you listen carefully:
Julius Caesar raised me most tenderly,
And lovely Morgan la Fée
Was my mother, so help me God.
These two conceived and engendered me,   3495
And I was their only child.
There was great rejoicing at my birth,
And they sent for all the barons in the land.
Fairies came to visit my mother;[27]
One of them was not happy with the way she was treated,   3500
So she gave me the gift you see,
That I would be a tiny hunchbacked dwarf,
And so I am, which grieves my heart.
I haven't grown since I was three years old.
When she saw the fate to which she'd condemned me,   3505

27. The presence of fairies at the birth of a child is an ancient folklore motif that appears in a number of Old French *chansons de geste* by the thirteenth century. They generally exercise their special powers to beneficent ends, as is the case with Auberon. See Laurence Harf-Lancner, *Les Fées au Moyen Age: Morgane et Mélusine: la naissance des fées* (Paris: Champion, 1984), 23–34.

She wished to make it up to me somewhat.
She gave me the gift you'll now hear about:
That I would be the most beautiful man
There ever was, except for Jesus.
And so I am, just as you can see: 3510
I am as beautiful as the summer sun.
A second fairy gave me an even greater gift:
I know the hearts and thoughts of man
And can tell him everything he's done,
As well as all his mortal sins.   3515
The third fairy wished to do even better
And gave me the gift you are about to learn:
No matter what borderland, country, or kingdom
As far as the Dry Tree or the Red Sea,
That I wished to go to in God's name,   3520
I would be wherever I wanted
As swiftly as I thought it
And with as many men as I could ask for.
And if I wished to build a palace
With thirty rooms and fifteen pillars,   3525
You can be sure that I'd receive it immediately,
Along with whatever I wanted to eat
And as much as I could ask to drink!
In truth, I was born in Monmur,
Which, I assure you, is far from here: 3530
Four hundred leagues, if you count them.
I can go from here to there and back
Before a horse has trotted four leagues."

27

Auberon said, "I was born in Monmur,
A city founded by my ancestor.   3535
I can go from here to there and back
Before a horse has run four leagues.
Huon, dear friend, you are most welcome!

You have not eaten in three days or more
What you could have downed in a single meal. 3540
But tell me now, for the sake of your soul,
Would you rather eat in this grassy meadow
Or in a great hall of stone or wood?"
"My lord," replied Huon, "for God in heaven,
I'll not object to whichever you prefer." 3545
"You have answered well," said Auberon.

28

Auberon said, "Huon, listen to me:
I have not yet related everything
That the fairies told and gave me.
The fourth fairy was most praiseworthy 3550
And gave me gifts such as you will hear:
There is no bird or beast or wild boar
So savage or brutally fierce
That would not come willingly and gladly to me
If I wished to tame it by my hand. 3555
In addition, she gave me another power:
I know all the secrets of paradise
And can hear the angels singing up there.
I will never grow old
And never die, unless it is my choice. 3560
At the end, when I am ready to die,
My throne is ready next to God's."
"My lord," said Huon, "you are greatly to be praised.
It is not wrong to brag when one has such a gift."
"Huon, my friend," continued valiant Auberon, 3565
"When you spoke to me, I was overjoyed
Because, by the One who suffered on the cross,
No finer day ever dawned.
You have not eaten in three days
What you could have downed in a single meal. 3570
Now you will dine abundantly

With as much food as ever you could imagine."
"My God," said Huon, "where will we find bread?"
"You will have an abundance," said Auberon.
"But first tell me truthfully,   3575
Do you wish to dine in the forest or meadow
Or in a great hall or splendid palace?"
"My lord," said Huon, "as God is my Savior,
I don't care, as long as I can eat!"
Hearing this, Auberon began to laugh   3580
And said to Huon, "Listen to me, friend:
Take your places on the ground in this meadow,
You and the men you've brought with you.
Everything you will see comes from God."

29

Said Auberon, "My lords, sit upon the ground."   3585
And they did so gladly and willingly.
Then Auberon began to make a wish,
And before you could go as far as a bow can shoot,
Auberon said to them, "Stand up!"
So they got to their feet,   3590
And before them they saw a magnificent palace
With numerous floors and rooms.

30

King Auberon was most praiseworthy.
"My lords, stand up!" he commanded.
And Huon's men replied, "Willingly and gladly!"   3595
They leapt to their feet and looked around.
Before them they beheld a beautifully constructed palace
With thirty rooms and fifteen pillars.
It seemed to them that it had always been there.
The knights went up to the palace   3600
And found the tables all prepared.

The servants brought them large golden basins
For washing their hands,
And then they all sat down for the meal.
Valiant Auberon was seated on a throne.   3605
Would you like to hear it described?
Its feet were made of pure gold
And carved with images of Cupid's bows.
Fairies had crafted it on an island
And sent it to King Alexander,[28]   3610
Who founded and established tournaments.
He handed it down to Cæsar,
Who left it to his beloved son.
This throne had many magical powers:
It could be placed on a fire without burning;   3615
Anyone who sat upon it could rest assured
That he could never be poisoned
Or harmed by any venom,
For he could detect any poison as soon as it was brought to him,
Thanks to the power of the golden throne.   3620
The king was wearing a tunic
Of natural silk,
Richly decorated with pure gold
And sewn up the sides with golden thread.
Young Huon sat beside him,   3625
Eating well, for he was quite hungry.
Auberon observed him carefully
And cordially prepared his bread
As well as the rest of his dishes.
While the others ate, however, Geriaume was weeping,   3630
For he feared he might be obliged to remain with Auberon.
"Geriaume, what is the matter?" asked Auberon.
"For the love of God, do eat and drink,
For as soon as you have finished your meal,

28. Alexander the Great is said here, anachronistically, to be the creator of tournaments in order to celebrate his acclaim as an unparalleled warrior and conqueror.

I will give you permission to leave."   3635
Geriaume was thus reassured,
And you may be sure that all were impeccably served.
There were many courses accompanied by old wine and claret.
When they had eaten and drunk their fill,
Huon said to Auberon: 3640
"My Lord, if you please,
We would gladly take our leave."
"Wait just a bit, Huon," said Auberon.
"First I wish to give you some of my treasures."
He immediately summoned Gloriant.   3645
"My friend," he said, "bring me my goblet."
"As you wish, sire," he replied.
Gloriant found the goblet and brought it to Auberon,
Who took it with both hands.
"Huon, look at this goblet," he said.   3650
"As you can see, it is completely empty."
"Indeed, sire, that is true."
Auberon set the goblet on the table and continued:
"Huon, you can now behold
The great power that Jesus gave me.   3655
In the fairy world, I do as I wish,
As you are about to see for yourself.
You see that this sparkling golden goblet
Is completely empty, but it will soon be filled."
With his right hand he traced a circle around the rim three times,[29]   3660
Then made the sign of the cross upon it for God in majesty.
The goblet was immediately filled with clear wine.

29.   The precise nature of Auberon's magical gesture is unclear in our manuscript.
The verb used is *heürez* (from *augurere*), meaning to guide the goblet's destiny,
i.e., compel it to produce wine. See William W. Kibler and François Suard, ed.
and trans., *Huon de Bordeaux. Chanson de geste du XIIIe siècle, publiée d'après le
ms. Paris BNF fr.* 22555 (Paris: Champion, 2003), 203 n.1). We have preferred
the more specific reading from manuscript *M, enviré*, which likely means to trace
circles. See Pierre Ruelle, ed., *Huon de Bordeaux* (Brussels: Presses Universitaires
de Bruxelles, 1960), 407 n.3678).

Auberon said, "Huon, listen carefully:
You saw what I just did.
This goblet's power comes from God.   3665
I assure you, it is so potent
That if all men born of women
And all of the dead resuscitated
Were to be assembled here,
This goblet would provide enough wine   3670
Or whatever beverages they could want,
Provided that a virtuous man possessed it.
For I tell you truly,
None can drink from this goblet but the virtuous,
Those who are pure, innocent, and free from mortal sin.   3675
As soon as an evildoer touches it,
The goblet loses all of its powers,
Regaining them only when a virtuous man reclaims it.
As God the King of majesty is my witness,
If you are able to drink from it, the goblet is yours."   3680
"Sire," said Huon, "may God reward you!
But I do not believe I am worthy
Of drinking from it or even touching it.
Never in my life have I witnessed such a marvel.
I believe you are a magician!   3685
Listen to me, sire:
I tell you truly that I confessed
To the pope in Rome.
I have repented of all my mortal sins,
May God save me!   3690
And I no longer hate any man born of woman."
The young knight stepped forward,
Took the wine-filled goblet with two hands,
Brought it to his lips
And took a long, full drink.   3695
When Auberon saw all this,
He was overjoyed and ran to embrace the young man.
"Huon, fair friend," said valiant Auberon,

"Thanks be to God. I have found you to be a virtuous man.
Now I will give you, in the spirit of holy charity,   3700
The fine goblet with all of its magical powers
Under these conditions:
If you remain loyal
And conduct yourself according to my advice,
I will help you faithfully.   3705
However, the moment you tell a lie,
The goblet will lose its magical properties,
And you will lose my friendship."
"My lord," replied Huon, "I will take great care to avoid lying.
Now, if you please, allow me to take my leave."   3710
Auberon said, "Wait just a moment.
I have one more treasure to give you.
I have in my possession a shining ivory horn
More valuable than the city of Paris.
Because I have found you to be a virtuous man,   3715
Pure and free from mortal sin,
And because you responded to my greeting in friendship,
I will give it to you, so help me God.
Noble and honorable man,
You may keep it in your alms purse.   3720
Now I wish to demonstrate
The great power that Jesus has given me
In the fairy kingdom where I reside:
As far away as you may be,
In whatever kingdom, town, city, or castle,   3725
If you sound this ivory horn,
I will hear it in my city of Monmur,
And I swear to you in all loyalty
That I will be ready,
With a hundred thousand armed men at my side,   3730
To assist you in battle against any man.
However, I will do this on one condition:
If you cherish my friendship,
Know this in all loyalty,

I forbid you, at the risk of having all your limbs cut off,   3735
To sound the horn without good reason.
So help me God, if you sound the horn
Without being in dire need,
You will find yourself in such a dreadful situation
That every man alive will pity you."   3740
"My lord," said Huon, "may God spare me this.
Now, if you please, I must take my leave."
"Huon, you may now depart.
I commend you to the Lord our God."
Huon and his men stood up.   3745
The servants packed their baggage,
And they all swiftly made ready to depart.
Our barons mounted their horses,
And Huon clasped the precious golden goblet.
He did not forget the ivory horn,   3750
Which he quickly hung around his neck.
All fourteen companions set out on their journey.
King Auberon embraced Huon
And began to weep.
Seeing this, Huon grew worried   3755
And asked him, "Sire, what is wrong?
You seem upset about our departure
I don't know why you are so despondent."
Auberon replied, "My friend, I will tell you.
By my faith, you have captured my heart.   3760
Go with God, for I will not accompany you any farther."
Then the fourteen knights departed.
Huon and the others rode through thick woods
Until they had covered fifteen leagues.
They then came upon a river   3765
That had neither passage nor ford.
They were quite frightened
Because they did not know where to cross,
But a messenger sent by the fairy Auberon
Was following them, and he was carrying a rod   3770

Made entirely of gold and endowed with magical powers
Such that any river in the entire world
Struck by this rod
Would split in two,
Opening a paved road   3775
So wide and so large
That seven hundred men could pass through it.
Auberon's servant was ready to act:
Without speaking to anyone,
He went right past them and up to the water,   3780
Where he struck a single blow with the golden rod.
The water split. The path was so wide
That it could have afforded passage to seven hundred men.
Then the enchanted fellow turned around and was gone.
Huon and all the other knights saw this   3785
And marveled at the extraordinary spectacle.
They proceeded to cross the river.
When they reached the other side, they looked behind them
And saw the water resume its normal course
By the grace of God.   3790
"By my faith," said Huon, "we have been under a magic spell.
So help me God, I am convinced
That the fairy Auberon is behind all this.
However, since we are out of danger,
I have no fear whatsoever   3795
That he will harm me in the future."
Thus, our noble knights rode off
Through the thick woods.
They often spoke of the fairy Auberon,
For Huon could not put him out of his mind.   3800
After a while, the young man looked to his right
And saw a garden. He turned and rode toward it.
In the garden flowed a stream from a spring.

31

Without pausing for an instant,
Young Huon rode swiftly,   3805
Covering a full fifteen leagues.
Having spotted a garden,
He headed in that direction
And dismounted without delay,
Along with his men.   3810
They gathered alongside the spring.
There was ample food sent by Auberon.
They spread out linens and proceeded to eat.
The goblet provided plenty of wine.
"By my faith," said Huon, "God showed his love for me   3815
By guiding me into those woods.
I found and experienced an amazing adventure
When Auberon greeted me
And gave me a marvelous horn
As well as this goblet.   3820
It is quite clear that God was with me.
Certainly, if ever I return to France,
I, the unfortunate one,
Will present this precious goblet to Charlemagne.
If he cannot drink from it, I will be delighted.   3825
Wait! What am I saying? What a foolish thought!
I don't even know what will become of me,
But by the One who created the world,
This gift from the dwarf is worth more
Than two of the greatest cities across the sea.   3830
However, I cannot believe his claim
That he can hear me sound the horn from any distance whatsoever.
May God curse me if I don't put this to the test."
Geriaume said, "That is pure folly!
If you sound the horn, the king will destroy us!   3835
He told you that very clearly as we were leaving."
"May I be damned if I let you stop me!" exclaimed Huon.

He seized the horn and blared it.
At the sound, old Geriaume and the others began to sing.
Who could blame them for it?   3840
Then old Geriaume cried out:
"Blow that horn, my friend, and blessed be the one who engendered you!"
And Huon sounded the horn over and over.
Auberon heard it as he was riding through the woods.
He swore to God that he would help Huon,   3845
But if it were a false alarm, Huon would pay dearly!

32

Huon sounded the shiny ivory horn.
His fourteen companions greatly rejoiced.
Old Geriaume cried out:
"Blow that horn, cousin, for God's sake!"   3850
Huon sounded the horn over and over
So violently and so forcefully
That Auberon heard it from the depths of the leafy forest.
"My God," he said, "I hear my friend sounding the horn.
He is the man I value most in this world.   3855
Oh God, who can be trying to harm him?
I wish I were in the very spot from where the horn is being blown
With a hundred thousand men wearing hauberks,
Or even more, if necessary."
In an instant, he was there.   3860
Huon looked down across the prairie
And saw the armed knights arriving.
Fair Auberon came before them.
Huon and his companions were terrified.
The young man called forth his knights, saying: 3865
"My lords, as God is my witness,
I see clearly that we are finished.
I am certain that we will all be slain."
"That is only just," said valiant Geriaume.
"Be silent," said Huon, "and let me speak."   3870

Behold the fairy Auberon,
Who cried out forcefully:
"Huon, may God strike you down!
Where are those who wish to harm you?
How could you have disobeyed my command?"   3875
"My lord," said Huon, "have mercy on me, for the love of God!
I will tell you what happened:
I was sitting here in this prairie.
I had eaten and drunk quite well
And experienced the powers of your goblet,   3880
But I hadn't yet tested your horn.
I would never have dared enter a great battle
Had I not first put it to the test.
Now I see that everything you told me was true.
Noble lord, I beg you to have mercy on me!   3885
Here is my sword: cut off my head."
Auberon replied, "Huon, be on your way
And follow the path you must take.
You will come upon the city of Tormont,
Where the proven traitor Dudon lives.   3890
He is your uncle and was born in France.
He is your father's brother, I assure you.
In France he was called William.
Because he tried to strangle and murder the king,
He was exiled from the land.   3895
He went across the sea to the Holy Sepulcher,
But he renounced holy Christianity.
Now he believes in Mohammed and crazy Tervagant.[30]
Whenever he captures a Christian,
He has him dragged to the gallows   3900
Or thrown into prison.
I am certain that if he captures you,
He will shame and destroy you.
I forbid you, on pain of death,

30. Along with Apollo and Mohammed, Tervagant is a member of a pagan
"trinity," modeled by Europeans, likely on the Christian one.

To set off in that direction."   3905
"My lord," said Huon, "your words are in vain,
For, by the One who hung on the cross,
I will go to see my uncle.
If he is as you describe him,
I will have all his limbs cut off.   3910
If necessary, I will not hesitate to sound the horn,
For I know you will come to my rescue."
Auberon said, "That is true.
But I command you, in the name of all you hold dear
And at the risk of losing my friendship,   3915
Not to blow the ivory horn
Unless you are gravely wounded.
As God is my witness, if you do sound the horn
Without being in mortal danger,
And I am obliged to hasten to your side for no reason, 3920
I will make you suffer for it."
"My lord," said Huon, "fear not.
I will not sound the horn for all the gold in a city
Unless I am gravely wounded
Or in mortal danger."   3925
Then young Huon took his leave,
But King Auberon called him back.
Tears began to flow from his beautiful eyes.
"My lord," said Huon, "for God's sake, what is wrong?"
Auberon replied, "I am filled with pity for you,   3930
For I assure you in all loyalty,
No man could express,
No ear could hear, and no heart imagine
The great hardships that you will endure, Huon."
"My lord," said Huon, "you promise me much misfortune." 3935
Auberon replied, "You will have even more
Hardships to bear,
Thanks to your foolishness.
Go with God. I will say no more."
Auberon turned to leave, and Huon remained.   3940

When the noble young man was sufficiently rested,
He and his men quickly mounted their horses
And set out on the proper road.
I shall not recount the details of their voyage.
Suffice it to say that they traveled quickly 3945
Until they arrived one evening at Tormont.
Fair Geriaume looked around him
And observed Tormont closely.
He called out to Huon, saying:
"So help me God, my lord Huon, 3950
We have come to an evil place!
There before us lies Tormont.
Without God's help, we will all be slain."
Huon replied, "My lord, do not lament.
God willing, nothing will happen to us." 3955
Thereupon, they set off without delay
And rode rapidly, for it was almost evening.
Just as they were about to enter the city,
They encountered a servant
Carrying a bow, for he had just been hunting. 3960
Huon greeted him, saying:
"My friend, may God save you,
He who sought to redeem us all."
When the servant heard him speak of God,
He looked at the companions with astonishment 3965
And said to the well-born knight:
"My lord, you who greeted me
In the name of the Lord who hung on the cross,
May you also be greeted in his name.
But I beseech you, speak carefully 3970
To avoid notice by the duke who governs this city,
For I tell you in all loyalty,
If he recognized you and knew you were here,
He would have you torn limb from limb.
You may trust me, however, 3975
For I have believed in God for over seven years now.

I cannot reveal my secret because of the duke."
"My friend," said Huon, "in the name of God,
Tell me who rules the city."
The servant replied, "My lord, I will tell you: 3980
A proven traitor rules it.
His name is Dudon, and he used to be a Christian,
But he renounced holy Christianity.
Now he is so cruel and unrestrained
That any Christian he captures   3985
Will be martyred.
But tell me, where are you trying to go?"
"My friend," replied Huon, "I will tell you:
I am headed straight for the Red Sea.
I wanted to lodge for one night   3990
In this city, for we are all tired."
"My lord," said the servant,
"I advise you, by God in majesty,
Fair lord, not to enter the city,
For if the duke knew you were there,   3995
He would have you thrown into a dungeon.
He has already imprisoned one hundred forty men,
But if you wish to take another route,
In the name of the Lord in whom I believe,
I will gladly lead you a different way."   4000
Geriaume said, "My lord, take the second route."
But Huon replied, "In the name of God, I will not!
It is nearly nightfall, and the sun is about to set.
It would be a shame to miss out on such a good city."
The pagan said, "You are right,   4005
And for the love of God in whom you believe,
I wish to take you to a lodging place
Where you will be honored and well served.
It is the home of the provost Hondré,
Who has believed in God for a very long time."   4010
"May God reward you, my friend!" said Huon.
They then entered the fine city,

Guided by the pagan.
They went directly to their lodgings,
Where they found Hondré on his bridge.					4015
Huon greeted him in the name of God.
When the provost heard God's name,
He was truly filled with wonder.
He said to Huon:
"Noble lord, welcome.						4020
For the love of God, speak carefully
So that the duke does not learn of your presence.
If he knew you were here, you would be in harm's way,
But if you wish to take lodgings with me,
For the Lord in whose name you addressed me,				4025
All of my possessions will be at your disposal:
Marten furs and collared ermine cloaks,
Bread, meat, old wine, and claret.
Even if I had to house a hundred knights for a year,
I would not have to leave my house					4030
To satisfy any demands that might be made."
"My lord," said Huon, "may God reward you!"
They proceeded to dismount.
The servants removed the harnesses from the horses,
Put them in the stables,						4035
And gave them an abundance of hay and oats.
As for our knights, may Jesus protect them,
They entered the bourgeois's dwelling.
The provost treated them most honorably.
When they were seated and had rested a bit,				4040
Huon spoke to bearded Geriaume:
"My lord," said Huon, "rise quickly
And run through the streets
Announcing on every corner
That I invite every jester, minstrel,					4045
And penniless scoundrel
To come and dine in my lodgings.
I will give them an abundance

Of bread, meat, old wine, and claret,
None of which will cost them a penny.   4050
Next, go to the butcher shop
And have them send all the meat in their stock,
And all the fish, both fresh and salted."
Geriaume replied, "Just as you wish."
The host intervened, saying, "My lord, if you please,   4055
There are great quantities of food in my household,
And I have already placed everything I have
At your disposal, most willingly."
Huon replied, "That is out of the question.
I do not wish to cause you any expense,   4060
For we have a great deal of money.
I also have a goblet worth an entire city,
Capable of providing wine to all the men in the world."
His host took this claim for pure madness.
He found it to be unbelievable,   4065
And yet he thought about it for a long time.
Then Huon did a very foolish thing:
He took the ivory horn
From the pouch where he had carefully wrapped it
And handed it over to his host.   4070
"My lord," said Huon, "please listen to me:
Guard this horn for me until tomorrow
And return it to me if I need it."
His host replied, "By all means, just as you wish."
He took the horn and placed it in a case.   4075
The day would come when brave Huon
Would bitterly regret this action.
Meanwhile, old Geriaume wasted no time.
Fluent in the Saracen language,
He quickly mounted his horse,   4080
Found a servant, and had him announce
Throughout the streets of the entire city
That all jesters, vagrants,
Scoundrels, and poor knights

Should go immediately to the home of the provost Hondré,   4085
Where they would find an abundance of food,
None of which would cost them a penny.
When all the ragged and barefoot vagrants
Heard this invitation, they were filled with joy.
They all ran around spreading the news.   4090
You should have seen the riffraff gather!
You could not go for half a league
Without seeing four hundred of them assembled,
All wanting to dine with Huon.
Brave Geriaume went to the butcher shop,   4095
Where he ordered all the meat,
As well as all the fish, fresh and salted,
To be delivered to his host.
He engaged in no bargaining, I assure you.
He then came back to Hondré's dwelling.   4100
When the meal was ready,
The tables were set, and all sat down to eat.
There were poor people seated everywhere.
Huon served them their meal,
Along with their host and brave Geriaume.   4105
Huon carried the pure gold goblet:
No matter how much he poured
To quench the thirst of all the guests at all the tables,
His goblet was always full to the brim.
Everyone who saw this was amazed.   4110
The traitor Dudon's seneschal
Went to the market to buy food,
But he could not find a single soul
Who could provide him with provisions for his lord.
Angry and outraged,   4115
He called out to the vendors:
"What is going on? Have demons been here
Stripping the market of all its goods?"
They replied, "My lord, we will tell you:
An old man with graying hair   4120

Bought up everything in the market."
When he heard this, his blood boiled.
"Where is he?" asked the wretched scoundrel.
And they replied, "At the home of Hondré the provost."
"By my faith," he declared, "I will pay them a visit!"   4125
He turned on his heel, angry and outraged.
He returned to the palace,
Where he found the duke and called to him:
"My lord, something is up.
There are people seeking to wrong you,   4130
For they have emptied out the market
So that I couldn't find a soul
To sell me a single piece of food for your dinner.
They are now at the home of Hondré the provost."
"By my faith, they will be sorry!" said the duke,   4135
"For, by Mohammed whom I worship,
I will go and pay them a visit!"
He cried out, "Go and arm yourselves,
And bring me my hauberk!"
And they obeyed, for they dared not refuse.   4140
They quickly armed themselves
And brought the duke his hauberk.
He donned the armor
And girded his sword on the left side.
His knights were properly equipped,   4145
All wearing their hauberks.
I shall now leave these traitors
And tell you about fair Huon:
He was serving food to the poor,
Along with his host and brave Geriaume.   4150

33

That night Huon was lodged
In the home of Hondré the warrior,
Where he served a meal to the poor.

They had their fill of old wine and claret,
For the goblet used by proud-faced Huon   4155
Contained enough to satisfy everyone,
Provided that a virtuous man poured from it.
But there was a spy eating in the house.
He left the table as soon as he could
And slipped out of Hondré's dwelling.   4160
He went directly to the palace,
Where he found Dudon.
The traitor immediately shouted:
"My lord, please be quiet and listen to me!
In the home of your provost, there is a knight   4165
Eating with a large crowd of people.
They are all eating and drinking their fill,
For the noble young man has a goblet of pure gold
That serves enough to satisfy everyone.
It gushes forth, by Mohammed whom I cherish,   4170
Just as a spring flows on the sand.
They can draw from it as though from a river,
As much as they please,
Without diminishing its contents one bit."
"By my faith, I can't believe my ears!" exclaimed Dudon.   4175
"I could certainly use such a goblet.
By Mohammed, to whom I pray,
I will go after them immediately.
They will come away with neither palfrey nor warhorse."
He quickly departed, may God bring him misery!   4180
He brought with him at least thirty knights
And rode swiftly until he reached Hondré's residence.
There they found the drawbridge lowered and the gate closed.
The noble provost spotted them first
And said to Huon, "This doesn't bode well.   4185
The duke is here, and he is furious.
You will be slain and dismembered,
You and your men, unless God takes pity on you."
Huon replied, "Have no fear.

Let me plead my case before him."   4190
Proud Huon approached the duke directly
And called out to him loudly, saying:
"My lord, in the name of God, welcome!"
"Lowly vassal," replied Dudon, "do not come any closer!
You are a Christian, and I am a pagan.   4195
I can have no affection for you whatsoever.
And, by Mohammed to whom I pray,
You will leave here with neither palfrey nor warhorse.
Instead, I will have your head lopped off.
You and your men will all be slain."   4200
"My lord," said Huon, "what do you stand to gain
If you have me slain and dismembered?"

34

"My lord," said Huon, "you are quite wrong.
For the love of God, what do you want from us?"
"Lowly vassal," said Dudon, "I'll tell you at once: 4205
Because you believe in the Christian God,
You will have your head cut off at once
And not return with a fighting steed or packhorse.
Now tell me truthfully:
Why are so many men gathered here?   4210
You have quite a crowd for supper!"
"My lord," replied Huon, "I'll tell you at once:
I am going to cross the Red Sea.
I've prepared a meal in God's honor
For all these poor people you see here,   4215
So that He will let me return joyfully."
Dudon responded, "You've made a terrible mistake.
You will never escape from here,
Because I'll have you torn to pieces."
"My lord," said Huon, "stop this quarrel,   4220
And go disarm yourself immediately.
Here is what I propose:

You and your men go wash your hands,
And I will give you plenty to eat:
Bread, meat, old wine, and claret,   4225
Fish, both fresh and salted.
After eating, state what the law requires.
If anyone has done wrong, I will make it good.
For I tell you, as God is my witness,
You will gain little by harming me,   4230
But I think you would do well
To act properly and spare my life,
For I have heard that you were once a Christian."
Dudon responded, "You have spoken well.
We will gladly do as you have requested."   4235
He said to his men, "Take off your armor.
Let's eat, since we've found food
And have nothing for supper at home."
His men replied, "You have spoken well."
Quickly they removed their armor,   4240
Washed their hands in a large basin,
And sat down to dine at the high table.
Huon and valiant Geriaume sat down,
Along with their noble host and the other barons.
Across from them sat bearded Dudon   4245
Accompanied by his men, who were all pagans.
It goes without saying that all were well served.
Then young Huon rose to his feet
And cast off his fine silk cloak.
He crossed quickly in front of Dudon   4250
And grasped the golden goblet.
"My lord," Huon said, "in God's name, look.
You can see that this goblet is completely empty."
"You are right," said the madman Dudon.
Without hesitating, Huon made the sign of the cross   4255
And the goblet was immediately filled.
He offered it at once to his uncle,
But as soon as Dudon took it, the wine disappeared.

"Lowly vassal," said Dudon, "you have cast a spell over me!"
"Not I," replied Huon, "but your sins have.   4260
Put it down, for you cannot drink from it.
Thieving traitor, you are cursed
Because you've slain many good men
And the evil of it lives inside you.
You have never confessed to a priest   4265
Because you were cursed from birth."
"Lowly vassal," Dudon said, "you insult me
Here in my own city!
As Mohammed is my god, you are crazy.[31]
I could kill you and cut you to pieces,   4270
And no one would dare defend you!
So, tell me now without deception,
I entreat you on your word of honor
To tell me the honest truth:
From what land do you come? From which kingdom?"   4275
Huon responded, "Indeed, I'll tell you,
For I would never hide it from you.
In faith, I was born in Bordeaux."
"In Bordeaux?" — "Yes, so help me God."
"Who was your father, your progenitor?"   4280
"Upon my word, it won't be hidden from you:
He was called Seguin. May God have mercy on him,
Because he died more than seven years ago."
Dudon heard this and began to weep.
"My brother's son! Welcome to you!   4285
So why are you not staying with me?
Tell me, nephew, where are you going?"
"Uncle," replied Huon, "I'll tell you:
I am going across the Red Sea
To deliver my message to King Gaudisse.   4290
I've been sent there by valiant Charlemagne

31. We have chosen to use uppercase for the Christian deity and lowercase for
the Muslim deity. This choice is entirely dictated by the original intent of the
medieval Christian authorial voice.

Because I killed his son Charlot,
And he has confiscated all my lands
In such a way, so help me God,
That I'll never be able to return to them   4295
Until I have spoken with Gaudisse."
"Fair nephew," said Dudon, "by God,
Like you, I too was exiled from France.
I came here across the sea
And, I swear, I never wanted to return,   4300
So I renounced my Christian faith.
I settled here and became engaged.
I now have great lands, castles, and citadels
As a result of my marriage.
Now I'll tell you what you must do: 4305
You will come at once to my house
And remain there until sunrise tomorrow.
I will summon some of my men
And have you escorted to safety,
For you have a very dangerous road ahead."   4310
"My lord," Huon said, "may God bless you!
I will come at once, since you desire it."
But Geriaume said, "You will regret it!"
"That's for certain," added the provost Hondré.
But Huon went off without delay;   4315
All his belongings were brought
To Dudon's house, including the good goblet,
But the horn with which he was to summon Auberon
Was left at Hondré's place.
He spent this night with his uncle,   4320
Who was powerless to do him ill that night.
The next day, at dawn,
Young Huon rose early
And came to ask leave of his uncle.
"Fair nephew," said Dudon, "wait a bit longer,   4325
And I'll summon some of my men."
"My lord," replied Huon, "just as you wish."

The tables were set, and they sat down to dine.
The traitor sent for Jeffrey,
A knight who'd been born in France.   4330
Dudon had brought him here with him
And made him renounce his Christian faith.
Here is what he said to him:
"Jeffrey, listen to me:
Go immediately into that great hall   4335
And have five hundred pagans arm themselves.
Kill my brother's son while he is eating.
If he escapes, you will have lost my friendship."
Jeffrey replied, "Just as you wish!"
He entered the room at once   4340
And found seven hundred hauberks there.
On seeing them, he began to reflect:
"Alas! Miserable, unhappy man that I am!
The more evil one does,
The more one has to repent before God!   4345
This wicked traitor is crazy:
That's his brother's son he wants to kill!
His father Seguin once did me a great favor
At a tournament I attended:
Had it not been for him, I'd have been killed.   4350
Since the father did me such a favor,
I must repay it to the son.
May God damn me if I harm Huon.
Instead, I'll make Dudon pay!"
Then he headed for the dungeon;   4355
You'll soon hear what he had in mind.

35

Jeffrey left after formulating his plan.
He came to the dungeon where he found seven hundred Frenchmen.
Jeffrey spoke very softly to them:
"My lords, listen to what I have to say: 4360

This very day Jesus will help you,
And if you take heart, He will free you."
They answered, "In the name of God who created everything,
Each one of us will do as you will have us do.
We will follow you even to death   4365
If we can get out of here."
On hearing this, Jeffrey was overjoyed.
"My lords," he said, "now listen to me,
And I'll tell you everything that is in my heart.
In this palace is a noble young man,   4370
A Frenchman from that fine land.
He was born in Bordeaux, the son of Seguin.
His uncle Dudon says that he will kill him,
But if it pleases God, the traitor will be thwarted,
And blessed be anyone who will help me!   4375
Take vengeance for the evils you have endured!
Soon I'll see who will be the bravest,
And I will love him from this day forward."
They all answered, "Don't you worry.
The least among us will shine   4380
And fight bravely against the pagans."
Hearing these words, Jeffrey freed them at once
And led them out of the dungeons
And into the upper room
Where he had found the seven hundred hauberks.   4385
Then he spoke to them as follows:
"My lords, come here
And arm yourselves quickly!"
Every one of them donned his armor:
They put on the hauberks, laced up the helmets,   4390
And attached swords to their sides.
Jeffrey led them into the palace.

36

The barons were fully armed.
Jeffrey led them into the palace,
And Huon questioned his uncle: 4395
"My lord, for God in majesty,
When are you going to summon your barons?"
"Lowly vassal," replied Dudon, "don't be concerned.
By Mohammed, you are not one of my men,
And you can be sure that if you leave here,   4400
It will be one of the best days you'll ever see!"
He shouted, "Strike, my knights!
If he gets away, you'll all die!"
Hearing this, Huon was very shaken.
He quickly got to his feet   4405
And seized the sword at his side.
Suddenly there was Jeffrey with his men:
"Monjoie!" he shouted in his loud, clear voice.
"Strike, barons, as God is your Savior,
These are people I can never love!"   4410
And they did so ceaselessly,
Splitting the sides and lopping off
The heads and arms of those Saracens.
When Dudon realized that they weren't pagans,
You can be sure he was not pleased!   4415
The coward turned tail and ran
Into a nearby room.
Huon followed him, his engraved blade unsheathed,
But the traitor escaped cleanly:
He leapt from the window into the moat.   4420
It's a pity he didn't break his neck!
Jeffrey remained in the palace,
Slaughtering pagans
Until not a single one remained.
He threw over two thousand into the moat.   4425
When he saw this, Dudon nearly lost his mind.

Our Frenchmen occupied the splendid palace.
They bolted the gates, raised the drawbridges,
And then embraced and congratulated one another.
After they had recognized one another,   4430
The brave men rejoiced.
But soon their happiness turned to sadness,
Because the traitor had blown a horn.
Before you could have gone half a league
Four thousand men had gathered,   4435
Who all asked, "Noble lord, what is it?"
"My lords," replied Dudon, "I'll tell you:
The French have occupied my palace,
Wresting it from me by their overwhelming numbers.
Bring up my war machines at once!"   4440
They dared not refuse and did as he ordered.
They aimed the machines high
And attacked the palace from all sides.
They pummeled and assaulted it
Until one of its towers collapsed.   4445
On seeing this, Huon's blood surged.
"Dear God, who was nailed to the cross,
Are we to be captured here like this?
We can be certain
That if we are trapped and captured here   4450
We will all be dragged to the gallows and hanged."
"Huon, why don't you sound your horn?" asked Geriaume.
"I can't, by God," said Huon,
"Dudon has deceived us from the start!"
Just at this moment I've told you about,   4455
The good provost Hondré arrived.
He approached Dudon and said:
"My lord, you are a complete fool
To destroy your own palace this way!
That's your brother's son you're attacking.   4460
Do what's right, if you will:
Go to him and promise

Upon your word of honor
That if he surrenders your splendid palace to you,
You will let him go free."   4465
Dudon replied, "Provost, go to him."
"As you wish," said Hondré.
As he turned away, the traitor stayed behind
And said in a low voice, so as not to be heard:
"By the lord who makes the wheat grow —   4470
That is to say, Mohammed, whom I adore —
If I catch him, I'll have him dragged to his death!"
The provost did not forget his duty:
He approached the palace
And shouted from across the moat: 4475
"Huon, my lord, let me speak with you!"
"My God," said Huon, "who is coming there?"
"It is I, my lord," replied the provost Hondré.
"Dear host, for God's sake, what do you have to tell me?"
He replied, "My lord, I'll tell you at once: 4480
I beg you, my lord, for God in majesty,
To hold the palace as long as you can,
Because, as God is my Savior, I say to you
That if the traitor can trap you in there,
He will have you dismembered!"   4485
"Dear host," said Huon, "for God in majesty,
I beg you, my lord, for blessed charity,
To have pity on me and save me,
For I am a dead man if you fail me!
I left an ivory horn with you.   4490
If I had it, I would have everything I need.
You would suddenly see so many men come forward
That this whole city would be filled with them.
So, dear host, give it to me,
Because if you don't, my end is near!"   4495
"Here it is, my lord," said the provost Hondré.
He took the shiny white ivory horn
That he had hidden in his alms purse

And had his servant carry it at once to Huon.
Huon took it and rejoiced.   4500
He put it to his lips and was about to blow it
When noble Geriaume shouted:
"Huon, fair sir, what are you thinking?
So help me God, the King of majesty,
You are about to reveal your secret like a fool.   4505
Unless you are crazy, you are well aware
That if this provost were up to some evil
When you told him about the powers of your horn —
If he were a traitor and full of evil —
He would have immediately told Dudon everything,   4510
And we would be destroyed.
For God's sake, dear sir, keep your secret to yourself,
Because we don't know whom we can trust!
Huon, fair sir, for the love of God,
Who was nailed to the cross,   4515
Don't blow the shiny ivory horn.
I don't see a single wound upon you!"
On hearing this, Huon was greatly angered:
"What is this? The devil's to pay!
Am I to wait until I'm killed?   4520
I'll blow the horn, no matter what anyone says!"
He took the shiny white ivory horn,
Raised it to his lips, and blew it
So loud and hard
That bright blood flowed from his mouth.   4525
Those who were attacking the splendid palace
Began to sing when they heard the horn,
While the men in the palace started to dance.
And Huon kept blowing and blowing.
Auberon heard him in his city of Monmur.   4530
"My God," said the little king, "I hear my friend,
The most loyal born of woman, sounding his horn.
By Jesus, whom I must adore,
I love him so much for his great loyalty

That I want to protect him from all his enemies.   4535
I wish to be where he has blown the horn,
Accompanied by a hundred thousand men at arms —
And even more, if need be!"
No sooner had he made this wish than he was there.
Through magic and the will of God,   4540
They came to Tormont, the marvelous citadel.
They filled the streets from end to end,
And the pagans and Saracens could only wonder
Where so many men had come from.
Auberon entered the palace,   4545
And Huon, on seeing him, ran to embrace him.
"My lord," he exclaimed, "we are glad to see you!
I thank you five hundred times in God's name
For coming to help me in such a distant land."
Auberon said, "It's because we are friends.   4550
I will not fail to help you as long as I live
So long as you are loyal to me."
"My lord," said Huon, "may God be gracious to you!"
Our barons entered the citadel
And slaughtered the pagans,   4555
But Auberon issued a solemn decree:
Whoever believed in God would be spared.
When the pagans heard the decree
That good King Auberon had issued,
More than five hundred were baptized.   4560
They then seized Dudon, the wicked traitor,
Took him up into the high palace,
Brought him before Huon,
And turned him over to him in front of all his men.
"Fair nephew," Dudon said, "have pity on me!"   4565
"Upon my word," replied Huon, "may God strike me dead
If ever again you betray anyone as you did me!"
Without waiting an instant,
Huon drew the sword that hung at his side
And struck a mighty blow   4570

That swiftly cut off Dudon's head.
He then had it hung on the city walls.
The country was well rid of him.
Then Auberon called to Huon:
"My friend, listen to what I have to say: 4575
You have now done all that you desired.
I am returning to Monmur, may Jesus be with you!
But I must not hide from you the fact
That I will not see you again
Before you have suffered so much   4580
That no man could tell it all.
This will come to pass because of your great folly."
Upon hearing this, Huon was greatly frightened.
"Noble sir, in God's name, you are mistaken.
Order me, fair sir, to do anything at all,   4585
And I will do whatever you wish."
Auberon replied, "Now you have spoken well!
Huon, dear friend, for God's sake listen carefully.
Hold in your heart what I am about to say.
That would be a good thing, and I would be grateful."   4590
"My lord," said Huon, "tell me,
For I am ready to do anything you command."
"So now I will tell you," said Auberon.
"I forbid you, on pain of death,
Ever to turn your steps toward Dunostre,   4595
Which is a tower beside the sea.
I tell you, and you must believe me,
That Julius Caesar, who raised me well,
Founded it and had it constructed.
It took over twenty years to build,   4600
And no one has ever seen a more beautiful tower:
You can count three hundred windows,
Twenty-five rooms, and five grand halls.
No one has ever heard of a finer one!
At the entrance there stand two men   4605
Entirely constructed of copper.

Each of them holds a mace,
Made entirely of iron and much to be feared.
They swing them constantly, in winter as in summer,
And I assure you in all honesty   4610
That even a swift-flying lark
Could not get past them into the palace
Without being cut to pieces and killed.
Within lives a huge, mad giant
Who is called Arrogant.   4615
He stole the tower and palace from me,
And along with them a fine gilded hauberk,
Which is whiter than the flowers of the field
And weighs less than a loaf of white bread.
I tell you in all honesty   4620
That whoever wears it on his back
Can never be wounded by any enemy.
Should he fall into water, he will never drown,
And there is no fire that can ever burn him.
Huon, dear brother," valiant Auberon continued,   4625
"I forbid you, on pain of death,
And on the love you have for my friendship,
Ever to turn your steps in that direction,
Because if you go there you will surely die!
I assure you, you cannot escape.   4630
Therefore, I wish to forbid you categorically
To go there. You would be wise to heed my advice."
"My lord," said Huon, "you are wasting your breath,
Because there is no man alive
Who could keep me from visiting this giant,   4635
Since I came from the kingdom of France
In quest of adventure.
You have told me about one I want to try
And, in the name of the God we must adore,
I tell you in all truth and openly: 4640
I will go to win the white gilded hauberk.
If it is as you have described it to me,

139

I will need it, I am certain.
And should the giant get the better of me,
If need be, I can sound the horn   4645
And be sure that you will come to my aid."
Auberon said, "I won't, by God!
Huon, dear friend, don't trust the horn,
Because, in the name of the One who suffered on the cross,
You can blow all you wish   4650
But you will not be rescued by me!"
"My lord," said Huon, "you may do as you like,
And I will do what I have in mind."
With that they separated;
Auberon returned to his woods   4655
And Huon remained in the city.

37

King Auberon left Huon
And returned to his own country.
Huon remained in the city.
He made all the Saracens convert.   4660
He gave all of Dudon's lands
To his host and Jeffrey to hold,
Making them both lords of the land.
Next the marquis made preparations to leave:
He took a great amount of gold and silver,   4665
Enough to weigh down ten packhorses.
Huon and his men mounted and set off.
They took leave of the barons of the land,
Commending them to the God of paradise.

38

Valiant Huon departed.   4670
The young man did not stop for anything.
He and his men traveled all day
Through the woods and deep valley.

They saw wonders and wild beasts
Everywhere they looked.   4675
The princes rode so long — may Jesus watch over them! —
That evening was drawing near.
As the day ended and night fell,
The weather grew troubled,
And they halted in a meadow.   4680
There were a great number of wild animals,
Deer and other beasts, grazing there.
Our men — may Jesus watch over them! —
Stayed quietly there all night long
While their horses grazed on the grass.   4685
When dawn appeared,
They mounted up without the least delay.
They rode toward the sea without stopping
Until they were about a league distant
From the giant's tall tower   4690
That the good and valiant King Auberon
Had forbidden Huon to seek on pain of death.
The sun rose, and the day grew brighter.
They had gone but a short distance
When Huon beheld directly in front of himself   4695
The tall tower and sparkling palace.
He spoke to the men around him:
"My lords, by almighty God,
It was not very wise of us, to be sure,
To stay in that meadow over there,   4700
Because now I see a high and mighty tower
Where we could well have spent the night."
Old Geriaume looked at the tower
And recognized it at once.
He was so frightened that his blood heaved   4705
And his beautiful eyes shed tears.
He began to lament woefully:
"Oh God! Almighty Father!
We will suffer this very day.

I see the tower that valiant Auberon   4710
Forbade us to seek on pain of death."
Seeing Huon, he told him frankly:
"Look! My lord Huon,
So help me almighty God,
As everyone knows, I've often said   4715
That only a fool takes a child's advice.
Look! Good sir, what can we do now?
So help me God, we are in dire straits,
And I tell you, as God is my witness,
That what you've shown us is Dunostre.   4720
I swear to you that a giant lives there!
If every man who ever died were resuscitated
And joined together here
With everyone who's now alive,
Still the giant wouldn't fear them all   4725
As long as he had his armor.
Oh, noble sir, don't you remember
When we left valiant Auberon,
The good gentlemen we love so dearly,
That he forbade us on pain of death   4730
Ever to approach Dunostre?"
"Sir Geriaume," said honest Huon,
"For the love of God, what are you saying?
Ever since the day I left France,
So help me God, I have never sought anything   4735
Other than adventure, I assure you.
Stop complaining, dear sir,
Because, by the One who shed his blood for us,
I will go up into this shining palace,
And if I find the giant up there,   4740
I'll attack him with my sharp sword.
Unless he is harder than a diamond,
I'll run him through with my steel sword!
You will stay here and wait for me
In this green meadow."   4745

Geriaume replied, "As you wish it."
Then the brave young man donned his armor:
He put on his hauberk, laced on the shining helmet,
And strapped his sword to his left hip;
He hung the ivory horn from his neck,   4750
But did not carry the valuable goblet.
He embraced his men as he left
And commended them to almighty God.
They wept tenderly as he departed.
Huon turned and strode   4755
Courageously toward Dunostre.
May the Redeemer Jesus be with him!

39

Young Huon strode directly to Dunostre,
Carrying with him the ivory horn.
He walked all the way.   4760
He walked so steadily that before long
He reached the tower.
Right at the entry he found the two automatons,
Just as Auberon had told him.
Each of them held a mace   4765
Made entirely of iron, which frightened Huon.
They swung them constantly, in winter as in summer.
God never created a bird swift enough
To get past them alive into the palace
Without being sliced to pieces.   4770
Young Huon stared steadily at them
And begged them repeatedly in God's name
To stop, but neither of them did.
Seeing this, Huon called upon the Lord God
And the Virgin who gave him birth.   4775
Huon wondered
How he could ever enter the palace.
Huon looked to his right and saw

A golden basin hanging from a pillar.
Whoever put it there had attached it tightly.   4780
Huon went over to it.
Listen now to what he did:
He drew the sword that Seguin had given him
And struck the basin three times.
The sound resonated loudly throughout the palace.   4785

40

The son of Seguin of Bordeaux
Struck the pure gold basin
Three times with great vigor.
There was a maiden in the splendid palace,
A great beauty named Sebile.   4790
As soon as she heard the golden basin resonating,
She rushed to the window, looked down,
And saw Huon, who was trying to enter.
Though she did not recognize him, she began to weep.
She turned away, then looked back.   4795
Grieving bitterly, she began to cry.
She lamented to herself, saying:
"Alas! God, true God in majesty,
Who is this man trying to enter the palace?
Woe is me!" she said, "if the giant finds out,   4800
He will want to strangle and murder him.
Even if there were a thousand men gathered below,
He would waste no time cutting them to pieces and killing them.
Alas!" she said, "I don't know the truth of the matter,
Whether or not the knight was born in France.   4805
I will go and take another look."
She hastened to the great gate
And thrust her head out the window.
She saw Huon's armor
Emblazoned with a magnificent gold cross.   4810
It had taken three years to fashion it.

When she saw this, the fair-faced maiden
Knew that the knight was from France.
"Alas!" she cried, "he was certainly born
In sweet France, the land I love dearly.   4815
Now I will be destroyed if the giant finds out."
Immediately, she hastened
To the room occupied by Arrogant.
He was sleeping — may he never get up!
Seeing this, the fair-faced lady   4820
Turned around and sighed deeply.
She quickly opened the door.

41

The young lady opened the door,
Producing a gust of wind that stopped the automatons:
The figures swinging their maces were immobilized.   4825
As soon as the door opened, their arms stopped moving.
Young Huon entered the palace,
And the damsel withdrew in haste,
Immediately entering another room.
When Huon realized that she was not speaking to him,   4830
You may be sure that he was deeply troubled.

42

When Huon saw that he could not speak to her,
He was downcast and distressed.
He was so upset that he did not know where to turn.
There were so many rooms, floors, and staircases   4835
That young Huon did not know which to enter.
He began to wander about the palace,
And his attention was soon drawn to one spot:
He saw fourteen decapitated men
Lying beside a pillar.   4840
After he had observed them carefully,

He went to shake them one by one,
But cursed be the one who could speak to him!
"By my faith," said Huon, "this was an ill-fated stop.
It was devils who made me enter this place! 4845
I'll leave now, because I don't want to stay here."
He went to the door, intending to make his escape,
But the automatons were back in movement,
Swinging their maces.
"By my faith," said Huon, "now I'm trapped! 4850
I fear — God help me! —
That I'll never be able to leave this place."
He turned around and reentered the palace.
Listening carefully, he heard the lady crying
And followed the sound of her lament. 4855
He entered a room where he found the young lady
And greeted her, saying:
"My lady, may God grant you honor.
Do you know how to speak my language?
My sweet lady, what is wrong?" 4860
"My lord," she replied, "I am overcome with pity for you.
If the one who guards this castle awakens,
So help me God, you'll die."
"What?" said Huon. "My lady, for God in majesty,
You speak French?" 4865
"My lord," she replied, "yes, so help me God,
For I was born in France.
That is why I feel such pity for you.
I noticed the cross you are wearing.
I am deeply saddened because of you." 4870
"My lady," said Huon, "for God's sake, tell me truly,
In what region were you born
And into what family?"
"My lord," she replied, "I will tell you:
I was raised in Saint-Omer. 4875
I am the daughter of Count Guinemer
And the niece of Seguin of Bordeaux."

When Huon heard this, he ran to embrace her.
He kissed her three times with great affection
On the cheek and then exclaimed: 4880
"My lady, may God save me,
You are my cousin, I assure you,
For upon my word as a Christian,
I am the son of fair-faced Seguin.
But tell me, on your honor,   4885
Who brought you here, my lady?"
"My lord," she replied, "I will explain:
My father came on pilgrimage to the Holy Sepulcher.
He loved me so much that he put me in his boat
To bring me along to Jerusalem.   4890
When we reached the high seas,
A great storm struck our boat.
The high winds and the squall brought us
All the way to this tower, where we dropped anchor.
When the huge giant who guards this dwelling   4895
Saw us arrive below,
He came down to meet us, mightily armed.
He killed my father and all of his men
And then brought me to this palace.
I have been here for more than seven years,   4900
Without hearing a single mass.
But tell me, where do you come from?"
"My lady," replied Huon, "I will tell you:
I come from the noble kingdom of France,
And I am going to cross the Red Sea   4905
To bring a message to King Gaudisse
On behalf of valiant Charlemagne.
My men are below in the meadow,
And I came here to see this dwelling
And to meet the raging giant."   4910
"Fair cousin," she said, "what were you thinking?
In the name of God, if five hundred men like you
Came and gathered here,

As long as he was fully armed,
He would not fear them any more than a piece of bread.   4915
Fair sweet cousin," implored fair-faced Sebile,
"Take your departure, if you please,
And I will go and stop the automatons."
"My lady," said Huon, "that is out of the question.
By the faith I owe the soul of my father,   4920
The good Seguin of Bordeaux,
I will see the giant before I leave this place."
The maiden replied, "Fair cousin, you must not!
You and I would both be in great danger."
"You are wasting your breath," said Huon,   4925
"For even if I were to be torn limb from limb,
Nothing would stop me from seeing the giant."
"I am absolutely certain," said Sebile,
"That you and I will both be devoured.
However, since you insist,   4930
I will tell you where to find him:
Enter here, fair sweet cousin.
In this first room, you will find clear wine;
In the next, quantities of fine furs;
In the third, you will see the four gods;   4935
And in the fourth, you will find Arrogant.
That is where he sleeps — may he never get up —
For he was not fathered by a man!
My noble lord, if you find him asleep,
Cut off his head while he slumbers,   4940
For if he awakens, you are doomed.
He just returned from hunting in these woods.
I saw him bring back those fourteen men.
When he gets hungry and wishes to dine,
He will eat one of them and another at supper."   4945
"By my faith," said Huon, "that is out of the question!
I will never be reproached in high court
For striking a man without having challenged him."
Young Huon turned to leave,

His shield around his neck and his sword drawn.   4950
He entered the first room, but did not stop there.
He entered the second, and then the third,
Where he found the four raging gods.
Young Huon looked at them carefully
And dealt each one a mighty blow.   4955
In the fourth room he found Arrogant.
There slept the huge raging giant
On a luxurious bed:
The coverlet was made of an elegant fabric from across the sea
And the sheets were of natural silk.   4960
The pillow where he laid his head
Was worth a hundred pounds.
The feathers came from an exotic red bird
And were more fragrant than macerated balsam.
The chandeliers were extraordinary.   4965
The feet of the bed were made of pure gold
And its edges of carved ivory.
At the four corners of the bedstead, all in gold,
Were four sculpted birds
That sang in winter as in summer   4970
And announced the break of day.
The harp and the fiddle lost their charm
Compared to the song of these golden birds.
There slept the huge raging giant.
Would you like to hear me describe this devil?   4975
He was eighteen feet tall,
With stout arms and large, solid feet.
His eyes were as red as burning coals,
And a good six inches separated his eyes from his nose.
Brave young Huon observed him carefully   4980
And then exclaimed:
"Dear God! By your holy goodness,
If valiant Charlemagne were here,
He would see what I am up against.
Holy Mary, what will I do?   4985

If the giant wakes up, I am a dead man.
May God preserve me. I don't know what to do.
If I struck him without first challenging him,
It would be an act of vile treachery
That would earn me reproach in high court.   4990
God, what am I saying? I am an utter fool.
No one would know about it except God in majesty,
But in God's presence no man should plan an evil deed.
May God destroy me on this very day
If I strike the giant without challenging him!"   4995
He then began to shout:
"Son of a whore! Are you awake or asleep?"
Hearing himself addressed in this way,
The giant stretched out so violently
That he turned over the bedstead.   5000
Greatly alarmed, he leapt to his feet.
"Lowly vassal," he said, "who brought you here?
Whoever let you in cares nothing for you."
"By my faith," said Huon, "since you know French,
I will tell you what brought me here: 5005
It was my great audacity and my great madness!"
"That is true," said the giant,
"For if I were clad in my armor,
I wouldn't give three dice for five hundred men like you.
But I am not wearing armor, and you are armed to the hilt.   5010
No one could blame me for hesitating."
"Be quiet," said Huon. "May God strike you down!
Get up and ready yourself,
For, by the One who suffered on the cross,
I will never be reproached in high court   5015
For striking you before you are completely armed."
The pagan replied, "You have spoken well.
I will arm myself, since that is your wish."
He leapt up like a madman
And ran quickly to arm himself.   5020
He put on a gambeson

Made of thirty thicknesses of silken cloth
And placed over it a clavain.
He then donned a very long and very wide hauberk
Measuring fourteen feet in length: 5025
Four men could have fit inside it.
Over the hauberk he placed a tunic
Of tough leather from Cappadocia.
Rare was the sword that could pierce it.
He then seized a scimitar[32] with his two fists.   5030
When he was fully armed, he entered the great hall
Where brave Huon awaited him.
When the giant saw him,
He began to shout at the top of his lungs:
"Here I am, brother. Now I am fully armed!   5035
But I beseech you, upon your honor
And the faith you must defend,
Tell me who your father is —
He was a worthy man, I am sure of it —
And tell me in what land you were born,   5040
What you seek, and where you wish to go.
When I have killed you and cut you to pieces,
Your head will be placed on this ornamental ball.
Whom will I have the pleasure of naming to my men
As the knight who allowed me to arm myself?   5045
Clearly, you are not the son of a coward."

32.   The Saracen weapon is named *faulz* in Old French, which is the same as modern French *faux*, or "scythe." Due to this obvious similarity, it is not even glossed in Godefroy or Greimas (see Bibliography), and is regularly translated "scythe." It was considered a peasant weapon and was indeed frequently used as such. Godefroy does gloss *faulque* as a "*sorte de faux*" in the citation "*une faulque de fer.*" A scythe has a long, curved blade and is used even today for mowing or reaping. We believe that *faulz* in our text refers to a *scimitar*, a broadly curved Eastern blade introduced as early as the eighth century, but then widely employed during the Mongol invasions of the thirteenth century. Whereas a scythe has a long wooden handle, the scimitar is held by a short grip, more like a sword. And, whereas the scythe was made of iron (see quotation above), the scimitar of our text is twice described as being of steel, a stronger and more expensive metal (lines 6505 and 6754).

Huon replied, "You are completely mad!
I am still in perfect health, thank God,
And entirely whole, yet you boast of my death.
Nonetheless, I tell you truly: 5050
If you kill me, you will be able to boast
That you have killed an unfortunate wretch
Whom Charlemagne deprived of his inheritance.
Thus, I am obliged to cross the sea
And bring a message to King Gaudisse.   5055
I was born in Bordeaux,
And my name is Huon.
Now I have told you the whole truth.
But I entreat you, upon the faith you must defend,
To tell me the truth in turn: 5060
What land are you from, and who are your family?
When I have killed you and cut you to pieces,
Whom will I have the pleasure of boasting to my men
That I have slain, killed, and cut to pieces?"
The giant replied, "You have spoken well.   5065
If you kill me, you will be able to boast
That you have vanquished Arrogant,
The great giant who lives beside the sea.
I have fifteen brothers, and I am the eldest.
Every pagan, Saracen, and Slav   5070
From here to the Dry Tree, or as far as one can go,
Owes me four pure gold pennies per year
In tribute as the price of his freedom.
I attacked the emir Gaudisse —
The one you are going to see —   5075
And took fourteen cities from him,
The poorest of which had ten thousand knights.
He is my liege man through ransom.
He gave me a fine gold ring
To free himself from servitude.   5080
I also attacked the fairy Auberon:
All of his magic and marvelous knowledge

Could not harm me in the slightest.
I took this castle away from him,
Along with a fine gilded hauberk: 5085
Any man born of a mother
Who can fit his head through its opening
Can never be wounded by any weapon.
However, it is not available to just anyone.
According to the inscription on its collar, 5090
In order to don this hauberk,
A man must be virtuous, free from mortal sin,
Innocent, pure, and loyal.
And if the mother who carried him
Ever thought about being with a man 5095
Other than her husband,
He would not be able to don this armor.
Thus, I assure you that the man able to wear this hauberk
Has not yet been born.
But I declare to you most faithfully 5100
That the hauberk's magic is so powerful
That the one who wears it
Will never sink if he falls in the water;
If he falls into a fire, he will not burn,
As I have verified, by Mohammed.[33] 5105
Because you permitted me to arm myself,
I will permit you to try the hauberk.
I have long kept it safe in a case."
He ran to the spot where the hauberk was kept
And grabbed it without delay. 5110
I assure you, it was quite light.
When he came back, he cried:
"Here it is, brother, by my god Mohammed!
It weighs no more than white bread made of fine flour.
If you wish, you may put it on. 5115

33. Kibler and Suard, 283, n 1, interpret this line to mean that the giant has tested the hauberk's properties by throwing it into water and fire; he has not, however, been able to wear it.

By Mohammed, no harm will come to you."
Huon replied, "As you wish."
He took the hauberk
And went to stand beside a pillar.
He began to pray fervently, asking God   5120
To allow him to don the hauberk.
He unlaced his green-gold, gem-studded helmet
And unbuckled his engraved sword.
He removed the hauberk he was wearing
And took the one that was brought to him.   5125
He lowered the front section,
Lifted up the back,
And fit his head through the opening,
Which was neither too long nor too wide.
He then laced up his green-gold helmet   5130
And grasped his fine sharp blade.
The giant said, "Now you are properly armed.
Give it back to me at once, as is right and fitting."
"Be quiet," said Huon, "may God strike you down!
I wouldn't give it back to you for fourteen cities.   5135
How very ugly you are.
May the One who suffered on the cross curse you!
You were never begotten by a man."
The giant replied, "That is true.
The demon Beelzebub is my father,   5140
And Lady Murgale, a sea-dwelling giant,
Bore me in her womb.
Every devil and demon in hell
Belongs to my extended family.
If you return my shining hauberk,   5145
I will let you leave willingly,
And you will have the precious ring of pure gold
Given to me by the emir Gaudisse.
Here it is, brother, on my finger.
It is small enough for my little finger,   5150
But you could fit it on your arm.

The ring could be useful when you deliver your message,
For you have a dangerous voyage ahead of you, by Mohammed!
I must tell you in all loyalty
That when you have crossed the Red Sea   5155
And entered the fine city —
Before you arrive at the splendid palace —
You will find four porters
And four bridges, all raised.
If you tell them that you are French,   5160
They will cut off one of your hands at the first bridge;
You will lose the other hand at the next bridge,
And at the third bridge you will leave one of your feet,
And at the fourth you will lose the other one.
When you are in this sorry state,   5165
All of the porters will grab hold of you
And carry you to the emir,
Who will have your head lopped off.
But if you want to avoid all this,
Return to me my fine gilded hauberk.   5170
I will give you my precious ring of pure gold,
Then you will be able to go safely
About the palace whenever you wish.
Even if you killed five hundred men
And struck the emir in the nose   5175
So that blood gushed to the ground,
You could show them this fine ring of pure gold
And never fear a living soul."
Huon replied, "Never mind all of that,
For, by the One who suffered on the cross,   5180
This hauberk will never leave my body
Until I have killed you and cut you to pieces.
And I will have that ring, whether you like it or not!"
The giant replied, "You are determined, then?"
"Indeed, in the name of holy charity," said Huon.   5185
"I challenge you in the name of almighty God."
The giant replied, "And I challenge you as well!"

He raised his scimitar high into the air
And then threw it toward Huon.
The young man dodged it, for he was quite agile.   5190
He missed the blow, and the scimitar hit a pillar,
Penetrating four feet into the marble.
The giant pulled it out furiously
And began to mock and insult Huon:
"Lowly vassal," he cried, "by my god Mohammed,   5195
I do believe that my blow frightened you!
If this scimitar had struck you,
You would no longer have had any desire whatsoever
To insult me: that is what I think.
There is one thing you must do, if you please: 5200
Renounce that fool Jesus.
He could never defend you against me.
How could he possibly help you, when he allowed himself
To suffer on the cross and be killed by the Jews?"
"Be quiet," said Huon. "May He dishonor   5205
And destroy you but save me!"

43

Huon was angered by the giant's words;
He was trembling with fury and wrath.
Raising his arm and his sword,
He approached the giant with great ferocity   5210
And struck him so violently
That the giant's shiny golden headgear
Protected him about as much as a little vine-shoot.
The blow sliced into his basinet and coif.
Reeling with pain, the wretch swerved to one side,   5215
And the blade pierced his flesh above the hip,
Slicing off a handful of skin
That dangled from his body.
The giant screamed in agony.
Seeing this, Huon gave thanks to God, then said: 5220

"Scoundrel! Little do I esteem your bravery
After the things you said a moment ago.
I value you no more than a vine-shoot!"
The giant replied, "You will soon learn
The cutting power of this scimitar!"   5225
Brandishing the scimitar ferociously,
He rushed at Huon with great fury.
He tried to strike him hard on the head,
But God the almighty Father did not allow it.
As it came down, the scimitar hit a bench   5230
And sliced it in two like a little vine-shoot.
The bench and the scimitar both fell to the ground.
The bench struck Huon so hard
That it knocked him down
And caused him excruciating pain.   5235
He fainted from the agony.
When the giant saw him
Lying on the ground, he nearly exploded with anger.
He vowed to Mohammed, by whose law he was bound,
That he would not touch Huon until he stood up,   5240
For he feared him not one bit.

44

Young Huon regained consciousness
And saw the giant, who esteemed him so little.
No wonder he was afraid!
He implored God and his most holy name: 5245
"Glorious God, who created the entire world,
You fashioned Adam out of clay,
And you created Eve from Adam's rib.
All of paradise was at their disposal,
Except one apple tree, which was forbidden to them.   5250
Spurred by the devil, Eve ate of the apple
And gave some to Adam her companion.
For this, they were driven out of paradise.

Because of their sin, the whole world was damned:
Every prophet and every holy man   5255
Had to take up lodging in hell.
Then you took pity on them, dear Lord:
You sent Gabriel, one of your angels,
To hail the Blessed Virgin
Through whom we are all saved.   5260
We know truly that you were born of this Virgin.
For thirty-two years you traveled throughout the land,
Converting St. Peter,
St. Andrew, St. Paul, and St. Simon.
On Palm Sunday, you were welcomed joyously,   5265
And you took lodging in the home of Simon.
You pardoned Mary Magdalene,
Who lovingly anointed your feet.
Judas felt such indignation
That he committed a foul crime: 5270
He sold you for thirty pennies to the treacherous Jews,
And those vicious traitors nailed you to the cross.
You were then placed in the sepulcher to redeem us.
You descended into hell
And released Adam and Eve,   5275
Moses, David, and King Solomon.
You rose into heaven on Ascension Day.
Your companions were in great despair,
But you came to grant them pardon,
Ordering them to preach your name;   5280
They obeyed and were richly rewarded.
Just as I believe all of this, dear Lord,
Protect me from this cruel giant:
Do not let him kill me, almighty Lord!"

45

When young Huon had finished his prayer,   5285
He turned toward the giant,

Who was facing him, about to strike.
But Huon landed the first hard blow:
He drew his bright shining sword,
And before the giant could raise his weapon,   5290
Huon had hit him so mightily with his steel sword
That he cut off his arms at the elbows,
Leaving the forearms still holding the scimitar.
The monster fled — he had no wish to stay and chat!
Huon pursued him, brandishing his sword.   5295
Hearing this, Sebile turned toward them.
Carrying a large club,
She came toward the commotion
And encountered Arrogant,
Who was running for his life.   5300
The maiden raised the club
And thrust it between the monster's legs.
The evil giant was tripped up
And fell on his back in the middle of the palace.
Huon climbed up upon his belly   5305
And struck him fourteen mighty blows,
Then with the fifteenth cut off his head.
Now the land was free of him!
Huon came to the palace window
And shouted to his men who were outside: 5310
"My lords, quickly now, come forward!
Now you can safely enter."
Hearing him, his men were overjoyed.
They came directly to the castle's entrance.
The maiden hastened to unlock the gates   5315
And knock down the mechanism
Controlling the two automatons
That were still swinging their maces.
The men strode up into the palace
And rushed to embrace Huon   5320
And ask him how he had done this.
"My lords," replied Huon, "I am very tired.

Step forward, by God, and look
At what I found guarding this castle."
Then he led them to where the huge giant lay.   5325
When they saw it, they stared
And wondered how fair-featured Huon
Could have defeated such a man.
Geriaume said to Huon:
"My lord, for the sake of almighty God,   5330
Who is the lady that we found here?"
"My lord, I'll tell you at once:
She was born in the town of Saint-Omer
And is the daughter of Count Guinemer.
She is my cousin, have no doubt about it.   5335
She and her father came into this kingdom
To see and visit the Holy Sepulcher.
A great storm hit their ship,
And they had to anchor below this tower.
This huge giant that I've slain   5340
Killed her father and then his men as well,
Then brought the lady to this castle."
Upon hearing this they went to embrace her.
There was great merriment that night:
There was much to eat and drink,   5345
And the barons rejoiced that night.
But this joy would soon turn to sadness.
The next day at dawn
Young Huon rose early.
He summoned his men at once: 5350
"My lords, listen to me.
You know well where I must go.
I cannot stay with you any longer.
I must leave, and if you love me,
You must await me here in this tower   5355
For two weeks, so help me God.
If I am not back with you in two weeks,
Go to France, greet Charles in my name,

And tell him all that I have done."
They replied, "Listen, Huon,   5360
Instead of the two weeks you ask for,
We will stay in this place for an entire year.
We will await you both winter and summer."
"My lords," replied Huon, "may God be with you."
Then the young noble equipped himself: 5365
He donned his hauberk and his gem-studded helmet
And girded his sword at his left side.
From his neck he hung the shiny ivory horn
And tucked the goblet under his belt.
He took the ring from the huge giant   5370
And put it immediately on his arm.
Then he went to embrace his men one by one,
Urging them repeatedly to watch over the lady.
There was great grief at his parting
As Huon commended them to God's care.   5375
He left the palace, strode down the staircase,
And headed straight down to the sea.
My God, how pitifully the lady wept!
Old Geriaume and the other knights
All went to the window   5380
To observe and watch Huon.
My God, how they grieved for him!
Meanwhile Huon arrived at the sea,
Which was quite near the castle.
He stopped on the shore,   5385
But he could find neither path nor ford,
Plank nor bridge, rowboat nor ship,
By means of which he could cross over.
He drew his sword from its scabbard,
Thrust it quickly into the sea   5390
But could not touch bottom.
"By my faith," said Huon, "I'd be crazy to step in,
And I don't dare trust this hauberk,
Because if I went in, I'm afraid I'd drown.

Holy Mary, please save me!"   5395
With that, the young warrior sat down
On the shore and began to weep.
He dearly missed the fairy Auberon,
Who was in the woods with his own men.
Auberon began to think about young Huon   5400
And tears began to flow from his beautiful eyes.
His men said, "Noble lord, what is it?"
Auberon replied, "My lords, I'll tell you:
I am remembering the noble young man,
Huon, who is so faithful   5405
And who defeated the huge mad giant,
Arrogant, who was so fearsome
And who held Dunostre, which he had stolen from me.
Now the young man is wearing the enchanted hauberk
And sitting on the seashore   5410
Where he has no idea how to cross the sea
Or find Babylon on the other side.
His weeping has touched my heart."
Malabron[34] responded, "There is no reason for that.
You can easily help him,   5415
Because, if you wish, I can help him cross."
Auberon said, "Thank you!
Go, brother, I urge you to,
But on the following condition:
Your penance will be doubled,   5420
And you must remain a sea creature for twenty-eight years,[35]

34. Malabron is a sort of double for Auberon. His magical powers are complementary to Auberon's, and he is able to act independently. Most Old French *lutons* (which we translate as "sea creature") are nefarious, whereas Malabron, like Auberon, is beneficent.

35. The penance that Malabron is given is a bit confusing. We understand that an initial penance of thirty years for incorrectly mixing a magic potion (vv. 5467–70) was "doubled" by adding twenty-eight more years when Malabron helps Huon cross the Red Sea. An additional twenty-eight years are imposed when Malabron comes to Huon's rescue a second time (lines 7344ff).

And I command you on pain of death
Not to promise anything to Huon,
Except that you may tell him
To stay true and loyal."   5425
Malabron said, "I will do all that you command."
Then he put on his fish skin at once,
Began to run, and did not stop
Until he reached the sea.
He leapt feet first into the water   5430
And swam faster than a stag through the meadow.
Huon was still on the seashore
Weeping, without knowing what to do.
As he was lamenting so,
He looked to his right   5435
And saw a beast approaching,
Swimming faster than a wild salmon.
It appeared to be a sea creature.
It leapt up onto the shore beside Huon,
Shook itself off, and shed its skin.   5440
There stood the most beautiful man
That anyone had ever seen or beheld!

46

Young Huon looked at the sea creature
And saw that he was handsome and fair-featured.
He spoke to him courteously, without malice: 5445
"My friend, in the name of God,
From what land and region do you come?
Are you a follower of Pilate or Nero?[36]
I saw you swimming rapidly
Through the water like a sea creature,   5450
But now I see you with noble features.
I believe you are one of King Auberon's men.
In the name of God, please don't harm me!"

36. Pilate and Nero are evoked as embodiments of evil.

He replied in a friendly manner:
"My good lord, sir," said the sea creature,   5455
"I am well aware that you're named Huon,
Son of fair-featured Seguin,
Who held Bordeaux and its environs.
Do not be afraid, son of noble Seguin,
For by my head, I'll never harm you.   5460
I've been sent to you by a famous king,
By my faith, and his name is Auberon."
"What?" said Huon, "May I know your name?"
"You will, brother: my name is Malabron.
I come from Auberon's household,   5465
And I'm his liege man, so help me God.
I once mixed up a powerful potion for him,
But since it went beyond his commands,
My lord condemned me to spend thirty years
In the form of a sea creature."   5470

47

"Dear friend and brother," said valiant Huon,
"For the love of God who saves us all,
Do I dare trust you?"
Malabron replied, "Have no fear.
I'll carry you across the Red Sea   5475
Without wetting your shoes or feet.
I'm going to reenter my fish skin.
You must get up on my back
And make the sign of the cross
So that the true God will help us to cross safely."   5480
Then young Huon exclaimed:
"May almighty God, who lives in majesty,
Have pity and watch over us!"
Then Malabron reentered his fish skin,
And Huon clambered onto his back   5485
As Malabron dove into the sea.
I cannot tell you how long it took to cross,

But no man, young or old,
Could have swum half a league
In the time it took Malabron to cross   5490
The sea and carry Huon to the other shore,
Where he laid him gently on the grass
And spoke kindly to him:
"Huon, I'm sorry you were ever born,
For no one could find the words to tell you,   5495
Nor could any ear hear nor heart conceive
The great sufferings you must undergo.
Even I must suffer on your account,
For I am condemned to double my penance:
I must remain a sea creature for twenty-eight more years,   5500
In addition to the thirty of my initial sentence.
I will suffer much grief for having helped you.
Now I will tell you what you must do:
You see before you the town you must enter.
Remember well what orders you've received: 5505
Be true to yourself, remain loyal,
For the moment you tell a lie,
You will lose Auberon's friendship.
Go with God's blessing; I can tell you nothing more."
He leapt feet first back into the sea,   5510
Young Huon remained alone
And commended himself to God.
Then he headed for the noble city.
Emir Gaudisse was holding court
At the feast of St. John in summer.[37]   5515
When Huon entered the city,

---

37. The feast of St. John in summer is celebrated June 24. Celebration of this feast by Saracens is also mentioned in other *chansons de geste*, including *Aye d'Avignon*, lines 2241-42 (*Aye d'Avignon, chanson de geste anonyme*, ed. S. J. Borg (Geneva: Droz, 1967)); *Vivien de Monbranc*, lines 19-24 (*Vivien de Monbranc*, ed. Wolfgang van Emden (Genava: Droz, 1987)), and *Lion de Bourges*, lines 3490-91 (*Lion de Bourges, poème épique du XIVe siècle*, ed. William W. Kibler, Jean-Louis G. Picherit, and Thelma S. Fenster, 2 vols. (Geneva: Droz, 1980)). John the Baptist is mentioned in the Qur'an as a significant prophet, and therefore it is not surprising that medieval Saracens might have honored him.

There were so many pagans assembled
That no one could have counted them.
He headed straight for the splendid palace
Where he found a thousand pagans returning from   5520
Hunting with falcons and another thousand setting forth.

48

He found a thousand shoeing horses
And another thousand helping with the hobbles.
He found a thousand men playing chess
And another thousand throwing dice.   5525

49

He found a thousand entering the palace
And another thousand returning.
All these thousands looked at Huon.

50

Because of the many pagans,
Huon forgot about the ring on his arm.   5530
He moved on, not wanting to stop.
In the middle of town, a pine tree
Was planted upon fifty pillars,
All of which were made of purest gold.
It was from here that the emir Gaudisse   5535
Instructed his pagans how they should behave
And should serve and honor Mohammed.
Young Huon looked closely at them
But moved on and did not stop.
Valiant Huon came to the first bridge   5540
And called to the porter as you will hear:
"Friend, dear brother, let me enter."
The porter replied, "Willingly,

If you will tell me where you were born.
If you are French, you must lose a hand,   5545
But if you are a Slav or Saracen,
The bridge will gladly be lowered for you."
Huon replied most unwisely.
The time would come, by almighty God,
That even for a hundred marks of pure silver   5550
He would prefer never to have thought of it.
"I'm a pagan," said valiant Huon.
He had lied, and Auberon knew it.
Now he had lost Auberon's love
And would deeply regret that he would not see him.   5555
A man is a fool to lie and swear to untruths
When he would be honored
By speaking the truth. He behaves foolishly.
But this is what Huon did through his stupidity.
His reckless lie allowed him to cross the bridge.   5560
Before he reached the second bridge,
He noticed the ring upon his arm
And remembered the fairy Auberon.
He was so upset that he thought he would go mad.
He swore to God, who suffered on the cross,   5565
That he would never lie again,
Even were he to undergo great suffering.
The young warrior reached the next bridge
And immediately shouted out
To the porter in a loud voice: 5570
"Son of a whore, are you asleep or awake?
May you be damned by the One who suffered on the cross!"
Hearing him, the porter was angered
And replied, "Where were you born?
How did you get across the first bridge?"   5575
Huon answered, "You'll soon find out!"
He took the ring that he had shoved on his arm,
Proudly raised it high,
And said to the porter, "Look closely

At this sign I showed him. 5580
Do you recognize it? Don't try to hide it."
He looked and recognized the ring.
He opened the gate and went to embrace Huon.
"Young man," he said, "you are welcome here.
And how is my lord, fair-featured Arrogant?" 5585
Huon said nothing. He dared not speak
Because he was afraid of lying.
Without saying a word, he crossed the bridge.
The noble warrior came to the third bridge,
And the porter approached him. 5590
Huon stopped. The porter asked him
How he had crossed the previous bridge.
Huon showed him the good ring of pure gold,
And the porter rushed to open the gate.

51

Huon stepped forward, but he was deeply saddened, 5595
For he realized he had behaved foolishly
When he had broken faith and lied.
"Alas," he said, "what will become of me?
My poor mother, who bore me in her womb
For nine months, will never see me again!" 5600
With these words he crossed the third bridge.
The porter spoke not a word to him.
Huon advanced to the fourth bridge.
When he reached it, he shouted to the porter:
"Open the gate, damn you!" 5605
As soon as the guardian of the gate
Heard him, he got to his feet.
He was an evil, ferocious man, prone to anger.
Seeing Huon was armed, he filled with ire,
And fear rattled his blood. 5610
He swore by Mohammed that as long as Huon was armed
He would not set foot upon the bridge.

Staring down at Huon, he boldly stated:
"Lowly vassal! Listen to me:
I'm asking you how you managed   5615
To cross over those previous three bridges,
Since you are French and don't believe in our god.
By Mohammed, who created and formed everything,
Be assured that whoever placed this green-gold helmet
On your head had little love for you.   5620
If he saw you before, he'll not see you again,
But if he does see you, he'll feel great pity for you.
You will be painfully destroyed.
I'll rip every limb from your body
And then burn them in a fire.   5625
With the beginning of the feast of St. John,
The emir gave us this command:
By my head, no armed man
Can pass through this gate alive.
Since they let you pass, the three previous porters   5630
Will be covered with shame.
And what would happen to you if you got through?
I am positive that the emir would kill you."
"Shut up," said Huon, "and cursed be your mother!
May your entire lineage and the one who engendered you   5635
Be accursed by the God who created everything.
Look at this sign I'm about to show you!"
Huon took the ring and raised it high.
The porter recognized it well.
He immediately opened the gate   5640
And lowered the bridge. Huon entered.
The porter embraced him at once
And kissed his legs more than twenty times.
"My lord," he said, "blessed be the one who bore you!
I swear to you: don't worry,   5645
The emir will cause you no harm.
If you want his daughter, surely he'll give her to you.
But how is our lord? When will he come?

By Mohammed who formed and created everything,
I'm very surprised he has not come to greet you."   5650
"Lowly vassal," replied Huon, "he will never come."
He said no more and passed on,
But to himself he lamented:
"By my faith, the almighty Lord was with me
When I slipped this ring upon my arm,   5655
But I'm sure that the devil deceived me
When I lied at that first bridge."

52

Now Huon has crossed over the four bridges.
Next he headed toward the splendid palace.
He entered the emir's orchards.   5660
God has not created a fruit tree
That was not planted there.
A spring flowed forth from its source,
Whose waters, no doubt, came from paradise.
No matter how old, white-haired, or gray,   5665
Anyone born of woman
Who washed his white hands in it,
Would immediately become a youth again.
Huon came to it and paused.
He washed his hands and drank from the spring.   5670

53

It is the spring of Emir Gaudisse.
Its waters flow from the river of paradise.
God has not created a woman so promiscuous
Who, were she to drink even a drop of its water,
Would not be as pure as the day she was born.   5675
Huon, the noble youth, came to it,
Washed his hands, then sat beside it.

54

This spring was guarded by a serpent.
No commoner could put his finger in the spring,
And if he tried, he would die at once. 5680
Huon came to it, and the serpent bowed to him
Because of the power of his hauberk.
He drank the water and washed his white hands.
He promptly forgot what he was supposed to do.

55

Huon had entered the orchard. 5685
The noble youth sat down to rest
Beside the spring of Emir Gaudisse.
He began to lament and weep tenderly:
"Oh God, please comfort me!
Holy Mary, please help me! 5690
Father of glory, what will become of me?
Oh Auberon, what will you do?
Will you fail me or help me?
Soon I will find out, by holy charity!"
He took hold of the bright ivory horn, 5695
Put it to his lips, then blew it so mightily
And with such force and power
That blood flowed from his nose and mouth.
Auberon heard it in his leafy woods.
"Oh God," he said, "I hear the rascal 5700
Who lied at the first bridge blowing his horn.
But by the One who died on the cross,
He can blow and sound his horn all he wants,
Because he won't be rescued by me
This time, so help me God. 5705
Instead, he'll have to suffer great distress
And endure starvation and terrible hardships.
The little scoundrel will be sorry he lied!"

And young Huon continued to sound his horn.
The emir was seated for dinner   5710
Among his close followers and peers.
They were being served wine and claret,
But at the sound of the horn they began to sing
And the emir started to dance.
The close followers, counts, and peers   5715
Danced until the horn stopped.
Emir Gaudisse cried out immediately
And addressed his men:
"My lords," he said, "listen to me.
Whoever is sounding that horn in our leafy orchards   5720
Has come to bewitch us.
I order you on pain of death
And by all the love you bear me,
To put on your armor and take up arms
As soon as he stops blowing his horn."   5725
They replied, "Don't worry.
Even if there are four hundred of them,
You will not see even four escape alive."
When Huon realized that no one was coming to comfort him,
He stopped blowing and set down the horn.   5730
Tears began to fall from his beautiful eyes.

56

When Huon saw that Auberon was not coming,
You can be sure he was greatly upset.
"Alas!" he said, "what can this poor boy do?
Oh, sweet mother, this sad, sorrowful boy,   5735
So filled with grief, will never see you again.
Ah, King Charles, may the God who created all things
Forgive you for the injustice you've done me,
Because, though I've done no wrong, you've banished me from your land.
Ah, noble Auberon, what will you do?   5740
If you don't help me, by God who made everything,

I'll never be able to return and —
Woe is me — I'll never see you again.
Ah, King of glory, I sinned most grievously
When I told a lie at the first bridge.   5745
I was heedless, and I know that I'll suffer
Much grief and will never escape it
Unless the One who created the world has mercy on me."
Then he said, "No more crying!
If Auberon fails me, then Holy Mary   5750
Who bore God in her womb, will save me.
Whoever trusts in her will not be abandoned.
In the name of the One who created this world,
I'll go there, no matter what might happen,
And deliver the message I was sent to give."   5755
He donned his armor without further delay,
Girded on his sword, relaced his helmet,
And headed straight for the palace.
May the One who formed the universe be with Huon,
For he knows not what will become of himself.   5760

57

Valiant Huon set off for the palace
But did not enter
Until the emir was seated at his noon meal.
Then he turned and started up the stairs,
Wearing his hauberk, with his gem-studded helmet laced,   5765
And his sword at his side shining brightly.
Now young Huon was in the palace.
A statue of Mohammed had been carried into the room:
It sat upon two magnificent pillars
With four candlesticks before it,   5770
Each bearing a lit candle.
Every Saracen and Slav bowed to it
As it passed before the other barons.
But young Huon refused to bow

And turned his back to the statue as he passed by.   5775
The Saracens stared at him
And said to one another, "It's easy to see
That this man does not believe in our god."
Others said, "Let him go.
He's a messenger from another kingdom.   5780
Perhaps he wants to speak with the emir
And hand over his engraved steel sword."
Fair-featured Huon heard what they said.
He remained silent and passed on.
A noble was serving Emir Gaudisse.   5785
All eyes were upon him
Because he was engaged to marry Esclarmonde.
He was a wealthy man with vast land holdings.
"Woe is me," declared Huon. "This is the man
I must kill if I don't want to break my oath to Charles.   5790
But, by the One who died on the cross,
No man alive will prevent me
From doing what I've been ordered to do.
May God do with me as He will!"
He stood at the table before the emir;   5795
He drew his sword with its golden pommel
And struck the suitor such a blow
That his head landed on the table
And spattered blood all over the emir.
"A good start!" said fair-featured Huon.   5800
"I believe I've killed the first man I met
And made good my promise to Charlemagne."
The emir began to shout:
"Barons, seize this man!
If he escapes, you are dead."   5805
Saracens attacked Huon from every side;
He clearly needed to defend himself.
He gripped his sword with its shining blade
And struck mighty blows to all sides.
He killed four pagans in front of the emir,   5810

But his defense would not last long
Because the dastardly unbelievers were too strong.
Seeing this, Huon was worried.
He retreated toward the emir,
Removed the ring from his arm,   5815
And tossed it instantly upon the table.
"Emir, my lord," said Huon. "Look:
By this sign, you must not harm me."
The emir looked at the ring
And recognized it as soon as he saw it.   5820
He shouted to his men:
"Pagans, get away from him!
By Mohammed to whom I pray,
If any Slav or Saracen here,
No matter how high-born, does him any harm,   5825
He will be hanged from a wide-branched tree!"
The pagans immediately ceased attacking,
For they were afraid to disobey the emir's command.
Huon stood tall
And addressed the emir at once: 5830
"My lord, by all that is holy,
I've not yet accomplished everything."
The emir replied, "Young man, you may
Stride through my hall from one end to the other,
And even if you killed five hundred men   5835
You need not fear any man alive."
Huon stepped forward,
Came up to Emir Gaudisse's daughter,
And kissed her three times as everyone watched.
Touched by the young man's kisses, she fainted.   5840
Seeing this, Gaudisse was incensed.
He said to his daughter, "Has he hurt you at all?"
"My lord," she replied, "I'll heal quickly!"
She saw a maiden there beside her
And said the following to her: 5845
"Do you know why I fainted?

His sweet breath has so wounded me
That if I don't have him beside me tonight,
I'll go mad before morning!"
Young Huon stepped away from her   5850
And spoke to Gaudisse.

58

"Emir, lord," said noble Huon,
"I do not believe in your Mohammed.
I have no more belief in him than in a stinking dog.
Instead, I believe in Jesus, who shed his blood   5855
And who was born to the Virgin in Bethlehem
And died on the cross at the hands of tyrants.
I was born in France, the land of the Franks,
And am a liege of noble Charlemagne.
The emperor is very sad of heart   5860
Because there is no prince from here to the East,
From Acre to Bocidant in Persia,
As far as the seas and heavens extend,
Who does not submit to him,
Except yourself, whom I see here before me.   5865
The brave emperor gives you notice
That since the creation of Adam
And since the terrible battle of Roncevaux,
Where he lost Roland and Olivier,
Our king has not assembled a mightier army   5870
Than he will next summer.
He intends to cross the sea at the next feast of St. John
And ride out against you.
If he captures you, by God the Redeemer,
He will hang you without recourse.   5875
If first you do not convert to Christianity,
You will die cruelly, you and your people.
If you wish to avoid this torment,
You will have yourself baptized at once."

The emir replied, "Nothing of the sort!   5880
Your God is not worth a penny!"

59

"Emir, sire," said Huon, "listen.
Charlemagne has another demand:
He orders you to send a thousand molted sparrowhawks,
A thousand goshawks — never doubt it! —   5885
A thousand bears, a thousand hunting dogs leashed together,
A thousand young men,
A thousand beautiful maidens.
And, so help me God, he demands even more:
He wants a thousand powerful horses,   5890
Along with the white hairs of your mustache,
And four molars pulled from your filthy mouth!"
The emir said, "Your lord is crazy!
As far as I'm concerned, he's not worth a penny.
If he gave me everything he owned   5895
I wouldn't let him pull out my white beard
Nor four of my molars.
He has sent me fifteen messengers,
And I've not seen a single one escape alive.
I've had them all skinned and salted   5900
And, by Mohammed, you'll be the sixteenth!
But your ring has kept anyone from touching you.
Now I want you to swear by your God
And by the religion you practice:
Since you say you were born in France,   5905
What living devils gave you that ring?"
Huon could not lie or retreat
Because he was too afraid of the fairy Auberon.
"Emir, sire," said noble Huon,
"I'll tell you the truth, so help me God.   5910
By St. Denis, what good would it do to hide it?
I killed and beheaded your lord Arrogant."

Hearing this, the emir began to shout:
"Pagans, are you going to let him go?
You're dead if he escapes!"   5915
When they heard this, the pagans ran toward him
And attacked him from every side.
He defended himself as best he could.
He caught sight of a vaulted arch
And backed himself up against its pillar   5920
So that he could not be attacked from behind.
The Saracens yelled insults at him,
And Huon, with his engraved sword in his hand,
Injured every man he could reach.
No need to call a doctor; Huon gave swift medicine!   5925
Damned was anyone who dared approach him:
He destroyed and killed fourteen of them!
Seeing this, the pagans were greatly frightened.
The emir began to shout:
"If he gets away, you are all dead!"   5930
Hearing this, the pagans started shouting
And moved toward Huon as one.
A particularly strong pagan
Had a sharp steel faussart
With which he tried to strike Huon in the side.   5935
When he saw this, Huon feared the blow
And stepped aside. The faussart missed
And struck deep into a pillar —
Some two feet, by my reckoning.
Swollen with confidence, Huon advanced upon him   5940
And gave such a mighty blow to his gem-studded helmet
That it split him in two down to his belt.
He had slain him in front of the emir.
The emir then cried out:
"My lords, listen to me: 5945
By the lord who causes grain to grow —
I mean Mohammed with all his power —
If this man is not seized and caught,

You will all be hanged and dragged by horses!"
Hearing this, the pagans gained heart: 5950
They attacked Huon on every side,
And he defended himself mightily.
He grasped the sword with which he was knighted
And wounded many a pagan that day.
Whomever he struck met his end.   5955
The young man proved himself in this fight:
More than fourteen were slain.
But then a great misfortune struck:
His engraved steel sword flew from his hand
And was retrieved at once by a Saracen,   5960
Who fled away with it
And kept it for many days in a chest.
The pagans moved toward Huon as one
And knocked him down in spite of himself.
One Saracen stepped forward   5965
And took from his shoulder the bright ivory horn
He used to summon Auberon.
Another Turk seized the goblet,
And others disarmed him.
They removed his fine gilded hauberk,   5970
And Huon was left with only his tunic.
They led Huon thus arrayed before the emir.
He was young and in his prime,
With a shining face and handsome countenance,
Though it was a bit disfigured   5975
From having worn his hauberk.
The Saracens stared at him,
Saying to one another, "This is a handsome youth,
Made only to be admired.
It would be a great pity to cut him to pieces."   5980
The emir called to his pagans:
"My lords, quickly, come here!
How will we put this prisoner to death?"
"My lord, hang him," the pagans answered.

The emir replied, "It will be as you say,   5985
If my greatest noble barons agree."
There was among them a Saracen infidel,
An emir some one hundred forty years of age,
Who was a counselor to the emir Gaudisse
And full of good advice.   5990
When he saw Gaudisse, he spoke to him:
"My lord emir, listen to me,
And I will tell you how you must act:
Today is the summer feast of St. John,
And you must not hold an execution in your palace   5995
If you do not wish to go against your religion.
He must not be executed.
Rather, you should throw him into your dungeon
And give him enough to eat.
You must keep him there for a full year.   6000
When next summer is at its height,
And it is time to celebrate the feast of St. John,
Then you must free him
And find a champion
He can face in closed combat.   6005
And if he can defeat your champion,
You must let him go willingly
And accord him safe conduct
So he can return home safely.
But if your champion can defeat him,   6010
This prisoner must be hanged and dragged by horses."
Said the emir, "I have heard you clearly.
If this was the practice of my ancestors,
I dare not go against my religion."
The wise counselor said, "Yes, so help me god."   6015
Huon was immediately seized
And taken down into the dungeon.
The emir ordered this
And also said Huon should be well fed.
"Alas," said Huon, "these are sad quarters!"   6020

Now I will tell you about the bright-faced damsel
Who was the daughter of Emir Gaudisse.
She was lying abed but could not find rest,
Struck as she was by an unceasing love.
Unable to sleep, she rose from her bed,   6025
Took a candle she had lit,
And went down to the dungeon where she found
The jailer sleeping beside a pillar.
She skillfully stole his keys,
Quickly unlocked the cell door,   6030
And entered carrying the lit candle.
When young Huon saw the light,
He was surprised and quite afraid.
"My God," he said, "what is causing this light?
Holy Mary, is it already morning?"   6035
The maiden said, "Don't be afraid.
Sweet brother Huon — so I've heard you called —
I am the daughter of Emir Gaudisse,
And you kissed me this morning during breakfast.
Your sweet breath has so wounded my heart   6040
That I will love you for as long as I live.
If you agree to do as I desire,
I will arrange for you to be freed."
"My lady," answered Huon, "don't say that.
You are a Saracen, and I can never love you.   6045
I cannot deny that I kissed you,
But I did it to keep my promise,
For I had sworn to Charlemagne to do so.
Even were I to be confined for life
In this dungeon, as long as I live   6050
I could never consent to be with you."
When the maiden heard him speak this way,
She thought that she would go mad with grief.
"Huon," she said, "can you not do otherwise?"
"No," said Huon, "for the love of God."   6055
"By my faith," she said, "you'll pay for this!"

She called the jailer at once:
"My friend, listen to me:
I forbid you to give this Frenchman
Anything to eat for the next three days,   6060
Or you will have your limbs chopped off!"
And he replied, "It will be as you command."
She let Huon fast for three full days,
And on the fourth, he grew desperate.
"Alas," he said, "there's no bread or wheat!   6065
Ah, Auberon, little hunchbacked dwarf,
May He who suffered on the cross curse you!
I've hardly done anything to merit your anger.
So help me God, I didn't even realize it
When I lied to get across the first bridge.   6070
Holy Mary, please rescue me!"
The maiden heard
Everything that Huon said.
She came to the dungeon and spoke to him:
"Lowly vassal, have you had second thoughts?   6075
Do you want to do what I asked?
If you are willing to promise and swear
To take me with you into your kingdom
If you can escape from here,
By Mohammed, I'll ask no more of you.   6080
If you will promise and swear to me
That you will treat me honorably,
I'll see that you have plenty to eat."
"My lady," replied Huon, "as God is my Savior,
Even if I were to burn forever after   6085
In the deep pit of hell,
I'll do everything you ask."
"On my word," said she, "you've spoken well!
For love of you, I'll believe in your God."
Then she had food brought to him,   6090
Which he ate, for he was extremely hungry.
The lady summoned the jailer:
"Friend," she said, "do you know what to do?

182

You must go to my father in his palace
And tell him — don't fail me! —   6095
That the Frenchman he imprisoned
Has died of hunger and fatigue.
After that, give him enough to eat
Of the best food you can find."
He replied, "Just as you wish."   6100
He came to the palace and found the emir.
"Sire," he said, "by my faith, do you know
That the young man you imprisoned —
The Frenchman — is dead?
He died of starvation in your dungeon."   6105
Hearing this, the emir was upset.
"I'm sorry to hear that, by Mohammed my god.
But since he's dead, let's not worry about it.
Let Mohammed take his soul and have pity on him."
In this way, Huon was saved from death.   6110
The jailer returned to the dungeons
And came to Huon. He stayed with him
And gave him plenty to eat,
Everything he could possibly desire.
Now I shall cease speaking about Huon.   6115
When the time comes, we shall know what to sing.
Now I would like to tell you about his men,
Who were awaiting him across the Red Sea.
They had been in the tower four months
Without hearing any word of Huon.   6120
You can be sure they were quite upset.
One morning they arose together,
And all thirteen left the tower fully armed.
They set off to enjoy themselves
And were armed to the hilt.   6125
Geriaume looked off toward the sea
And saw a large ship approaching.
There were thirty pagans on board,
And they were transporting a load of gold and silver.
Geriaume called to his companions at once: 6130

"My lords, for God's sake, look there!
It seems to me, I see a ship approaching.
Let's go meet it, if you agree,
And see if we can get word of Huon.
They responded, "Just as you wish."   6135
The thirteen armed men went down,
And the ship arrived in port.
Old Geriaume went to greet it
And spoke immediately to the sailors:
"My lords, in what land were you born?"   6140
They responded, "You will hear at once:
We are from the magnificent city of Mecca.
We come here to speak with Arrogant
And pay the duties we owe him.
Show us where we can find him."   6145
Geriaume replied, "He is dead.
But, by my head, I've got other news for you:
You will surrender your gold and silver
And leave your heads as hostages."
Then he shouted, "My companions, attack them!"   6150
They drew their good steel swords
And swooped down on them as they docked,
Slicing open their sides and flanks.
The sailors were unarmed and not prepared to fight,
But our barons were ready for them.   6155
Before you could have run half a league,
They were all slaughtered and dead,
And not a single one was left alive.
They tossed them all into the deep waters
And captured the ship and all it was carrying.   6160

60

Now that the thirteen had captured the boat,
They had gold and silver aplenty.
They carried everything into the shining palace

And then sat down at once to eat.
After they had eaten and drunk all they desired,   6165
Old Geriaume addressed them:
"My lords, listen now to my advice:
When we have returned to France,
To Charlemagne, who is lord over all France,
He will ask about our young lord Huon,   6170
But we will have nothing to tell him.
If we tell noble Charlemagne
That he is dead — we don't know that.
If Huon returns afterwards, by almighty God,
We will forever be accused of treason,   6175
And after us fathers, then our sons as well.
It's possible for a man to be in prison fourteen years
And still return to see his wife and children.
My lords, in the name of God who shed his blood,
Let us do what is right, if you agree: 6180
Now we have red gold and white silver,
So let us board this ship at once
And cross the sea at God's command.
Let us go seek news of the young man
And see if he is dead or still alive."   6185
They answered, "We will do as you wish."
Weeping tenderly, they left the tower,
Carrying all the gold and silver they needed.
They placed it all on board the ship at once.
They loaded sea biscuits, bread, meat, and white wine,   6190
Along with their war horses.
They took the young woman with them
And then entered the large boat.
They weighed anchor, spread their sails,
And set out across the Red Sea.   6195
May God guide them by his worthy command.

61

The knights were sailing the high seas,
May God, who judges all things, guide them!
Garin served as their pilot and captain.
They had a favorable wind, may God be thanked!   6200
They sailed together across the high seas —
No need to tell you about their days.
They traveled so quickly
That they reached the grassy shore on the other side
And left the ship. They were fully armed   6205
And immediately mounted their warhorses.
They loaded three pack horses with gold and silver.
They had the lady mount up without delay
And set off along the path to Babylon.
May the supreme Judge watch over them!   6210

62

The renowned barons took their departure.
Just as they were entering the city,
Old Geriaume called out to them:
"My lords," he said, "listen to me!
We are about to enter the splendid palace   6215
Where we will hear news of fair Huon.
When we appear before the assembly of barons
And before the emir,
I will do the talking, and you will listen.
Be sure to agree with everything I say."   6220
And they replied, "Just as you wish."
Then they entered the worthy city.
"Dear God, by your holy goodness," said Geriaume,
"Let us hear news of the young knight
That will gladden our hearts!"   6225
Then they approached the splendid palace
And crossed over the four bridges

Thanks to Geriaume's knowledge of the language.
They dismounted in front of the staircase to the great hall,
And then all thirteen of them went up to the palace,   6230
Bringing the young lady with them.
They found the emir surrounded by his barons.
Geriaume was the first to speak.
He spoke Saracen, for he was fluent in the language:
"May Mohammed, savior of all,   6235
Who created the skies, the earth, and the sea,
Who makes the meadows flower and the wheat grow,
Who makes the fish swim and the birds fly,
May he preserve and protect the emir Gaudisse.
May he see to it that the emir   6240
Never sees or encounters God in heaven."
The emir said, "I wish the same for you.
Tell me, friend, in what land were you born?"
"You will find out straightaway," said Geriaume.
"I was born in Monbrant,   6245
And I am the son of the emir Yvorin."
Hearing this, Gaudisse cried out:
"My brother's son! Welcome!
How is he? Tell me everything."
"He is very well, my lord," said valiant Geriaume.   6250
"I am to express his greetings and affection.
He also sends you as a gift
The twelve Frenchmen you see before you.
Be assured that he captured them the other day
As they were returning from the Holy Sepulcher.   6255
He asks through me that you throw them in prison
Until the feast of St. John in the summer,
When my father will come to see you.
At that time, you will release them from prison
And dump them in the middle of this meadow.   6260
You will then summon your archers,
Who will shoot them in front of your barons.
Whoever is most skilled in this exercise will earn the most praise.

As for the lady you see before you,
Place her with your daughter: 6265
She will teach her to speak French fluently."
The emir said, "As you wish,
But first tell me your name."
"My name is Tiacre," said Geriaume.
"Tiacre, my friend," said the emir,   6270
"Here is what you must do:
I will give you the key to my entire prison,
Which I place in your charge from now on.
You will throw the Frenchmen in there,
For I know that you speak French.   6275
Give them plenty of food,
So that they don't die of hunger and exhaustion
As did Huon, a young knight
Sent to me by valiant Charlemagne."
Hearing this, Geriaume nearly lost his mind.   6280
His blood surged from his feet all the way up to his face.
He looked down and found a club.
He nearly struck the emir with it,
But instead dealt such a violent blow to each of the Frenchmen
That bright red blood streamed to the ground.   6285
He was seething with rage,
All because of Huon, the young knight.
He could not relieve his anger any other way.
He also wished to deceive the emir Gaudisse
By beating the Frenchmen, which outraged them,   6290
But they dared not speak out,
For they were terrified of the emir Gaudisse.
As they quietly cursed bearded Geriaume,
The emir called out to him, saying:
"My friend, you are beating those men cruelly."   6295
Geriaume replied, "I have no affection for them.
And by Mohammed, to whom I pray,
For as long as I live and endure,
I will do my best to humiliate Christians.

My family has always despised them,   6300
And I cannot bear to set eyes on them."
Geriaume led them off to the dungeon, beating them all the while.
Along the way, he met Lady Esclarmonde,
Who spoke to him, saying:
"Noble knight, allow me to address you.   6305
You are my cousin, and it is your duty to hold me dear.
If I dared place my trust in you,
I would tell you my story."
"My lady," he said, "tell me anything you wish."
"My lord," she said, "here is my secret: 6310
In this dungeon, you will find a Frenchman.
I have led my father the emir to believe
That he is dead and gone,
But I tell you in all honesty
That he has amply partaken of every dish   6315
My father has eaten at his meals.
I beg you, do not expose him."
Geriaume thought she was lying.
He went past her without saying a word,
For he was convinced that her story   6320
Was meant to deceive him. He dared not trust her.
Geriaume threw the Frenchmen into the dungeon,
But did not enter himself;
Rather, he turned back, filled with anger and sadness.
Valiant Huon began to shout: 6325
"My God!" he cried, "who is coming to visit me?
Living devils threw me into this place!"
The others lamented bitterly, saying:
"Oh God, cursed be the day we were born!"
They began to mourn for Huon: 6330
"Look, Huon, noble and generous lord,
Because of our devotion to you, we are reduced to misery.
May the Lord God have pity on your soul!"
Young Huon heard them lamenting.
He moved closer to them and asked: 6335

"My lords, where are you from?"
And they replied, "We will tell you at once.
We are from the honorable land of France."
"And where were you born?"
They replied, "In the city of Bordeaux.   6340
We were the vassals of a young knight
Named Huon — may God have pity on him!
King Charlemagne took away his inheritance
And sent him across the Red Sea
To deliver a message to King Gaudisse.   6345
He brought all of us with him.
We stayed on the shore
In a tower, where he secured lodging for us,
But we eventually crossed the sea out of devotion to him.
Just now, in the splendid palace, we learned   6350
That our lord is dead and gone.
To top it off, we were mistreated by one of our companions,
Who threw us into this dungeon."
Hearing this, Huon was overjoyed.
"My lords," he said, "in the name of God, come forward!   6355
Quickly, let us kiss and embrace each other,
For I am Huon, your long-lost friend.
Thanks to your story, I recognized you.
There is no light in here right now,
But we will have plenty before nightfall."   6360
When they heard this, they were ecstatic.
Filled with joy, they all reached out
To touch Huon as best they could.
They kissed and embraced him, saying:
"My lord, are you in good health?"   6365
"Yes," he replied, "God be praised!
The king's daughter has fallen so deeply in love with me
That she gives me anything I ask.
Soon she will come and visit us."
"My lord, have you remained loyal?" they asked.   6370
"Quiet," he replied, "doubt me at your peril!

My lords, tell me truly, by almighty God,
Where is Geriaume?"
"My lord, he is up in the splendid palace.
That old man has renounced God.   6375
Now he's trying to convince the emir Gaudisse
That he is his nephew, a member of his lineage.
In the palace, he goes by the name Tiacre.
He beat us so mercilessly
That bright red blood streamed to the ground.   6380
It is because of him that we are in prison."
Hearing this, Huon burst out laughing, saying:
"My God, what a schemer!
All of this is aimed at our deliverance."
Now I shall return to valiant Geriaume,   6385
Who had not forgotten the prisoners:
He took plenty of bread, meat, and wine —
Enough to satisfy twenty men —
And went straight to the dungeon.
The young lady, daughter of the emir Gaudisse,   6390
Approached him, saying:
"Dear cousin, have you decided
To do as I wish?
I swear to you, by my god Mohammed,
That I would do anything under the sun   6395
If you commanded it."
Geriaume replied, "What is it that you want?"
"My lord, I will tell you at once:
If you agree to renounce Mohammed,
That idol fashioned of pure gold,   6400
And to serve and adore God,
And also to follow my advice,
We could go to the kingdom of France.
The Frenchman you will find in the dungeon
Assured and promised me that this was possible."   6405
When Geriaume heard this,
His heart leapt with joy,

But he dared not show his true feelings.
Instead, he responded as follows:
"You little hussy, do you believe in God, 6410
Who suffered such torment and hardship,
Who was hung on the cross by the Jews,
And pierced in the side with the lance?
Had he really been God, he would never have endured it.
By Mohammed, how dare you even think such a thing? 6415
I will tell your father the emir,
Who will have you burned to a crisp
After he has that Frenchman hanged!
He's your lover, I am sure of it."
When Esclarmonde heard Geriaume speak in this way, 6420
She thought she would go mad with sorrow.
She wept so bitterly that she was unable to stop.
Turning to Geriaume, she implored him:
"My lord, by my god Mohammed,
Do me at least one little favor: 6425
Please, take me with you
So that I might say goodbye to the young knight."
"My lady," he replied, "this I cannot deny you."
The two of them entered the dungeon,
The lady carrying a large glowing candle. 6430
As soon as Huon saw Geriaume,
He recognized him and ran to embrace him,
Kissing him with great affection.
All the barons embraced one another.
When the lady saw them rejoicing, 6435
She was quite moved by the happy reunion.
"Huon," she said, "tell me truly:
Are these your men?"
"Yes, my lady," said Huon, "so help me God.
All those you see before you are my men: 6440
You may trust them completely."
"My lord, they will be dear to me for your sake."
"In the name of God, barons," said Huon, "leave me now

And entertain this noble lady.
She saved me from certain death   6445
And has served me well, providing everything I asked.
I have amply partaken of every dish
That her father had at his meals."
"My lord," they replied, "may God reward her!"
And the lady said, "My lords, now listen to me,   6450
And I will tell you what to do,
For I wish to help you escape.
I can no longer have any affection for my father,
Who believes only in crazy Mohammed.
God help me, I hate him for this.   6455
However, if he agreed to worship God,
I would never betray him.
Now I will tell you how to proceed:
We will wait until evening,
When my father is sound asleep.   6460
I will give each of you a fine shining hauberk,
A good sword, and a gem-studded helmet.
When you are armed and equipped,
I will lead you to my father's bed.
By the One who suffered on the cross,   6465
I want to strike the first blow.
Then, after you kill him and slice him to pieces,
We can leave the country."
"My lady," said Huon, "that is out of the question.
May it never please God, who suffered on the cross,   6470
That we harm your father in any way.
We will be freed before too long."
With that, the discussion ended.
Bearded Geriaume and the maiden left the dungeon,
And the others remained behind.   6475
Geriaume entered the great hall of the palace,
Where he was welcomed as master:
No one dared refuse him anything.
He often visited the prisoners

In the company of the lady.   6480
Now I shall cease speaking of the lady.
When the time comes, we shall sing more about her.
Instead I shall tell you about crazy Agrapart,
Brother of the giant from across the sea
Whom Huon had killed and cut to pieces.   6485
When he heard that his brother had been slain,
Agrapart summoned and assembled his men.
They mounted their horses at once
And set off for Babylon.
I cannot tell you the details of their journey,   6490
But they rode and traveled
Until they dismounted in a meadow near Babylon.
Agrapart said to his men:
"My lords, wait for me here,
While I go speak to the emir."   6495
"My lord," they replied, "just as you wish."
The giant donned his armor — may God destroy him!
The devil was fourteen feet tall
With eyes as red as burning coals.
His eyes and nose were separated by a good six inches,   6500
And his eyebrows were a foot apart.
He donned a hauberk brighter than wildflowers:
It too measured fourteen feet,
And it was wide enough to fit three men.
He held a steel scimitar in his hand,   6505
Exactly like his brother.
He set out on foot across the land,
And when he arrived in the fine city,
He went directly toward the palace,
Crossing all four bridges.   6510
Not a single pagan dared to stop him.
He did not pause until he arrived at the splendid palace,
Which he entered at once.
The emir was seated at his meal,
Served by bearded Geriaume.   6515

Agrapart burst in, puffed up with rage.
He stomped through the room so vigorously
That wine spilled all over the table.
He spoke loudly so as to be heard by all —
Not a single man dared make a sound —   6520
"May Mohammed, creator of all things,[38]
Who gives us bread, wine, and wheat,
Who created the world and preserves all,
Confound the emir Gaudisse,
That evil slave and proven traitor!"   6525
"Agrapart," said the emir, "how dare you
Insult me like this in my own court!
What do you want from me?"
Agrapart replied, "By god, I'll tell you:
I hold you responsible for my brother's death.   6530
By all accounts — and I am convinced of it —
The one who killed him and cut him to pieces
Is here, in this very palace.
You threw him into your dungeon,
Which you should never have done.   6535
He should have been dragged by horses and hanged!
By Mohammed, whom I worship,
If it weren't beneath me,
I would punch you in the nose
Until bright red blood spurted all over.   6540
You traitor, you scoundrel, may Mohammed destroy you!
Get up from that throne!
You aren't worthy to be emir!"
He stepped forward and pulled Gaudisse toward him
So violently that the emir's cap flew off.   6545
He almost knocked him to the ground.
The emir was most dismayed.
Agrapart snarled, "Scoundrel, now you will serve me!
I am outraged at my brother's death.

38. Demonstrating once again his ignorance of Islam, the poet conflates the
prophet Mohammed with Allah, the Muslim God.

I insist on taking possession of all of your lands.[39]   6550
From now on you will be called my slave
Or else be tortured and martyred.
However, I will proceed according to custom:
Have one of your Turks armed immediately:
Even if two come forward, I won't refuse them.   6555
We will face each other in closed combat.
If one of your Turks can defeat me,
I won't claim my inheritance,
But if I am the victor,
You will give me four molars   6560
And four golden coins
As tribute, to save your head,
And you will forever be my liegeman."
The emir replied, "I have no choice but to accept.
I am lucky to get off so easily."   6565
Raising his voice, he cried, "Where are my men?
Where are those I lavished with fine furs?
If one of them is brave and daring enough
To defeat this giant,
I will give him fair-faced Esclarmonde   6570
As well as half my kingdom."
When the emir finished speaking,
No one dared utter a single word,
Such was their fear of crazy Agrapart.
Seeing this, Gaudisse began to weep,   6575
But Agrapart said, "It's no use lamenting.
You will have to turn over the four coins.
No one will exempt you from it."
You should have seen the emir carry on!
Watching her father weep, Lady Esclarmonde   6580
Was deeply saddened, I can assure you.
She spoke to her father tenderly, saying:
"My lord, listen to me:
If it would not displease you,

39. Gaudisse was the vassal of Arrogant, Agrapart's brother.

I would speak openly and frankly." 6585
The emir replied, "Not at all, so help me God!
You may say whatever you like
Without fear of reprisal."
"My lord," she said, "by Mohammed,
The Frenchman who brought you a message 6590
Is still here in prison under my watch,
Alive and in good health.
If you wish, I can bring him to you.
You would do well to let him go free
If he agrees to fight in closed combat." 6595
The emir replied, "Bring him here, then.
If he agrees to do battle for me,
I will be most generous with him."
Esclarmonde left at once,
Accompanied by old Geriaume. 6600
They went down to the dungeon
And freed the young knight Huon
As well as all of his men — not a single one remained.
They brought them to the splendid palace,
Where Huon presented himself to the emir. 6605
He was plump, robust, and sturdy,
Though a bit pale from the time spent
In the great dungeon.
The emir said to him:
"Vassal, prison seems to have agreed with you." 6610
Huon replied, "My lord, may God be praised!
This is all because of your daughter, who came to visit me.
I have amply partaken of every dish
That you have had at your meals.
But tell me why you have summoned me here." 6615
The emir replied, "I will tell you at once:
Do you see that armed Saracen?
He has challenged me in combat,
But not one of my men is brave or daring enough
To take up the gauntlet. 6620

I am therefore asking if you would be willing
To be my champion against this Turk.
If so, I will allow you to return to your country
And provide you with safe conduct
All the way to Acre, I swear by Mohammed.   6625
And the Frenchmen who have been imprisoned
Throughout my land, far and wide,
Will all be freed because of you.
I will provide you with a good pack horse
Laden with the best gold I can find.   6630
You will present it to King Charlemagne on my behalf,
And every year, as long as I live,
I will send him another horse laden with gold
As payment for your saving my life.
I will also give you a letter confirming these terms.   6635
If Charlemagne is ever at war, let him summon me,
And I will provide assistance by land and by sea,
Accompanied by a hundred thousand armed men.
This is what you will gain from your sojourn.
I would rather be considered a slave in France   6640
Than pay a tribute of four pennies in my own country.
And if you wish to remain in my household,
You will have my daughter as your wife,
As well as half of my kingdom."
"My lord," said Huon, "I have listened to you carefully.   6645
I accept, on these conditions:
That you return my hauberk,
My ivory horn, and my sparkling gold goblet."
"They will be returned to you," said the emir.
He then shouted, "Give them back to him!"   6650
The pagans obeyed his command
And brought the fine gilded hauberk,
The ivory horn, and the sparkling gold goblet.
Seeing this, Huon greatly rejoiced.
Agrapart said, "Now I can return   6655
To my knights, who await me in the meadow,

For I see you have found a champion.
But see to it that he is armed quickly,
For I will not take off my armor
Until I have slain him and cut him to pieces."   6660
With that, he turned and descended the staircase.
Huon seized the goblet
And the ivory horn and handed them to Geriaume.
"My friend," he said, "guard this horn.
I trust you more than any man alive."   6665
Then he took the hauberk and turned to one side
To confess his sins, saying his "mea culpa"
And imploring God's forgiveness.
Gazing at the hauberk,
He was terrified of the fairy Auberon,   6670
Whom he had cursed in the deadly dungeon.
"My God!" he exclaimed, "will I be able to put it on?
Fair Auberon, what will you do?
I'm a dead man if you refuse to help me."
He took up the lightweight hauberk.   6675
Lifting the rear panel
And lowering the front,
He put his head through the opening,
Which was neither too long nor too wide.
"May God be praised!" said Huon.   6680
"Now I know that I am reconciled
With the noble fairy king Auberon,
I no longer fear that huge crazed giant."
Meanwhile, the Saracen,[40] who had taken
Huon's sword when he was captured   6685
And imprisoned following the mighty battle,
Returned it to him, saying:
"Here, take this sword.
I have kept it in a special case for a long time."
Huon took the sword joyfully   6690

40. This Saracen is the same person who earlier (lines 5960-62) had taken Huon's
dropped sword and kept it in a chest.

And then laced on his helmet with its gleaming carbuncle.
The emir ordered his men to saddle Bassant,
A gray dappled horse
More rapid than any in Christendom.
He gave it to Huon,   6695
Who mounted swiftly, with no need of stirrups.
The horse was equipped magnificently
With a saddle made of fish bones
And a headstall worth a thousand gold marks.
When Huon had mounted,   6700
Thirty bells jingled in such beautiful harmony
That the sound was more pleasing than a harp or fiddle.
Young Huon rode out of the city.
He spurred his horse, giving him free rein
And charging around the meadow.   6705
He executed three turns within the space of about seventy-five yards
And then circled back with a French turn.
The emir, who was watching from the battlements,
Observed Huon carefully, saying to his men:
"Look at that young man!   6710
How well he carries his shield!
It would have been a terrible shame if I had killed him."
He had the field guarded by a thousand Saracens,
All armed to the hilt,
To prevent any sort of treachery.   6715
As Huon proceeded to the battlefield,
The emir commended him to Mohammed:
"Go forth, may Mohammed preserve you!
And if the God you worship
Is more powerful than the one I just named,   6720
Let the truer God return you safe and sound!"

63

Noble Huon rode straight to the enclosure
Where Agrapart awaited him for closed combat.

He shouted loudly at Huon:
"Lowly vassal, where are you from? From what people? 6725
Are you related to the emir Gaudisse?"
"Not at all," Huon replied, "may God damn him!
No, I'm from France, I'll not hide it!
I killed your brother, may God damn him!"
Agrapart said, "Now I'm even more enraged! 6730
By Mohammed, you are of good lineage,
So abandon your God for mine,
And I'll give you lands and fiefdoms.
You can follow me into the East,
And you'll receive the lands from here to Bocident. 6735
What's more, I'll give you a fabulous gift:
My sister, who's as black as pitch.
She's taller than I am, and her teeth are a foot long!"
"By my faith," said Huon, "let a hundred devils have her!
I didn't come here to get married. 6740
Be on guard and defend yourself against me:
I defy you in the name of almighty God!"
"As I defy you!" responded the pagan.
"In the name of Mohammed, I challenge you for this land."
At that, they drew apart the distance of about seventy-five yards. 6745

64

They challenged one another,
Drew apart the distance of about seventy-five yards,
Then charged rapidly one toward the other.
They struck mighty blows to their shields
That shattered and broke them at the boss 6750
But did no damage to their hauberks.
Each man fell to the ground in the meadow
And just as quickly leapt back up.
The pagan seized his tempered steel scimitar
And hurled it mightily at Huon, 6755
But the agile youth easily dodged it,

And the scimitar passed by without touching him.
It struck the ground with great force
A good six feet beyond him, had one measured.
When he saw this, Huon was frightened. 6760
The giant said, "You'd have been in a bad way
If this scimitar had struck you!
By Mohammed, who is so powerful,
Who created the heavens and the light,
Who formed man and woman from clay, 6765
If you don't abandon your witless God,
I'll cut off your head with this scimitar!
Nonetheless, I really do want
You and me to be reconciled.
I'll give you the emir's lands — 6770
Those of the powerful king Gaudisse —
And you will be king over all he ruled."
"By my faith," said Huon, "this is disloyal!
I would be ashamed to do such a thing
And be considered a traitor the rest of my days. 6775
You are not worth a penny,
And by the God who dwells in the Trinity,
You won't see the sun set today!"
With these words Huon raised his sword
And struck Agrapart on his bejeweled helmet: 6780
He knocked off its precious gems and flowers
And sliced the coif from his fine gilded hauberk,
But his sword glanced aside, guided by devils,
Or else Agrapart would have been destroyed.
Nonetheless, noble Huon struck him so mightily 6785
As his splendid steel sword
Came down upon the giant's left side
That he knocked a hundred links from his gilded hauberk
And the sword cut into his left thigh,
Removing a huge handful of flesh. 6790
The giant howled like a chained bear.
"By my faith," said Huon, "now you've had a taste!

Wicked traitor, by God in majesty
And by Jesus Christ whom you've blasphemed,
You are about to have your head sliced from your body!"   6795
Said the giant, "I'll get you first!"

65

The battle was fierce and heavy:
You would never see two mightier combatants.
Agrapart was a wonder to behold:
The tyrant stood eighteen feet tall.   6800
He gripped his scimitar threateningly
And struck Huon on his shining shield,
Shattering it so that it was worthless.
His heavy blow hit Huon on the thigh
And broke off a hundred links from his hauberk.   6805
Huon stumbled under the weight of the blow,
And it was no wonder that he was frightened.
He called upon God, the almighty Father:
"Dear King of glory,
As you are truly all-powerful,   6810
Grant me, Lord, by your holy command,
The strength to defeat this haughty giant.
If he is defeated, I am sure and certain
That my peace will be made
With Auberon, who is so valiant."   6815
The giant said, "Huon, you are very strong.
By Mohammed, who is my witness,
Leave your God and follow my religion.
I feel very sorry for your suffering,
And I am about to give you a painful death."   6820
"Just listen to this poor, sad fellow!" said Huon.
"I don't care for a thing he says.
I trust in God, who created the firmament.
He who believes firmly in him
Will never be overcome."   6825

66

Huon's heart was swollen and weighed down
By what the giant had done to him.
He swore by God and his goodness
That he would rather die than fail to show
At once the "love" he bore him!   6830
The young man wielded his sharp sword
And gave the pagan a mighty blow
Upon his golden bejeweled helmet,
Which knocked off its precious gems and flowers
And utterly destroyed its rim.   6835
His white coif was ripped away
And all his armor was of no avail,
Because Huon had struck him straight on
With his burnished sword, as I have told you.
He trimmed the giant's hair down to the flesh.   6840
His sword then slid to the right
And cut off his right ear.
Said Agrapart, "You've landed a mighty blow.
By Mohammed, you've sorely wounded me!
If you strike again, you'll surely kill me.   6845
I'd rather give you four pennies
Than let myself be butchered and killed.
I surrender to you, don't harm me further!"
"By my faith," said Huon, "don't worry:
No man alive will harm you further."   6850
Huon seized him by the hauberk
And led him before his barons.
They entered the good city on foot.
When Geriaume saw that Huon had defeated the giant,
He called to Gaudisse: 6855
"My lord, listen to me:
When I came to your place the other day,
In the presence of your barons, I led you to believe
That I was a member of your high lineage —

The son of your brother — but it's not true.   6860
By the faith I owe you, I am no relative of yours,
But rather the liege man of young Huon.
I didn't know how to hear news of him
Except by claiming to be your nephew,
And all these other Frenchmen are his liege men as well."   6865
The emir replied, "It's certainly true
That you cannot be too careful of the French!"
After saying this, they went to seek Huon.
They found him at the foot of the great staircase
Where he was about to enter the palace.   6870
The emir came to meet him,
And they entered the palace together.
Huon seized hold of crazy Agrapart
And turned him over to Gaudisse.
"Lord emir," said Huon, "listen: 6875
He is yours. Do with him as you please."
The giant fell at his feet
And in sight of all the pagans cried out for mercy.
The emir returned his possessions to him
On condition that he remain his liege for all his days.   6880
Thus the man who wished to be called his lord
Became his servant to save his head.
They all sat down to have a festive meal.
Noble Huon sat next to Gaudisse.
The emir said, "Huon, what are your plans?   6885
Will you return to the kingdom of France?
Or do you wish to remain here with me?
I do not wish to break the promise I made you."
"My lord," replied Huon, "don't even think of it.
I would not stay here for anything you have."   6890
Then he said to Geriaume, "Bring me my goblet!"
"As you wish," he responded
And delivered it at once to Huon.
"My lord and friend Gaudisse," said Huon,
"Behold now how the Lord God is full of grace: 6895

This goblet is completely empty, is it not?"
The emir said, "You speak the truth."
Huon, that paragon of goodness, took the cup,
Made the sign of the cross over it,
And the goblet was filled with clear wine.   6900
"Take it, my lord, and drink," said Huon.
The emir seized hold of the goblet,
But as soon as he did, the wine disappeared.
Gaudisse said, "You have bewitched me!"
"No I haven't. It is the evil within you.   6905
Set it down, for you'll never drink from it.
The goblet has magical powers,
Such that only an honorable man can drink from it:
One who is pure, spotless, and devoid of mortal sin.
So, emir, noble and good man that you are,   6910
Have pity on your soul,
Believe in God who died upon the cross
And renounce Mohammed, who has no wisdom or power.
If you do not, by holy charity,
You will soon be in a bad way   6915
And see so many people arrive
That they will completely fill this good city."
Said the emir, "Listen to this bloody fool!
I've held him a full year in my prisons
Without anyone coming to inquire about him,   6920
And now he brags that he's going to kill me!
I wonder, by Mohammed my god,
Where are the men who are going to save him?"
Huon replied, "Is that your final choice?"
"It is, indeed, by Mohammed my god."   6925
"Upon my word," said Huon, "you will regret it!"
He took the white pure ivory horn,
Put it to his lips, then blew, and sounded it
So loudly and forcefully
That blood flowed from his mouth.   6930
The barons in the palace began to sing,

And the emir began to dance.
Auberon heard it in his leafy bower.
"Oh God, I hear my friend blowing the horn.
I've made him suffer so much pain,   6935
But now I forgive him all his transgressions,
For I have found no more honorable man —
If only he weren't so flighty!
I will transport myself to where he sounded the horn
Along with a hundred thousand armed men,   6940
Or even more if necessary."
He was there as soon as he said the word.
They entered Babylon at once
And soon filled all the streets from end to end.
Auberon went up into the palace   6945
Along with the men he had brought,
All of them armed to the hilt.
As soon as he saw him, Huon ran to embrace him.
"My lord," he said, "I'm so glad to see you!
In God's name, I thank you five hundred times   6950
For coming to such a distant land to rescue me."
Auberon replied, "Enough of this.
I will always help you faithfully
As long as you agree to heed my counsel."
Auberon's men went through the city   6955
Stabbing the pagans in their sides and flanks.
And the pagans — those who were armed —
Defended themselves as best they could,
But their efforts did not last long,
Because our mighty barons were too strong.   6960
Auberon had the emir seized
And turned him over to young Huon,
Who was happy to have him.
King Auberon proclaimed
That whoever believed in God would suffer no harm.   6965
More than two thousand were baptized,
And Huon asked the emir:

"Sire, have you thought it over?
Believe in God, the King of majesty,
Or else you will die now!"   6970
Said the emir, "I would rather be killed
Than abandon Mohammed, my god."
Then Auberon began to shout:
"Huon," he said, "you are a miserable fool!
Cut off this evil devil's head,   6975
And you can keep your promise to Charlemagne."
Huon seized his good steel sword
And promptly cut off Gaudisse's head,
Then he took the mustache below his nose
And took four molars from his mouth,   6980
Yanking them out of his jaw.
Huon had Gaudisse buried
Out of respect for Esclarmonde, his fair-featured daughter.
Auberon said, "Huon, listen to me:
You have the mustache as well as the molars.   6985
Keep them safe, in God's name,
Because they are your life or your death."
"My lord," replied Huon, "thank you, for the love of God.
I've always been a little careless,
So please put them somewhere   6990
Where I'll not lose them, if you are willing."
"You have spoken wisely," said Auberon.
"I wish them to be sealed in Geriaume's side,
Just above his hip,
Without his feeling any pain."   6995
And there they were, as quickly as he had wished it.
Auberon said, "Huon, listen to me:
I must return immediately to Monmur.
My dear friend, remember to act properly:
You are taking with you the emir's daughter,   7000
Esclarmonde, who is most worthy of praise.
I forbid you on pain of dismemberment,
Inasmuch as you love me,

Not to lie with her or fondle her
Until you have married her   7005
In Rome, the fabulous city.
If you do lie with her, so help me God,
You will suffer such torments
As no man alive could relate."
"My lord," said Huon, "I will be careful not to."   7010
"Then you will be acting properly," said Auberon.
Then he had a large boat prepared for them,
So splendid that no one could describe it.

67

The ship was beautiful, with fine lines.
It was so splendid it cannot be described.   7015
On it were carved the sea and its fish
And all the rulers of the kingdom of France
Since the most honorable Clovis.[41]
There were numerous rooms on board.
Within them were Gascon steeds,   7020
Bread and meat, red wine, claret, and fish,
Sea biscuits in profusion,
And fine furs for the barons.
Little Auberon took his leave
And embraced Huon as he departed.   7025

68

King Auberon asked for leave
And hugged Huon as he departed.
After embracing him, Auberon began to weep.

41. A warrior king, Clovis did much to expand the early Frankish kingdom by defeating the last Roman army at Soissons (486), the Alamans at Tolbiac (496), and the Visigoths at Vouillé (507). At the urging of his second wife, he was baptized in 498 or 499 by St. Remi, bishop of Reims, and ruled until his death in 511.

Seeing this, Huon inquired:
"My lord, for God's sake, what is wrong?"   7030
Auberon replied, "I feel very sorry for you.
I will never see you again
Until after you've suffered more pain
Than anyone's heart could ever imagine."
Then he turned away and left.   7035
Huon remained where he was.
He had the maiden he had discovered
In the mad giant's tower
Wed to a high nobleman of that land:
He was an emir who had become Christian.   7040
Huon the noble young man
Gave them power over all the land
That he had won from the Slav Gaudisse.
Next Huon made ready to depart.
They had a small boat reinforced with iron   7045
To take along with their large ship
So they could come ashore in small towns and cities.
Then Huon went aboard his ship
Along with all his men.
They weighed anchor and set out upon the sea.   7050
They sailed along all morning
Until it was afternoon,
When they sat down below deck for a meal.
They had an abundance to eat and drink,
For the goblet gave them plenty of wine.   7055
"My God," said Huon, "you have watched over me well!
I have a goblet worth as much as a city
And a hauberk worthy of praise,
Along with a bright white ivory horn.
When I wish to blow and sound it,   7060
I have as many men as I could ever ask for,
And I have the mustache and the molars,
As well as Emir Gaudisse's daughter,
The beautiful Lady Esclarmonde.

This hunchback dwarf is mistaken   7065
If he thinks he can keep me away from her:
By God, it won't be him
Who keeps me from having my way with her!"
Geriaume said, "You are a total fool!
You know very well that Auberon has spoken the truth,   7070
Yet still you want to disobey his command.
If you lie with her, so help me God,
You will be ashamed and humiliated."
"You are wasting your breath," replied Huon,
"For there is not a man alive   7075
Who could keep me from doing as I wish.
Sir Geriaume, if you are so afraid,
Climb into the small boat at once
And take along plenty of food."
"As you wish," replied Geriaume.   7080
Without any delay, Geriaume
And his twelve companions entered the iron-clad boat,
While Huon hurried to have a beautiful bed prepared.
Oh, you should have heard the maiden weep,
Wringing her hands and tearing at her hair!   7085
"My lord," she said to Huon, "for the love of God,
Wait until after you've married me!"
"No, my lady," he replied, "I won't, by God!"
Then he seized her and kissed her.
He lay down upon the bed at once   7090
And did as he desired with the maiden.
No sooner had he had his way with her,
Than a storm arose upon the sea.
The ship carrying Huon and the maiden
Began to swell and come all apart,   7095
Breaking into five hundred pieces.
Huon was left clinging to a plank,
With fair-faced Esclarmonde in his arms.
His barons, too, were afloat on the sea.
They floated along for over a hundred leagues.   7100

The plank to which Huon clung stayed afloat,
And through the grace of God,
Came ashore on an island.
Huon and his beautiful ladylove
Were as naked as the day they were born.   7105
They were both relieved to have escaped alive
And hid themselves among the rushes.
The young woman wept tenderly:
"Alas, we are both so shamed!"
"My lady," Huon said, "let it be.   7110
I swear to you there is no reason to weep.
Let us cling to one another, and we will die a gentler death.
Tristan died for love of beautiful Isolde,[42]
And in God's name, so will we."
"My lord," said she, "let it be as you will."   7115
Then they clung to one another,
But while both were overwhelmed with sadness,
Ten pirates were rapidly nearing the island
In a fast ship.
They planned to stop here to rest   7120
And soon reached shore.
They had brought along provisions
And sat down to eat at some distance from Huon.
The young man heard them talking
And said to his ladylove, "My lady, listen.   7125
So help me God, I hear someone over there."
He lifted his head and heard them speaking.
"My lady, they are eating, by God," he said.
"I will go and ask them for some bread.
Stay quiet. I'll be back soon."   7130
"My lord, may God be with you."

42. The reference is to the tragic love story of Tristan and Isolde, which originated
in Celtic myth and spread through French sources in the twelfth century, a
celebrated German version in the thirteenth, the British romantic poets in the
early nineteenth century, and has continued to resonate until modern times,
perhaps most famously now in the music of Richard Wagner.

Huon set off at a run,
As naked as the day he was born.
As he approached, he greeted them, saying:
"My lords, may the God   7135
Who rules over all save you!
I beg you to give me some of your bread."
They replied, "You will have plenty,
But first tell us what brought you here?"
"By my faith, a storm at sea."   7140
They gave him two loaves and let him go.
Huon returned straight to his love
And gave her some of the bread he had brought.
Meanwhile the pirates spoke among themselves,
And one said, "By Mohammed, my god,   7145
I wonder where this young man came from.
He surely didn't come alone.
Let's follow him to see where he went."
The whole gang followed after him
And reached the place where Huon was.   7150
They found the lady, who was completely naked.
When they saw her, they easily recognized her
And began to shout aloud:
"Lady Esclarmonde, you can't get away!
You had your father killed.   7155
We intend to take you back to Yvorin,
Your uncle, who will treat you as he sees fit.
He will have you tossed into a fire.
As for you, filthy man, you'll lose your head!"
"My lords," said Esclarmonde, "have pity, for the love of God! 7160
Do with me whatever you want,
As long as you don't harm this young man!"
They replied, "He won't be killed,
But he will have to suffer great anguish."
They immediately took hold of young Huon,   7165
Blindfolded his eyes, and tied his wrists together.
Then they all seized the lady

And brought her into their large ship.
You have never seen anyone sadder than she,
But they gave her a fine ermine dress   7170
And a fur-lined mantle.
They weighed anchor and raised their sail,
Leaving Huon lost and sad
And all alone on the island,
As naked as the day he was born.   7175
The young man was in great anguish.
They turned away, boarded their ship,
And set sail across the high sea.
A favorable wind blew their ship
To Aufalerne without stopping;   7180
They came to shore right below the tower.
The emir was in his splendid palace,
Leaning his head out of a window.
He saw the ship reach shore
And quickly came down from the tower.   7185
Taking a number of his barons with him,
He came to the port, where he encountered the sailors.
King Galafre called out to them:
"My lords, what are you bringing?"
They replied, "My lord, we will tell you: 7190
Expensive silk with ermine linings.
If we are required to pay a tariff,
We will be most happy to do so."
Galafre said, "I have another question for you:
Who is that lady I see weeping there?"   7195
"My lord, in the name of our god Mohammed,
She is a slave we purchased while at sea."
When she heard this, the lady began to cry out:
"My lord, that is not true!
By Mohammed, have pity on me,   7200
For I am the daughter of Emir Gaudisse.
My father was sent to his death
By a rascal from the kingdom of France,

And they are seeking to take me to my uncle.
If he gets hold of me, I know for a fact   7205
That he will have me burned alive."
Galafre said, "You will stay with me."
Then he said to them, "You will leave her with me."
The pirates replied, "By god, we will not!"
Hearing this, Galafre was incensed   7210
And said to his men, "Seize these devils!"
His barons leapt forward, thinking to capture them,
But they put up a strong resistance,
However, their resistance did not last long,
And they were all butchered and killed,   7215
Except for one man, who escaped them.
But they were unconcerned and let him go.
They seized the lady, for that was all they wanted,
And took her up into the splendid palace.
King Galafre was impatient   7220
And wanted to marry her at once.
Thereupon the lady said to him:
"My lord, have pity on me for the love of god.
I have sworn my vow to Mohammed:
For three years I cannot enter any bed   7225
Where there is a man — I'm telling the truth!
I was ill when I swore this to Mohammed,
And because of my love for you I'm sorry I did,
For I'm very happy that you have married me,
But if I go against my vow,   7230
Our lord Mohammed will be angry with you.
So, I beg you, my lord, to spare me."
"My lady," he replied, "as Mohammed is my god,
I would never wish you to betray your vow for me.
Instead, by the god I must adore,   7235
I would gladly keep you for twenty years or more
Provided that I might eventually possess you."
The maiden said, "Your wish will be fulfilled."
Then she added beneath her breath:

"By Jesus Christ, whom I adore,   7240
I will remain true to Huon
And endure any pain and suffering
Rather than lie with another man."
Now I shall stop telling you about the lady
And turn to one of the pirates,   7245
The one who had escaped from the ship.
He did not stop until he reached Monbrant,
Where he found Yvorin in his splendid palace
And told him everything he had learned:
That Yvorin's brother Gaudisse had been slain   7250
By a young man who was born in France
And who carried off fair-faced Esclarmonde.
"There were ten of us in a large ship.
We found them on an island in the sea,
Both as naked as the day they were born.   7255
We recognized the girl at once
And were attempting to bring her here
When our ship ran into a mighty storm,
And we had to anchor below Aufalerne.
King Galafre came to meet us   7260
And had all my companions killed —
Mohammed helped me escape —
And then Galafre married your relative."
Upon hearing this, Yvorin's blood boiled.
"Alas," he said, "my brother is dead,   7265
And Emir Galafre has taken my niece!
He is my liege and holds his realm from me:
He will agree to turn her over to me."
Yvorin had a messenger saddle up
And gave him an official letter   7270
Ordering Galafre to return his niece.
The messenger rode off
And entered Aufalerne one morning.
He found the emir amongst his noble barons
And spoke to him as you will hear: 7275

"Galafre, my lord, listen to me:
King Yvorin, so worthy of praise,
Has sent me to ask you to return his niece.
If you do not, you can know for certain
That he will have all your lands laid waste."   7280
Galafre responded, "Listen, my friend:
King Yvorin can do as he wishes,
But I would not return the fair-faced maiden
For all the gold in two cities."
The messenger said, "Is that your final decision?"   7285
"Yes, in the name of Mohammed, my god," said the emir.
The messenger set off to return.
He spurred his powerful steed along
Until he reached the city of Monbrant.
He recounted the news to Yvorin   7290
That King Galafre had clearly informed him
That he would not return
The beautiful maiden for any man alive.
Hearing this, Yvorin swore upon his beard
That he would capture Galafre's land and kingdom.   7295
I shall not sing to you any more about the war for now,
But shall return to it at the proper time.
Instead, I shall tell you about brave Huon,
Who was still lying miserable on the island
With his hands tied and both eyes blindfolded.   7300
And I want to tell you a little about Auberon,
Who was in the woods with his band of barons.
He thought once again of Huon,
And tears began to flow from his beautiful eyes.
His men asked, "My lord, what's the matter?"   7305
"I am thinking about a miserable soul — Huon —
To whom I've offered my friendship and love.
I helped him deliver his message,
And I helped him kill the emir.
Huon carried off the emir's daughter,   7310
And I forbade him on pain of dismemberment

Even to think about the maiden
Until after he was married to her.
But now the rascal has disobeyed my command
And is in such a miserable state   7315
That he has lost everything I gave him:
The ivory horn, the pure gold goblet,
And the hauberk he had won.
The poor soul is lying on an island in the sea
With his hands tied and both eyes blindfolded.   7320
May God confound him, for he has shamed me!"
Gloriant, a fairy knight, said:
"Lord Auberon, in God's name, you are wrong.
God created Adam and formed him from clay,
And He created the beautiful Eve, his wife.   7325
He gave them all of paradise
Except for a single fruit, which was forbidden them.
Eve, tempted by the devil, ate it
And then gave it to Adam.
By Holy Mary, can you not remember   7330
That this Adam, formed by God's own hands,
Disobeyed God's command
But was then fully pardoned by him?"
Then behold wise Malabron,
Who knelt before King Auberon.   7335
"Look, lord king, forget your cruel thoughts,
And go help free the young man!"
"In God's name, I won't!" said Auberon.
"Then I'll go, if you let me," replied Malabron.
"Go then," said Auberon,   7340
"But in the name of the One who suffered on the cross,
If you do, then I promise that you will remain
A sea creature for twenty-eight years in addition to
The thirty to which you are already condemned.
You must also bring back my hauberk,   7345
My ivory horn, and my pure gold goblet.
If you love him so much, you can ransom him.

Finally, I tell you in all truthfulness that you must
Neither give him anything, nor take anything from him,
But bring him back from the seashore   7350
Exactly as you will find him."

69

"Lord Auberon," said noble Malabron,
"Where will I find brave Huon?"
Said Auberon, "On the island of Moysan,
Just three short leagues from stinking hell.   7355
That's where you'll find the miserable creature."
Said Malabron, "May Jesus be with you!
Nothing will ever keep me
From rescuing the noble young man!"
Then he set off at a run for the sea   7360
And did not once stop
Until he came right to the roaring sea.
He immediately leapt feet first into the water
And swam faster than a bird flies.
He swam so fast and so far   7365
That he came to noble Huon
Where he was lying on the shore of Moysan island
With his eyes blindfolded and his heart grieving.
He cursed brave Auberon repeatedly.
Suddenly Malabron came swimming up!   7370

70

Malabron came onto the island
Where he found Huon overcome with grief.
He greeted him in the name of God in majesty:
"Huon, are you awake or asleep?"
"My God," said Huon, "who do I hear talking?"   7375
"I am a man who has loved you for a long while.
I love you, as God is my Savior,

Like a woman loves the child she has carried.
I am called Malabron,
And I am the sea creature   7380
Who bore you across the Red Sea
When you were on your way to Babylon."
"Malabron, dear brother," said valiant Huon,
"Please step forward, for God in majesty,
And remove this blindfold from my eyes."   7385
Said Malabron, "As you wish."
He came forward, took off the blindfold,
And then removed the bindings from his wrists.[43]
When Huon saw that he was free,
He could not have been happier with the gold from two cities.   7390
Seeing Malabron, Huon asked him:
"My friend, who brought you here?"
Said Malabron, "The fairy Auberon
Sent me on the condition
That I remain a monster on the high seas   7395
Twenty-eight years, in addition to the thirty years
To which I was previously condemned.
For your sake I have doubled my sentence.
In addition, I must bring back the hauberk,
The ivory horn, and the pure gold goblet.   7400
All this I have sworn to Auberon."
"By my faith," said Huon, "may God destroy him!"

71

"You must not speak like this," said Malabron.
"The little man knows everything you say."
"I really don't care at all," Huon said,   7405
"Because he has caused me so much pain and tribulation!"

---

43. Our manuscript has *lez .ij. piez denoiiez = untied his two feet.* The poet (or
copyist) has apparently forgotten that previously it was Huon's wrists that were
bound (lines 7166, 7300, 7320).

72

"Malabron, dear brother," said valiant Huon,
"Are you going to leave me or take me with you?"
Said Malabron, "Huon, listen to me:
I will take you safely across,   7410
But I can neither give you anything nor take anything from you.
Quick now, climb up on my back!"
"My lord, as you wish," said Huon.
Malabron got back into his fish skin,
And Huon climbed upon his back;   7415
He sat comfortably there with crossed legs,
As naked as the day he was born.
Malabron dove back into the sea.
I cannot tell you how long it took to cross
Nor the great sufferings that Huon endured: 7420
Blood oozed forth from thirty wounds
Because the sea was so cold.
But Malabron swam so far on the high seas
That he brought Huon to the other side
And cast him down upon the shore.   7425
"Huon," he said, "I commend you to Jesus.
I can neither give you anything nor take anything from you.
Now I must return for the hauberk,
For the horn, and for the gold goblet.
May God be with you, for I cannot comfort you."   7430
Thereupon he turned and leapt back into the sea.
Huon remained all alone on the shore.
He was so upset he thought he would lose his mind.
"Woe is me," he said. "Where can I go?
Holy Mary, please rescue me!   7435
If I had anything to cover my nakedness,
I think I would suffer no harm.
This wicked man has shamed me to death,
But by the One who suffered on the cross,
Since he has left me in such a miserable state,   7440

I'll lie as much as I want, if need be.
I'll never be loyal to him again,
Because I clearly see that he's abandoned me.
Let a hundred devils take his soul!"
Then he leapt up like a crazy man   7445
And began running through the meadows
As naked as the day he was born.
Listen now to the adventure
That God destined for the young man:
Whom God wishes to help, will never be destroyed.   7450
Huon found a man under a tree
Who was such as I shall describe:
He had his harp that he had learned to play
And his vielle[44] at which he was adept.
There was no better minstrel in all pagandom.   7455
He had stretched out a cloth before himself
Upon which were two loaves of white bread.
Near the bread were two pâtés
And a full keg of old wine and claret.
He was more than a hundred years old.   7460
He poured wine into his goblet but could not taste it
Because his eyes were filled with tears.
At this moment young Huon came forward,
As naked as the day he was born.
The minstrel was frightened when he saw him   7465
Coming through the meadow stark naked.
He began to shout loudly:

44. The vielle is a four- or five-stringed instrument played with a bow, similar
to a modern fiddle. It came into Europe from the east in the eleventh century.
Prior to then, all medieval stringed instruments were plucked. It could be used
to accompany both lyric poetry and *chansons de geste*. Other musical instruments
mentioned in *Huon* are the harp, the *rote* (a sort of lyre), and the *gigle* (a small
fiddle).

"Wild man![45] Don't hurt me!"
"By my faith," said Huon, "I am wild,
But I won't touch or harm you.   7470
But I beg you to give me some of your bread."
The minstrel replied, "You will have plenty,
But tell me first which god you believe in."
"Upon my word," said Huon, "whichever you want me to."
"I feel very sorry for you," said the minstrel.   7475
"Take an ermine cloak from my sack
And a silk mantle lined with fur —
You clearly need to cover your body —
Then come sit and drink this clear wine
And eat something, because I can taste nothing.   7480
Keep me company, if it pleases you,
On the condition I'm about to state,
Because you'll never see a sadder man."
"Upon my word," said Huon, "you and I are alike:
If you are sad, so am I.   7485
My lord, you seem to me an honorable man.
May God reward you for your words."
Then Huon stepped forward and opened the sack.
He took the ermine cloak and put it on,
Then placed the mantle over it.   7490
He found plenty of britches and shirts
And took as many as he desired.
The young man was fully dressed
As he sat down on the tablecloth to dine.
He ate some bread and drank the clear wine   7495
While the minstrel observed him
And then asked in a courteous manner:
"My friend, where were you born?"
When he heard this, Huon wondered to himself:

45.   The Wild Man is a worldwide creature of folklore. He appears as early as the epic of *Gilgamesh* (ca. 2000 BCE), as satyrs and fauns in classical antiquity, in art and literature throughout the European Middle Ages, on down to Sasquatch and the Abominable Snowman today.

"Lord God, King of majesty,   7500
Will I lie or tell him the truth?
I am well aware, so help me God,
That if I tell him the truth, I cannot escape.
Auberon, sire, you have failed me,
And I cannot love you.   7505
It was such a little thing that caused you to hate me
When you treated me so cruelly because of my ladylove,
But, by the One who suffered on the cross,
I will lie repeatedly to spite you.
If you've done me ill, I'll do worse to you!"   7510
Then Huon called the minstrel:
"My lord, what was it you asked me?
So help me God, I've forgotten."
"Friend," he said, "where were you born?"
"My lord," said Huon, "you will know at once: 7515
I'm from Africa — you'd be wrong to doubt it.
I am a merchant and was crossing the sea
When a great tempest hit our ship,
And all my companions were drowned.
Mohammed helped me escape alive.   7520
But tell me now, who was it,
By Mohammed, that has made you so upset?"
The minstrel replied, "My brother, you will know:
My real name is Instrument,
And there is no finer minstrel in pagandom.   7525
Here's my harp that I can play well
And my vielle at which I'm also adept.
I was attached to a most praiseworthy lord,
Gaudisse, the courtly emir.
A short time ago he was surprised in his lodgings   7530
By a young man born in France,
Whose rightful name is Huon.
He butchered and killed my lord.
Oh Mohammed, my lord, may you destroy him,
For he is the one who's caused my misery!"   7535

Hearing this, Huon hung his head.
The minstrel spoke to him again.

73

Said the minstrel, "What is your name?"
"My lord," said Huon, "I'm called Garinet."
"Garinet, my brother, by Mohammed,   7540
Don't worry, noble son of a baron:
A short while ago you were poor, but now you're rich.
You've donned a fine ermine cloak
With a silken mantle to put over it;
You have a great abundance of shirts and britches.   7545
You have good reason to take comfort:
You are handsome and in your youth;
Much good is still in store for you.
But I am an old man, and my mustache is turning gray.
I have lost a most noble baron: 7550
Gaudisse with the fine features.
May Mohammed forgive him all his sins!
He was surprised a short time ago in his house
By a youth from the kingdom of France,
And I believe that his name was Huon.   7555
Oh my lord Mohammed, bring shame to this Huon!"
When Huon heard this, he did not say a thing;
He kept silent and lowered his head.

74

"Garinet, my brother," said the minstrel,
"My lord is dead, may Mohammed have pity on him.   7560
Now I am going straight to the city of Monbrant,
To see Yvorin, the emir's brother,
To tell him this news.
If you wish to stay with me
And would be willing to carry these bags,   7565

I will swear to you by Mohammed
That you will be given half
Of every penny I am able to earn.
You will not have to walk far through this kingdom,
For I promise you on my word　　　　　　　　　　7570
That in every town and city we come to,
If I set out to exercise my trade,
You will see me give you so many mantles
That you'll be hard put to gather them all."
"Upon my word," exclaimed Huon, "you've found a servant!"　　7575
He took the sack and hung it from his shoulders;
He put the harp on top
Along with the vielle the minstrel played.
They headed straight for Monbrant,
With Huon ever in the minstrel's company.　　　　　　7580
But young Huon began to weep
And lamented to himself:
"Once so high, and now fallen so low!
I no longer have my fine gilded hauberk,
My ivory horn, nor my bright gold goblet.　　　　　　7585
Just the other day, I had my love at my side,
My thirteen men, and plenty of money.
Now I am the servant of a poor minstrel!"
When the minstrel heard him weeping,
He questioned him tenderly:　　　　　　　　　　7590
"Garinet, my brother, what's the matter?
My dear friend, stop weeping.
If you are poor now, before tomorrow evening
You'll be rich if you just accept your lot.
By the trust you owe me, stop your grieving."　　　　　7595
"Master," said Huon, "as you will."
As they were saying this, they looked to the right
And saw five hundred armed men approaching.
Huon was the first to see them.
He called his master and pointed them out:　　　　　　7600
"Master, for God's sake, look over there!

I see a mass of armed men approaching."
Said the minstrel, "Let's go meet them."
They came up to those in the lead
And Instrument asked, "Where are you going?" 7605
They replied, "To the city of Monbrant.
We are coming straight from Aufalerne on the sea,
Where the mighty emir Galafre
Has captured the niece of Emir Yvorin,
The beautiful Esclarmonde, 7610
Daughter of Gaudisse, who was just killed.
Emir Yvorin wants to get her back,
So now there is a war and great strife.
We have just been looting in Aufalerne
And are bringing back all this booty!" 7615
When Huon heard him mention Esclarmonde,
Blood surged from his feet to his face,
And he said to his master, "We ought to go there!"
Said the minstrel, "No more of this.
I don't wish to go where there's fighting." 7620
Then they set off at a fast pace
And came to Monbrant before the noon meal.
They hurried to the palace,
Climbed its marble staircase,
And found Yvorin among his barons. 7625
The minstrel was the first to speak:
"My lord, may Mohammed save you!
I have heavy news to bring you:
Your brother is dead and butchered."
"I was well aware of that," said the emir, 7630
"But I am even angrier about my niece
Being held by Galafre, who is my liege man.
He refuses to give her up, which angers me further!
But by Mohammed, whom I adore,
If I capture him, I'll have him dragged to his death 7635
And have Esclarmonde burned in a fire!"
Oh God, how Huon's heart leapt in his breast

When he heard mention of Esclarmonde.
He swore secretly to God
That even were he to be torn to pieces for it,　　　7640
He would go to see her within the month.
Then Yvorin spoke to the minstrel:
"My friend, listen to me:
Take up your vielle and play.
After this sadness, we need some joy!"　　　7645
"My lord, I will do everything you ask."
Ah, you should have heard him tuning his vielle
And plucking the thirty strings of his harp.
Music was resounding throughout the palace!
"Oh God," said Huon, "it's great to be here!　　　7650
There's no lyre or fiddle that plays sweeter."
The pagans said, "This is a good minstrel.
We must pay him handsomely."
You should have seen them removing their mantles
And tossing them in every direction!　　　7655
Huon went to collect them all
Because he was to share them with the minstrel.
The emir began to look at Huon
And said to his men, "See that handsome youth?
It's most unfortunate that he serves a minstrel."　　　7660
He called to the minstrel:
"Tell me, and don't keep it from me:
Where did you ever find such a boy?"
The minstrel said, "I'll tell you, sir:
When my lord was killed and butchered,　　　7665
I started for the city of Monbrant
To bring this news to your court.
After I had crossed the Red Sea,
I sat down under a tree to rest,
For I was very tired and worn out.　　　7670
I had stretched out my cloth under a tree,
And I had some bread and plenty of wine.
I had not even had a taste

When I saw this young man approaching,
As naked as the day he was born.   7675
He begged me politely for some bread,
Which I gladly and willingly gave him,
Then I had him put on an ermine cloak
And a mantle over it.
He had as many shirts and britches as he needed.   7680
I gave him so much that he remained with me,
And no one could find a better servant.
He carries my baggage and my harp as well,
And even my instrument if I want him to.
And when we had to cross dangerous places   7685
He immediately loaded me on his back
And carried me across like a gentle horse.
He's worth as much to me as a mule with a saddlecloth."
"Look, Instrument!" said the emir,
"I swear by my god Mohammed that he's only waiting   7690
Until you've amassed a lot of stuff, and then
He'll kill you when you're crossing a dangerous place.
Have him brought to me at once!"
Instrument could not disobey the emir,
So he went at once to bring Huon   7695
Into the palace before the emir.
King Yvorin spoke to Huon:
"Vassal, in what land were you born?
It's too bad! You are such a handsome youth,
You'd be better off guarding a castle   7700
Than serving a minstrel.
There is some other reason you are here.
Poor man, what are you up to?
Why are you serving this minstrel,
Who earns his living every day by begging?   7705
Don't you have some other skill
Through which you could gain a living?"
"My lord," replied Huon, "I do, by God.
I know lots of things I could do,

And I'll tell you, if you'd like to hear."   7710
Said the emir, "I'm ready to listen,
But be careful not to brag of anything
That you are not completely competent to do,
For I plan to test you at each."
"My lord," said Huon, "listen to what I can do: 7715
I know how to train a hawk[46]
And how to hunt the stag and the boar.
When I've caught them, I know how to blow my horn
And release the dogs.
I know well how to serve at table   7720
And am an expert at chess,
For there is no one who can checkmate me."
Said the emir, "Stop right there.
I'd like to test you in a game of chess."
"My lord," said Huon, "let me finish first,   7725
Then you can test me at whatever you wish."
Yvorin said, "You have spoken well.
Now tell me what else you have mastered."
"My lord," continued Huon, "I will tell you at once:
I know precisely how to put on a hauberk,   7730
How to carry a lance with a shield at my neck,
And how to run and gallop a horse.
I know well how to enter into combat,
And when it comes to giving heavy blows,
It's easy to find worse than me.   7735
And I certainly know how to enter bedrooms
To kiss and fondle young maidens!"
The emir replied, "Those are skills enough!
But I want to test you at chess.
I have a most beautiful daughter,   7740
Who is very skilled at chess.
I've never seen a man who could defeat her.
You must play against her, by Mohammed,

46. All the skills that Huon (in the person of Garinet) boasts of in the following
lines would identify him to any medieval listener as a member of the nobility.

With the provision that if she checkmates you,
You will immediately have your head chopped off.   7745
Now hear what will happen if you win:
If you can checkmate my daughter,
I will have a bed prepared in her room
Where you can lie with her all night
And do everything you wish with her,   7750
And in the morning, when dawn has broken,
You will receive a hundred pounds of my wealth
To do with as you please."
"My lord," replied Huon, "it will be as you please,
Though I do not care at all for this wager."   7755
Yvorin said, "By Mohammed my god,
It will not be other than I have stated."
A messenger headed at once to his daughter's room,
Found her, and told her everything:
"My lady, by Mohammed, you've not yet heard: 7760
A minstrel has arrived here,
Bringing with him a young man —
In all pagandom there is no youth more handsome.
Your father has sworn by Mohammed
That you must play against him at chess   7765
On the condition that, if you can checkmate him,
He will lose his head at once;
But if, my lady, he is able to checkmate you,
You will lie all night in his arms,
And he can do whatever he desires with you."   7770
The maiden replied, "My father is a fool!
Never, by Mohammed, whom I adore,
Will such a handsome man die on my account!
I would rather let myself be checkmated."
Then the emir sent for his daughter,   7775
And she came, not daring to disobey him.
Two counts were standing at either side of her.
The emir said, "My daughter, listen to me:
You must play against this young man.

If you are able to defeat him at chess,   7780
He will immediately lose his head;
But if he can get you to resign the game,
Then he can do whatever he wishes with you."
"My lord," she said, "since you wish it,
Whether I like it or not, I must obey."   7785
Then she said very quietly to herself:
"By Mohammed, how can I not love him?
Because he is so shapely and so handsome
I wish the game were already over
And he were holding me close   7790
And doing all he desires with me!"
Then they had a rug brought out
And thrown down in the middle of the room.
Huon sat down with the girl beside him,
And the barons took their places all around.   7795
Huon spoke to the emir:
"My lord," he said, "listen to me:
I request, my lord, that out of courtesy,
Neither you nor your barons say anything.
The game is critical, and no one must interfere."   7800
Said the emir, "Have no worries."
Then he declared that anyone who spoke
Would have his limbs cut off.
Then they had the chessboard,
Which was embossed in gold and silver, brought forward.   7805
The chess pieces were of solid gold.
"My lady," asked Huon, "which game do you prefer:
To move the pieces ourselves, or to throw dice?"[47]
"To move them ourselves," replied the young woman.

47.   Between the eleventh and fourteenth centuries, there is evidence from Europe that chess could be played by throwing dice. Before each turn they were thrown to determine which piece was to be moved. See Sunnucks, *The Encyclopaedia of Chess*, 97-98 and the note to line 7538 in Ruelle, *Huon de Bordeaux*. It could also be played as today by moving the pieces freely. Interestingly, "dice chess" is still sometimes played today.

Then they began to concentrate on their game.   7810
The pagans watched Huon closely,
But the young man was concentrating on his game.
He lost a number of his men
And began to grow quite pale.
The young girl stared at him and said,   7815
"Young man, whatever are you thinking?
You are close to being checkmated
And that would be a pity, by Mohammed,
Because then you will lose your head!"
"My lady," said Huon, "don't worry about that.   7820
The game is not over yet,
And you will be shamed and abased
When you have to lie naked in the arms
Of the servant of a poor minstrel."
The barons heard this and laughed heartily.   7825
But as the maiden stared at Huon,
Love struck her so hard that she was fully enflamed.
His great beauty was all she could think of,
So she lost her concentration staring at him.
When Huon saw this, he was delighted   7830
And immediately addressed the emir:
"My lord emir," he said,
"Now you can see how well I play!
If I had any shameful thoughts,
I could say 'checkmate' to your daughter."   7835
The emir said, "Get up, daughter.
You were conceived in an evil hour
When you have defeated so many noble men
And then been checkmated here by this boy!"
"My lord," said Huon, "don't be angry.   7840
Stop talking this way,
For I'll never do a shameful thing.
Let your daughter return to her room,
And I will go to serve my minstrel."
Yvorin said, "I'm most grateful to you.   7845

I will have you given a hundred silver marks."
"My lord," replied Huon, "I could use them!"
So Yvorin had Huon given the coins,
And his beautiful daughter
Returned to her room and complained angrily: 7850
"By my faith, may Mohammed destroy him!
If I had known that he wouldn't do anything,
By Mohammed, I'd have checkmated him!"
Meanwhile, Huon returned to his master.
Things remained this way all night long,   7855
But at dawn the next morning,
The emir ordered all his men
To arm themselves and take up weapons.
They rushed about putting on their armor,
Pulling on hauberks, lacing up their gem-studded helmets,   7860
And mounting their rapid, powerful steeds.
When Huon saw he had nothing to arm himself with,
He began to sigh deeply in his heart.
He would gladly accompany them into battle,
If only he had a horse to ride.   7865
When he saw the emir, he called to him:
"My lord emir, listen to me:
Please have someone lend me some arms
And a horse that I can mount upon,
Then lead me into battle   7870
So you can see how well I can fight!"
Said the emir, "You have spoken well."
Then he had Huon given good weapons.
A Saracen set out to mock Huon:
He hurried to his weapons chest   7875
And pulled out an engraved steel sword.
He approached Huon and gave it to him.
"Lowly vassal," he said, "carry this for me.
I have kept it in my chest for a great while."
Huon took it, pulled it from its sheath,   7880
And then went to stand by a pillar.

The engraving on the sword stated:
This is the sister sword of bright-handled Durendal
And took Galant[48] a year to forge.
It was dipped twenty times in fine steel.   7885
"By my faith," said Huon, "you have given me a great gift,
And I will repay you well if I am able."
The king called to his seneschal:
"Go and have a horse saddled,
The swiftest you can find,   7890
And give it to this young man."
A Saracen came forward —
He was wont to make disparaging remarks.
"My lord, what are you thinking?
This boy has been a minstrel's servant.   7895
He's been in low and scurrilous places
And knows every sort of evil and deceit.
By Mohammed my god, all he is waiting for
Is to be able to get away from you.
If you let him have a swift horse,   7900
He will ride off as soon as he mounts it."
"So, what would you have me do?" asked the emir.
The Saracen replied, "I'll tell you now:
Have them give him a lousy horse."
Said the emir, "That's a good idea!"   7905
They had a horse saddled for Huon:
It was long of neck and thin in the flanks;
It was worn out and had not been fed
Either oats or wheat in over seven years;
It limped on one foot and had lost an eye,   7910
And was seven years beyond its prime.
This was what they saddled for Huon.
He mounted it boldly
And pricked it firmly with his spurs,

48. Allusions to Galant, the mythical blacksmith who forged Roland's sword
Durendal, are ubiquitous in French *chansons de geste*. Durendal was the prototype
against which all subsequent swords were measured.

But there was no way to get it to run.   7915
"Alas," said Huon, "I'm so poorly mounted!"
The pagans left their good city
And rode toward Aufalerne.
Spurring on their powerful horses,
They began to pillage before they reached the moat.   7920
Yvorin began to pound upon the gate
As he shouted loudly:
"King Galafre, will you come out?
If I capture you, you'll be dragged to death
If you don't turn over my niece to me at once!"   7925
Hearing this, Galafre was filled with fear.
He saw Esclarmonde and said to her:
"My lady, listen to me: because of you,
They are laying waste to my kingdom."
"My lord," she replied, "I am very sorry for that.   7930
If you please, sire, turn me over to them,
And your land will be at peace again."
"You are wasting your breath," said Galafre.
"I would rather not have a foot of land left
Than to give you to any man alive.   7935
Even if I have to hang bearded Yvorin,
I intend to take my pleasure with you
Once the three years you have sworn to
Are all over and done with."
Within the city was a young man   7940
Named Sorbrun,
Who was the nephew of Emir Galafre.
When he saw how upset his uncle was,
He addressed him as you are about to hear:
"My uncle," he said, "let this be,   7945
And I'll tell you what you should do:
I will get my equipment ready,
Mount my good horse,
And go forth to challenge Yvorin,
Asking him to send forth   7950

The best warrior he has to joust against me.
If he can defeat and kill me,
You must give him bright-faced Esclarmonde,
But if I can kill his Saracen warrior,
He must quit your lands and country							7955
And leave Esclarmonde entirely to you.
It is better for the war to be decided by the two of us,
Than have so many men butchered."
"You have spoken well," said the emir.
Sorbrun, that bold warrior, took up his arms:						7960
He put on his hauberk, laced up his gem-studded helmet,
And strapped on his sword at his left side.
Blanchandin, a horse whiter than the flowers of the fields,
Was led into the square.
The horse was equipped magnificently						7965
With a saddle made of fish bones
And a headstall worth two gold marks.
The stirrups were of pure gold,
And one could find no fault with the harness:
Thirty bells had been attached to it.						7970
When Sorbrun mounted upon the horse,
The bells jingled so harmoniously
That the sound was more pleasing than a harp or fiddle.
Equipped thus, Sorbrun rode out of the city.
As soon as he reached the moat,						7975
He saw Yvorin and began to shout:
"My lord emir, be quiet and listen to me:
Emir Galafre has sent me to you.
Choose a Saracen from your entourage —
Or even two, I won't back off.						7980
If I can defeat or slay them,
Leave my uncle's properties in peace;
And if your champions can defeat me,
You will win back bright-faced Esclarmonde."
Hearing this, the emir looked about himself						7985
And saw no one who dared step forward.

They all had looked at the speaker
And recognized it was mighty Sorbrun.
Whoever awaited him would swiftly die.
When Huon saw that no one stepped forward,   7990
He came out of the crowd
And urged on his horse with both spurs,
But there was no way to get it to run!
The pagans said, "May the devil take him!"
But the minstrel began to shout: 7995
"Look here, Yvorin, may Mohammed damn you
For giving him such a terrible horse!"
But Huon would brook no delay.
He came up to Sorbrun and said:
"Saracen, my brother," he stated,   8000
"Speak to me if there is any mercy in your soul."
And Sorbrun asked, "My friend, what do you want?
Are you a pagan, Saracen, or Slav?"
"No indeed," replied Huon, "God confound them all!
Instead, I believe in the One who suffered on the cross.   8005
If I appear poor, don't hold it against me:
I am a knight and of high lineage,
And I ask you on your loyalty
And on the religion that you practice,
That you not let me depart without a fight."   8010
Said the pagan, "I've never heard such a thing!
It is your death that you are asking for.
I could kill you with a single blow.
If you believe me, turn back."
But Huon responded, "You are wasting your breath,   8015
For I would rather you killed me here,
Than turn back without jousting against you!"
These words ended the discussion,
And they both drew back about seventy-five yards.
Young Huon spurred his horse,   8020
But no matter how hard he spurred or struck it
There was no way to get it to run.

"By my faith," said Huon, "I am poorly served!
Holy Mary, come to my rescue
And help me win my enemy's horse." 8025
Would you like to hear what he did?
He positioned his lame horse sideways to the charge
And held his shield and buckler facing the pagan.
Sorbrun charged ferociously,
And his steed snorted like thunder from the sea. 8030
The pagan lowered his lance with its iron point
And struck Huon on his banded shield.
It split open and shattered above the boss,
But his hauberk held firm.
Sorbrun's lance broke and that was it: 8035
He was unable to move Huon aside
Any more than if he had attacked a tower.
The pagans in the meadow saw this
And said to one another, "This young man is amazing.
How wondrously powerful he is!" 8040
Said the emir, "He is full of might!
May it please my god Mohammed
That he were mounted upon my horse!"
Huon was gripping his good, bright steel sword,
Because he had thrown his lance into the meadow. 8045
He was very skilled at swordplay
And struck the pagan as he raced by.
He gave him such a mighty blow upon his helmet
That split it open — it was not worth a fancy glove!
His white coif? — not worth a penny! 8050
He cut Sorbrun in two, from his head to his waist,
And dropped him dead to the ground.
Huon seized Sorbrun's horse by the harness.
The young man dismounted from his own horse
In the meadow and climbed up on Blanchandin. 8055
He abandoned his poor horse there
And rode off on the one he had conquered.
He spun it around ten times within about seventy-five yards

And then approached the emir with a French turn.
Yvorin strode toward Huon 8060
And hugged him around the neck with both arms.
Pagans came pouring from the good city,
With Emir Galafre in the lead.
He found his nephew dead and butchered
And fainted four times over the corpse. 8065
Anyone who saw him grieving and weeping
Could not fail to have pity on him.
Then he left off his grieving
And entered the mêlée with his men.
They gave and received many a blow 8070
And overwhelmed Yvorin and his men,
But young Huon spurred Blanchandin.
He struck the first pagan he encountered
And separated his head from his body.
Then he struck a second pagan, slicing him in two, 8075
And with his third blow killed another.
He did not stop until he had slain a dozen.
Turks and pagans fled in all directions.
Galafre's men were terribly frightened
By the mighty blows that Huon could wield. 8080
They turned their backs and fled,
Sadly carrying the dead Sorbrun with them.
The youthful warrior Huon looked and saw,
Standing near him, the pagan who had given him
His engraved shining sword. 8085
When he saw him, the young warrior Huon
Spurred his horse, rushed at once upon the pagans
And caught up with them.
He gave one of them such a blow
That his head and helmet flew off. 8090
Huon seized his horse and turned back.
He came to the pagan and gave it to him.
"Here," said Huon, "take this powerful steed.
I present it to you because of the shining steel sword

You gave me this morning when I mounted my horse."   8095
The pagan replied, "I thank you five hundred times!"
Galafre retreated into Aufalerne.
He and his men were deeply saddened.
They had Sorbrun splendidly interred
At the foot of the altar with Mohammed's statue.   8100
Yvorin turned back
With Huon riding beside him,
And they rode along until they entered Monbrant.
They went up together into the palace,
And there they disarmed at once.   8105
Huon removed the green-gold, gem-studded helmet
And took off the fine gold-embroidered hauberk.
Once he had taken off and removed his armor,
He returned to be beside his master,
But Yvorin took him by the hand   8110
And said, "Friend, stand up,
And come sit beside me at my table,
For you have served and honored me well.
I offer you all the possessions I have here:
Fine fur, sable, ermine linings.   8115
And take whatever gold and silver you desire.
Go amuse yourself with the girls in their chambers,
And do whatever you wish with the most beautiful.
When I ride, you too will ride along;
When I drink wine, you will drink claret.   8120
I will not eat until you give the order.
May all my lands be given to you!"
"My lord," said Huon, "I thank you five hundred times."
He sat beside the emir for the meal.
Now Huon had everything he desired: 8125
Anything he commanded or ordered
Was done according to his wishes.
When they had dined, the cloths were removed,
And the minstrel tuned his vielle
And plucked the thirty strings of his harp.   8130

The sound filled the great palace on every side.
The pagans said, "This is a fine minstrel.
He should be richly rewarded."
You should have seen them stripping off their mantles
And tossing them all about.   8135
Huon remained seated beside the emir,
And the minstrel called to him:
"Vassal, you've climbed above your station!
I was your master, and now I'm your minstrel.
I don't think you hold me in much esteem.   8140
Come down, and gather up these mantles."
The Saracens all laughed heartily.
Now we shall stop speaking of Huon,
And I shall turn to telling you about his men,
About old Geriaume and the other barons.   8145
They sailed so long upon the high seas
And the tempest threw them so far off course
That they came to anchor below Aufalerne.
Old Geriaume looked around
And said to his men, "This is a dangerous place: 8150
That is Aufalerne we see in front of us.
Emir Galafre, who lives there, is ferocious
And he doesn't believe in God.
Without God's help, we'll all be killed!"
The emir, who had climbed to the battlements,   8155
Saw the French arriving at the foot of his tower.
He and his men went over to them,
And he asked, "My lords, where were you born?"
Geriaume replied, "We will not hide it:
We are from the honored land of France.   8160
We are returning from the Holy Sepulcher across the sea.
A great tempest beset our ship
And has forced us to anchor here beneath this tower.
If we owe a duty for coming into port here,
We will gladly pay it to you."   8165
The emir said, "Listen, my lords,

I assure you, I will cause you no harm,
Because if you wish to stay with me,
By Mohammed, you will be well received."
"And why is that?" asked valiant Geriaume.   8170
"My lords, I will tell you at once," said the emir.
"I am engaged in a terrible war, which is very troubling:
An emir who lives quite nearby
Is taking my land and laying waste my kingdom."
"Ah," said Geriaume, "if you are in the right,   8175
We will help you faithfully,
But otherwise we do not wish to remain."
Said the emir, "In the name of my god Mohammed,
I will tell you why I am in the right:
The other day, when I was at my battlements,   8180
I saw a ship coming to shore.
It was carrying ten pirates.
With them they were bringing a lady.
She was the daughter of the emir Gaudisse —
I don't know where they found her.   8185
They were obliged to anchor beneath this tower.
As soon as I saw them, I went to meet them
And took bright-faced Esclarmonde from them,
Whom they were taking to an uncle of hers.
I captured their wealth along with the lady   8190
And then had them all killed and butchered.
I have taken the lady as my wife,
And that's why Emir Yvorin is attacking me.
He's her uncle — may Mohammed damn him! —
And that's why he attacks me every day.   8195
They came yesterday with their catapults and lances
And pillaged all around my city.
King Yvorin had it all hauled away.
He has a young man with him —
I don't know what country he comes from.   8200
Yesterday he killed my nephew Sorbrun,
My sister's son, in a joust —

May Mohammed have pity on his soul!
This young man took Sorbrun's good horse with him —
Blanchandin, the most rapid and finest steed   8205
In all this kingdom.
I will take you on with the condition
That if the youth returns you will joust against him
And return the horse to me."
Said Geriaume, "I accept these terms.   8210
If he returns, and you point him out to me,
I will capture both the horse and its new master."
And Galafre said, "If you can return him to me,
I will offer you all my kingdom."
With these words they left the ship   8215
And bearded Geriaume led them into the city.
They did not waste any time
And brought all their belongings with them.
They came up to the palace and entered.
The emir would not let them take lodgings   8220
In the town nor at any other inn.
He had them stay with him in the palace.
Old Geriaume said to Galafre:
"My lord, if it would be pleasing to you,
Please let me see the young woman   8225
For whom you have undertaken such a terrible war."
Said the emir, "I won't refuse your request,
But if you were a young man or warrior,
By Mohammed my god, nothing would ever induce me
To let you speak to the lady.   8230
However, since you are such an old and decrepit man,
No maiden would ever want to love you."
Valiant Geriaume accompanied Galafre.
They both passed through a nearby chamber
And found the maiden in the adjoining room.   8235
As soon as she saw Geriaume,
She recognized him and grew suddenly pale.
She fell to the floor and uttered a cry.

Seeing this, Galafre asked her:
"My lady, by Mohammed, what is the matter?"   8240
"My lord, I have gout in my side,
Which makes me suffer night and day,
And I know for a certainty that this man
You have brought with you is from France.
I would like to speak with him in private   8245
To ask and inquire of him
If he can comfort me from my pain."
Said the emir, "As you wish."
Old Geriaume approached her,
And both went to stand near a distant pillar.   8250
"Geriaume, my lord," said the bright-faced lady,
"For the love of God, what brought you here?"
And Geriaume replied, "A storm at sea.
My lady, for God's sake, what can you tell me about Huon?"
"Upon my word, he has met his demise.   8255
When I was taken from him,
I left him alone on an island in the sea
With his hands tied and his eyes blindfolded,
As naked as the day he was born.
I am certain that he is dead and gone.   8260
May God almighty have pity on his soul!
Now Galafre has married me,
And I have led him to believe
That I have sworn to Mohammed
Not to let any man enter my bed for two full years.[49]   8265
He believes I am telling the truth,
But this is how I am saving myself for brave Huon.
And, by Jesus who is called God,
I intend to protect myself all the days of my life
From all other men alive.   8270
Dear man, for the sake of God in majesty,
If you could only manage

49. At lines 7225 and 7938 the term was three. Perhaps one of those years has
already passed, or perhaps the poet (or copyist) has forgotten.

To find a way for us to escape from here,
I ask you to take me with you
So that I can become a nun in some priory   8275
And pray for the young man's soul."
Geriaume replied, "Don't worry.
If I escape, you'll not be left behind."
At this moment Galafre shouted:
"Vassal, you are wasting time.   8280
You've been talking too long, by Mohammed.
Come on out! You two have talked too much."
At that, the two of them returned.
It was getting late, so they sat down to supper.
After the meal they went to bed   8285
And arose early the next morning.
Now I shall tell you about bright-faced Huon.
He immediately said to Yvorin:
"Sire, have your men arm themselves,
And let us go to meet Galafre.   8290
A man at war should not tarry.
By Mohammed, he disrespects you
By holding your niece against your will.
He should hold his possessions from you."
Said Yvorin, "You speak the truth."   8295
He immediately gave the order
That all were to arm themselves.
Young Huon did not delay:
He put on his hauberk, laced up his gem-studded helmet,
And strapped on his sword at his left side.   8300
Blanchandin was led forth from the stable
By the servant Huon had designated.
Huon mounted without touching the stirrups.
From his neck he hung a splendid shield
And held his strong spear in his fist.   8305
The barons assembled on the main square.
The emir's daughter was leaning
Upon the window ledge of the large palace

Accompanied by a number of young maidens.
Huon stopped just in front of the main hall,   8310
And the maidens all stared at him,
Saying to one another, "That is a handsome youth.
See how magnificently he wears his armor!
Fortunate will be the girl he chooses to love!
He is such a strong and brave young man: 8315
He killed Sorbrun the other day in a joust
And captured his powerful horse."
"To tell the truth," said the daughter of bearded Yvorin,
"I am quite upset with him, by Mohammed,
For what he did after he defeated me at chess: 8320
Had he been courtly, he would have embraced me
Or at least kissed me over and over,
And then, by Mohammed, whom I adore,
I would have been eternally grateful to him.
And if he had asked me for more,   8325
I would have given him my lovely body
For him to do with as he wished
In spite of Yvorin the bearded one."
Then the pagans went forth from the city.
King Yvorin and worthy Huon rode   8330
Side by side some distance from the others
In the direction of Aufalerne,
And at length they reached the moats.
Young Huon spurred his horse across,
Pounded on the gate with his engraved steel sword,   8335
And began to cry out in a loud voice:
"King Galafre, come joust against me!
I killed and butchered your nephew,
And by my head, I'll do the same to you
If I can get you to fight me.   8340
You will return bright-faced Esclarmonde,
And if you don't, you'll lose your lands
And be dragged through the streets and hanged."
When he heard this, Galafre's blood turned cold,

And he said to Geriaume, "What are you going to do?   8345
He's the one who's so ruined me!"
Geriaume replied, "Don't be afraid of him,
Because soon you'll have the horse and its master."
Geriaume immediately donned his armor,
Putting on his hauberk, lacing up his gem-studded helmet,   8350
And strapping on his sword at his left side.
King Galafre had them saddle Bausant,
The fine horse that he always rode,
And had them present it to Geriaume.
The old man leapt onto it without using the stirrups.   8355
With his lance in hand and gripping his shield,
The bearded one stood up so firmly
That the horse's spine sagged,
The iron in the fine gilded stirrups broke,
And the leather straps stretched four finger-lengths!   8360
The pagans said, "Here is a mighty warrior!"
King Galafre had his men arm themselves,
And he too was soon beautifully armed.
There you would have seen many a powerful steed
And so many lances and bucklers   8365
And gold and silver shining brightly.
They opened the gates and left the city.
Bearded Geriaume was in the lead,
Followed on every side by his companions,
Each one well armed upon his horse.   8370
Old Geriaume spurred his horse,
And it bolted out ahead of the others
The distance of about seventy-five yards, I believe.
He had his lance in hand and his shield in front.
His long beard hung below his gem-studded helmet   8375
All the way down to his waist;
He tossed it over the ventail of his hauberk.
When Huon saw him riding boldly forward,
He spurred Blanchandin in his direction.
Both were charging with such ferocity   8380

That they did not say or shout a single word.
They met with lances lowered
And struck mighty blows to their shields.
They split open and cracked beneath the bosses,
But the hauberks were not damaged.   8385
Their shields, bodies, and powerful steeds
Crashed together with such violence
That they were both thrown to the earth,
And their helmets plowed into the ground.
They both sprung to their feet angrily   8390
And drew their good steel swords.
Geriaume seized the sword at his side,
Came up to Huon, and struck him a mighty blow,
Sending bejeweled and flowered decorations flying
And splitting his helmet open to its metal lining.   8395
The white coif did not last long
And was not worth two pennies.
Geriaume trimmed Huon's hair down to the flesh,
And his bright red blood flowed down.
Fearing the blow, Huon had flinched.   8400
Had he not, and were it not for God in majesty,
Huon would have been sliced in two.
When Huon saw that he had been severely wounded,
The young man began to lament:
"Upon my word, I am done in!   8405
This pagan is terribly fierce —
I've never been hit so hard by any man!
Holy Mary, help me!
Ah, beautiful Lady Esclarmonde,
It is clear you'll never see me again,   8410
For I can tell that I've been wounded to the death.
Sir Geriaume, you'll never see me again!"
Hearing this, Geriaume was dumbstruck,
Because by these words he recognized Huon.
He took his sword and threw it to the ground.   8415
He was so overcome he could not speak.

When he saw this, Huon asked him:
"Saracen, what are you thinking?
Are you going to make peace or fight on?"
Old Geriaume humbly answered:					8420
"Ah, Huon, my lord," said valiant Geriaume,
"Step forward, for God in majesty.
Take my sword and cut off my head:
I earned as much when I wounded you so.
I didn't recognize you, and I'm heartily sorry."			8425
Hearing this, Huon was overjoyed.
Both unlaced their green-gold, gem-studded helmets
And embraced one another at once.
The Saracens and Slavs, who were watching them
On every side, were astounded,					8430
For they had no idea what they were thinking.
Geriaume said, "Huon, listen to me:
There is no time to waste,
Because we are surrounded by pagans.
I will tell you what we must do:					8435
Get back on your horse at once,
And I will do the same and then pretend
To lead you away against your will.
You will come now to Aufalerne,
Where you will find bright-faced Esclarmonde.			8440
For love of you she has remained faithful
In spite of having married Galafre:
He has never had his way with her.
Let's go now, and be welcome here,
For you are much desired by the lady."				8445
"My lord," replied Huon, "as you wish."
They swiftly mounted their horses.
Geriaume took hold of young Huon,
Seizing him by the hauberk.
They rode toward Aufalerne.					8450
Bearded Geriaume's companions
Quickly fell in behind them.

Yvorin began to shout:
"What are you doing, Saracens and Slavs?
Will you let this young man be led away?   8455
If we were to lose him, I'd be very upset."
Saracens rode up from every side
And spurred the horses after Huon.
Galafre likewise came toward him.
Old Geriaume went to meet him   8460
And shouted loudly to him:
"Sire," he said, "ride on!
So help me God, this is the young man
Who killed your nephew in the joust.
I am taking him as my prisoner to Aufalerne   8465
And will throw him into the great tower.
Ride forward and defend yourself.
I'll soon be back to help you fight."
Galafre said, "As you wish."
He immediately rode back into combat.   8470
Old Geriaume did not hesitate:
He brought Huon into the good city
Along with all of his men.
All fourteen entered the city.
As soon as they were inside, they had the gates shut   8475
And shouted "Monjoie" as loud as they could.
They killed and butchered
All the Saracens who had remained in the city:
They did not let a single one escape.
Next they had the gates secured and locked   8480
And the drawbridges raised.
Then they went up into the splendid palace
And found the beautiful lady
Who had wept so tenderly for Huon.
As soon as he saw her, Huon removed his helmet   8485
And ran to embrace her.
The maiden recognized him at once,
And they were both overcome with joy.

Everyone was happy to have found Huon.
Geriaume's men searched high and low   8490
Through the city and slaughtered
Every Saracen and Slav they found
And then threw them out into the fields.
Having conquered the entire marvelous city,
They returned to the palace   8495
Where all fourteen took off their armor
And joyfully celebrated their victory together.
Lady Esclarmonde embraced Huon and said:
"My lord, you are most welcome here!
I never thought I'd speak with you again."   8500
"My lady," said Huon, "I love you so much!
I am very happy to have found you again,
And I am eternally grateful to you
For having stayed faithful to me for so long."
With these words they had water brought up,   8505
For they had found food aplenty to eat.
They set the tables and sat down to dine.
The Saracens were locked out,
Fighting with their engraved steel swords.
There you could see a combat to the death   8510
With so many lances shattered and shields smashed,
So many feet, hands, and heads chopped off,
Bodies piling up on top of bodies,
And from one side of the field to the other
More than seven hundred butchered and killed.   8515
But who cared whether or not they died?
They were Saracens, may God damn them all!
But now two messengers went to Galafre.
"My lord," they said, "by Mohammed, did you know?
All the Frenchmen who were staying with you   8520
Are up there in your splendid palace
And have conquered your entire city.
There isn't a pagan or Saracen remaining
That they've not killed and butchered

And thrown out into the fields.   8525
They've secured and locked the gates
And raised the drawbridges.
The man who killed your nephew in the joust
And who was taken prisoner down on this meadow
Is their rightful lord, and they have recognized him.   8530
By Mohammed, my god, he's the young man
Who killed Gaudisse in his palace —
We recognized him easily yesterday and today,
Because we saw him enter Babylon
When he defeated crazy Agrapart.   8535
We wanted to tell you this, fair sire,
But we did not dare address you
Until the battle was over;
But it seems to us that he has escaped you,
Since they are ensconced and enclosed within.   8540
Your city is destroyed and laid waste,
And you have lost it beyond recovery."
When he heard this, Galafre nearly went mad,
And he said to his men, "What do you advise me to do?"
They replied, "Upon our word, you will hear: 8545
You must go to Yvorin
And beg him to take pity on you.
That is all the counsel we can give you."
Galafre said, "I will do what you wish."
Then he spurred his good horse   8550
Until he found King Yvorin.
As soon as he saw him, he dismounted,
Fell to his knees on the meadow, and begged for mercy:
"Take pity on me, noble king, for I deserve
To lose my head, since I've been disloyal to you.   8555
Take my sword and cut off my head
And do whatever you wish with me,
But if it pleases you, return my lands to me.
If I have wronged you, I wish to make amends,
Whatever you and your barons judge,   8560

But please help me to kill the scoundrels
Who have taken my wife and my city.
The young man you loved so dearly,
Who came here yesterday with your minstrel,
Is the Frenchman — I swear by my god Mohammed — 8565
Who killed King Gaudisse in his castle,
Your brother who was so good.
This is what two messengers told me,
Who recognized him at your court.
Thirteen Frenchmen were staying with me: 8570
They were his men, and they recognized him.
Now they are up there in my splendid palace
And have captured my admirable city."
When Yvorin heard this, he nearly went mad.
"Alas," he said, "what a mistake it was 8575
Not to hang him before he escaped!"
He said to Galafre, "Wait a while longer,
And I'll consult about what you've told me."
Yvorin called his barons to one side:
"My lords, what advice do you give me?" 8580
His men said, "My lord, you will know:
Since he has begged you to pardon him
And has humbled himself before you;
Since he has offered to make amends for any wrong,
Then give him back, my lord, all his lands, 8585
And then attack the French. If we can capture them,
Then drag them all behind horses to their deaths!"
Yvorin replied, "I agree to all this."
He said to Galafre, "Fair friend, come forward.
I will return all your lands and possessions, 8590
And I forgive you all your trespasses.
I will help you kill the Frenchmen."
Galafre replied, "I thank you five hundred times!"
He humbled himself at Yvorin's feet,
But Yvorin had him rise back up, 8595
And the two kings made their peace.

They swore to besiege the city
And not to leave for wind or storm
Until there was famine within.
If they could overpower the French,   8600
They would hang them to swing in the wind.
Meanwhile our Frenchmen had finished eating
And gone immediately to the battlements
To observe and watch the Saracen forces.
The emir was wasting no time: 8605
He quickly had a gallows erected
Above the moat at the main gate.
If our barons are captured or taken,
They will be hanged there.
May God who suffered on the cross watch over them!   8610
Yvorin summoned the minstrel
Who had brought Huon to his court.
"Vassal," he said, "come forward at once.
You brought me the proven traitor
Who killed and butchered my brother.   8615
You will rue the day you did that, by Mohammed!
You will be hanged on my gallows for it."
The minstrel replied, "Noble and generous lord,
For Mohammed, have pity on me,
Because I swear to you upon my word   8620
That when I brought the young man here
I had no idea in what land he was born."
"Traitor! You are lying," said the emir,
"And you will be hanged before nightfall."
He immediately had thirty pagans arm themselves   8625
And seize the poor minstrel.
He ordered them to hang his harp
From his neck and lead him to the gallows.
They did as he ordered, for they dared not refuse:
They seized the minstrel, who was in despair,   8630
And knotted a large rope around his neck,
Led him straight to the gallows,

And had him mount the steps
With his hands tied and eyes blindfolded.
The minstrel managed a glance toward the good city,   8635
Where he saw Huon and cried out to him:
"Huon, my lord, are you going to let me die?
Remember the great favor
I did for you on the shores of the Red Sea,
When you were wandering naked in the meadow?   8640
When I saw you, I took great pity on you
And gave you a fine ermine-lined cloak.
Huon, dear brother," said the minstrel,
"If you don't help me, I am sure to die!
I will be hanged because I cared for you."   8645
Huon heard him and recognized him well.
He said to his men, "Put on your armor!
That's my master I hear crying out.
So help me God, he once did me a great favor.
I would rather die than let him be killed."   8650
All fourteen hurried to take up arms
And mount upon their horses.
Lady Esclarmonde went to guard the gate,
And the barons issued forth from the city.
Huon did not rein in Blanchandin.   8655
He quickly reached the man holding the minstrel,
Who was about to raise him up on the gallows.
He lowered his lance and gave him a mighty blow
That his armor was unable to withstand:
He struck him dead with his lance through the body.   8660
Old Geriaume attacked another pagan
And wounded him so swiftly through the body
That he fell dead before he could even say a word.
All the others fought so well
That each slayed his man.   8665
Whether the Saracens and Slavs liked it or not,
They rescued the noble minstrel.
Huon took him and cut the rope

They had knotted around his neck.
Old Geriaume spurred his horse   8670
And brandished his bright shining sword.
He struck a pagan he encountered
Such a blow on his gem-studded helmet
That he split him down to his waist.
He took his horse and turned around,   8675
Handing it over to the minstrel,
Who grabbed it and mounted into the saddle,
Then fled at once back to the good city.
He came to the gate and entered.
The barons kept up the fight   8680
And killed and butchered the thirty Turks
Who had been about to hang the minstrel.
But their triumph was short-lived:
If the One who suffered on the cross abandoned them,
They would never reenter the city,   8685
For Yvorin, who had seen and watched them,
Had ordered a horn to be sounded.
Pagans took up arms on every side,
Mounted the horses they had had saddled,
And rode after the Frenchmen.   8690
Seeing them, Huon called to his men:
"My lords, stay together!
I beg you in God's name not to break ranks.
We will go back together into the city."
The barons took this advice and turned back   8695
As a group toward Aufalerne.
As they approached, the pagans shouted:
"Sons of whores! By Mohammed, you won't escape!"
Hearing this, Huon turned back
And struck the first pagan he encountered: 8700
He gave him such a blow on the top of his helmet
That he split his head down to his molars.
Then he struck off the head of another
And killed a fourth and a fifth pagan.

The young knight proved his worth: 8705
Pagans fled from him in every direction,
And no one was so naïve as to dare approach him.
His companions proved themselves as well:
Every one knocked his opponent from his horse.
But the emir Yvorin put on his armor; 8710
He and Galafre mounted their horses
And entered the skirmish with thirty thousand men.
When Huon realized that they could not hold out,
He shouted to his men:
"My lords, let's return to the city!" 8715
They obeyed him and turned back.

75

It was a mighty battle, though the two sides were uneven,
For there were thirty thousand armed pagans
Against a mere fourteen of our knights.
Unable to hold out any longer, 8720
They turned back and rode toward the city.
Lady Esclarmonde and Instrument
Opened the gates when they saw them coming,
And the knights entered eagerly.
Young Huon, however, committed a terrible oversight, 8725
For Garin of Saint-Omer remained outside the city.
Saracens attacked him from all sides
And killed his horse right under him.
He leapt to his feet with his shield in front of him,
Begging God, the King of paradise, 8730
To have mercy on his soul,
For he realized his body was failing.
Noble Garin refused to surrender alive,
Defending himself like a man enraged,
But he could hold out no longer: 8735
Pagans and Saracens cut him to pieces.
May God welcome his soul into holy paradise!

When young Huon realized
That noble Garin was not with him,
Bitter tears fell from his beautiful eyes.   8740
He climbed atop the battlements
And saw the vile Saracens swarming
Around the body of noble Garin.
Huon returned to the gate and was about to go out
When his knights shouted to him: 8745
"Huon, fair lord, have you lost your senses?
There is nothing to be done for the dead."
"Garin," said Huon, "because of you, I am deeply saddened!
For my sake, you left behind your land,
As well as your wife, daughters, and sons.   8750
May the Lord our God who pardoned Longinus
Have mercy on your soul."
Geriaume came forward and grabbed him by the hauberk.
His companions tried to reason with Huon:
"My lord," they implored, "in the name of God in paradise,   8755
Put aside your grief and your lamenting."
"Barons," said Huon, "my heart is heavy
Because such a noble man died this way."
Geriaume said, "You cannot bring him back."
They led Huon to the vaulted palace,   8760
Where all the knights removed their armor.
They set the tables and sat down for a meal.
Be assured that they wanted for nothing.
There was an abundance of claret and old wine.
When they had eaten their fill,   8765
Huon called out to the minstrel:
"Take up your vielle, fair friend,
For our grieving must be followed by joy.
Let us be glad, if you please.
Because of you, we are badly shaken."   8770
And the minstrel replied, "Just as you wish."

76

Without hesitating, the minstrel
Quickly tuned his vielle.
He plucked the thirty strings of his harp
So that the music resounded throughout the palace. 8775
The companions listened with great pleasure
And then retired for the night.
They feared no harm from any living being,
Since Aufalerne is situated on the coast:
The sea closes off access from one side, 8780
While crenellated walls protect it from the other.
For this reason, I assure you,
The city had no fear of attack.
The Saracens pitched their tents.
The next morning at daybreak, 8785
Our knights arose.
"My lords," said Huon, "what will we do?
We are completely closed in,
And I see no means of escape."
Geriaume said, "This is true 8790
Unless God comes to our aid."
"It's no use lamenting," said Huon.
"Let us wait for God to make his will known."
They then sat down for a meal,
Where they enjoyed an abundance of food and drink, 8795
For the city was well supplied with provisions.
When they had eaten and drunk their fill,
They removed the tablecloths and left the table
And then went off to the seashore
To relax and amuse themselves. 8800
Listen, my lords, in the name of God,
And hear the adventure the Lord sent them:
Huon looked off to the right
And saw a large ship marked with a gold cross
Sailing toward them. 8805

He showed it to Geriaume straightaway, saying:
"My lord, in the name of God, listen to me!
I see a ship approaching.
There are Frenchmen aboard, I am sure of it."
"I noticed them too," said Geriaume.   8810
"And I can see the cross on the side of the ship.
God, the King of majesty, has come to our aid."
The ship sailed steadily
Until it arrived beneath the tower.
The sailors looked up   8815
And prayed ardently to God.
They said to one another, "What a stroke of bad luck
To arrive in a place inhabited by Saracens and Slavs!
Their lord is the emir Galafre.
God help us, we are all doomed!"   8820
Hearing this, those inside the ship
Began to lament, weeping bitterly.
When he heard their cries, young Huon
Came to the port with his knights.
Geriaume was the first to speak, asking: 8825
"My lords, in what land were you born?"
And they replied, "Since you speak French,
We will tell you, if you guarantee our safety."
Geriaume replied, "Do not worry,
For we are all French and were born in France.   8830
Tell us the truth without fear."
"My lord," they said, "very well.
We are from France, may God save us!
Some are from Saint-Omer,
Others are from Paris,   8835
And still others come from lands I cannot name."
"My friend," said Huon, "may God save you,
Are any of them from Bordeaux?"
And he replied, "Yes, so help me God.
There is one man who is old and grizzled.   8840
He is over a hundred years old,

And his name is Guiret.
We offered to bring him across the sea for the love of God,
But we arrived at the wrong port."
"My friend," said Huon, "show him to me."   8845
"You will see him right away," he replied.
The sailor cried out:
"Where is the old man from Bordeaux?"
"Here I am," said the provost Guiret.
Rising quickly to his feet,   8850
He came to the prow of the ship.
Huon observed him carefully
And asked, "My friend, where were you born?"
"In the city of Bordeaux," he replied.
"What is your name?" asked Huon.   8855
"My lord, I am called Guiret."
"My friend," said Huon, "in the name of God,
Tell me what brought you here,
Where you come from, and where you are going."
"My lord," he said, "you are about to find out,   8860
For I will tell you the exact truth:
I had a lord who lost his inheritance.
His name was Huon, may God have pity on him!
He was banished by valiant Charlemagne.
Because he had killed his son Charlot,   8865
Charles sent Huon to Babylon, across the Red Sea,
To deliver a message,
While Huon's brother Gerard remained on their land.
Their mother died over three years ago,
And Gerard took possession of the entire fief.   8870
By my head, the scoundrel then married
The daughter of Gibouart of Viemez.
Gerard torments everyone throughout the land,
Poor people as well as knights.
He disinherits orphans   8875
And diminishes widows' lands.
He has done more evil than I can say.

I myself have suffered at his hands,
For I was once provost, charged with guarding the land,
But he stripped me of my duties.   8880
One day, the barons gathered
And asked me to go looking for Huon.
It has been a good two years since I crossed the sea.
I have gone to every country, borderland, and kingdom
As far as the Dry Tree and the Red Sea,   8885
Searching for the young man.
I never heard anything about him,
And thus I am returning, sorrowful and brokenhearted,
For I have nothing to tell or to relate,
And I have pawned all of my possessions.   8890
These merchants kindly allowed me in their ship
And offered to bring me across the sea for the love of God,
But they arrived in the wrong port."
When Huon heard this story,
He began shouting at the top of his lungs: 8895
"Lord Geriaume, come quickly,
And you will be able to embrace your brother!"
Hearing this, Geriaume came running.
He embraced his brother, saying:
"My brother, I'm so happy to have found you!"   8900
And Guiret replied, "May God bring you great honor!"
Huon embraced him as well:
"Guiret," he said, "do you recognize me?"
"My lord," he replied, "I do, so help me God!
I know very well that you are mighty Huon."   8905
"By my faith," said Huon, "it is true."
"Huon, fair lord," said Guiret,
"In sweet France they long for your return.
Will you come, or will you stay here?"
"By my faith," said Huon, "I am eager to return."   8910
Guiret then addressed Geriaume, asking:
"My brother, in the name of God, where are you coming from?
I haven't seen you for a very long time —

I've kept careful track — it has been sixty years
Since you left the city of Bordeaux."   8915
Then Geriaume told him the whole story,
Explaining how he had found Huon.
However, I do not wish to relate everything they said.
Huon called out to the sailors:
"My lords, in the name of God, listen to me: 8920
I beg you to speak softly,
For there are Saracens and Slavs out there.
Two emirs have besieged us,
And we have no means of escape.
If they see us, death is unavoidable.   8925
I beg of you, in the name of God,
There are fourteen of us in the city,
Along with a very beautiful lady.
Please take us aboard your ship.
I'll give you so much silver and gleaming gold,   8930
Taffetas, fine silken cloth, and fur-trimmed garments,
That you'll be rich for the rest of your days,
And as for the old man that you brought here —
The one from the city of Bordeaux —
I'll give you plenty of money for his passage."   8935
And they replied, "That is out of the question!
We won't take a single penny
Or even two gold marks if you offered them,
For we did this in honor of the Lord our God.
By the One who suffered on the cross,   8940
The entire ship is at your disposal.
You may bring on board anything you wish."
"My lords," said Huon, "may God reward you!"
All night long they carried aboard
Gold and silver, silks and taffetas.   8945
After waiting until dark,
All fourteen entered the ship.
They brought enough bread, wine, and wheat
To last them more than a year.

They also brought the young lady with them,   8950
As well as the noble minstrel.
They weighed anchor and set sail.
God gave them such good winds
That before daybreak they had sailed a hundred leagues.
The following day at sunrise,   8955
The Saracens advanced to the city walls
And began to attack from all sides,
But all their projectiles were in vain,
For not a single man born of woman remained inside.
When they saw that no one appeared   8960
And that their attack drew no response,
They abandoned their assault and turned back
To inform the emir.
"Sire," they said, "by Mohammed,
There is no one left in the entire city!"   8965
Hearing this, the emir's blood began to boil.
He had thirty pagans armed
And loaded into a boat.
He then ordered them to proceed
To the postern facing the sea.   8970
The Saracens set sail
And quickly reached the postern,
Where they found not a single man nor woman.
The pagans opened the gates
And entered the fair city,   8975
Rushing in from all sides.
The two kings went up to the palace.
They were both full of anguish
Because the Frenchmen had gotten away.
King Yvorin returned to Monbrant,   8980
And King Galafre remained in the city.
Thus the Saracens went their separate ways.
Now I shall tell you about our knights.
I cannot relate the details of their journey,
But they sailed across the high seas   8985

Until they arrived at the port of Brindisi,
Where they left their great ship
And went to take lodging in the city
At the home of Garin of Saint-Omer.
Huon said to Garin's fair-faced wife: 8990
"My lady, pray for wise Garin,
For you will never see him again in this world."
"Blessed Mary! What are you saying, Huon?
Is my beloved husband dead?"
"Yes, my lady. It grieves me to say so."   8995
Hearing this, the lady fainted away four times.
Huon lifted her up, and she began to weep softly.
"My lady," he said, "do not lament.
Since he is dead, it is no use weeping.
May God, by his grace, have pity on his soul!"   9000
Old Geriaume ordered water brought,
And they all sat down after washing their hands.
Our Frenchmen rested throughout the day;
They then purchased many horses and palfreys,
Had garments made of exotic silk,   9005
And clothed themselves most elegantly.
After spending five full days
With the wife of Garin of Saint-Omer,
They had at least thirty packhorses and mules
Loaded and prepared.   9010
Huon paid the sailors handsomely,
Giving them such an abundance of gold and silver
That they would always be wealthy and comfortable.
When the time came, they took their leave,
Commending one another to Jesus.   9015
Huon then set out on his journey:
He traveled through Puglia and Calabria,
Riding as quickly as possible.
I cannot tell you the details of his journey,
But he and his men rode so long and hard   9020
That they arrived in Rome one morning

And entered the city.
They went directly to the church of St. Peter,
Where Huon encountered a servant.
He questioned the man, as you will hear,   9025
Asking him to reveal truthfully
Where he might find the pope.
The servant replied, "You can find him
In his splendid palace, so help me God."
Huon spurred his fine horse,   9030
Followed by all of his knights.
They rode without stopping until they reached the palace,
Which they entered at once,
Flanking Lady Esclarmonde on all sides.
The pope looked carefully at Huon   9035
And recognized him immediately.
He rose to greet him, saying:
"Huon, I bid you welcome."
"My lord," said Huon, "may God bring you honor."
The pope said, "Fair nephew, tell me everything: 9040
How are you? Are you well?"
Huon replied, "My lord, I have suffered many hardships,
And we lost Garin of Saint-Omer."
The pope exclaimed, "May Jesus have pity on him!
I heard that you had taken him with you."   9045
"My lord," said Huon, "may God preserve me,
I have suffered many hardships,
And yet I accomplished what I set out to do,
For I have Emir Gaudisse's mustache
As well as his four molars   9050
And his very beautiful daughter.
I humbly request that you baptize the lady,
And then I will take her as my wife."
"Just as you wish," the pope replied,
"Provided that you stay the night here with me."   9055
"My lord," said Huon, "I will do as you please."
That evening, there was much rejoicing.

The next morning at daybreak,
Huon arose and got dressed.
The pope had the bells rung for mass,   9060
And they brought the young lady to the church,
Where they baptized her in honor of our Lord.
They did not, however, change her name:
She would always be called Esclarmonde.
Without any delay,   9065
The pope himself said the mass,
But before the service began,
He heard young Huon's confession:
The young man confessed all his serious sins,
Without concealing any of them,   9070
As far as he could remember.
The pope pardoned all his sins
And then married Huon and the maiden.
When the mass had been said, and the ceremony was over,
They returned to the splendid palace.   9075
That day there was much rejoicing.
You may be sure that the wedding feast was magnificent.
There were six minstrels, all well compensated.
When the day ended and the sun set,
The barons retired for the night.   9080
Huon lay beside his beloved,
Free at last to fulfill all his desires.
Auberon would no longer reproach him
As he had before on the Red Sea.
The next day at sunrise,   9085
Young Huon arose
And prepared for his journey,
For he greatly desired to return to France.
He had the lady mounted on a mule
And then went to take his leave   9090
Of the noble and valiant pope.
"My lord," said Huon, "I commend you to Jesus.
May God reward you as you have rewarded me!"

The pope replied, "Huon, go with God.
I only regret that you cannot stay longer."   9095
Then young Huon took his leave.
He and his men left the city
And rode unceasingly day and night,
Never stopping for wind nor storms.
I cannot tell you the details of their journey,   9100
But they rode so long and hard
That they soon spotted the walls and moats of Bordeaux.
This sight filled Huon with great joy.
He eagerly showed the city to his wife, saying:
"My lady, behold your inheritance!   9105
This is the city I wish to offer you.
At the present time, it is but a duchy,
But if I am able to return from France,
It will become a kingdom, so help me God."
Geriaume said, "This is no time for boasting,   9110
For you have no idea what's in store for you.
For now, ride on without delay
Until you reach Saint-Maurice-des-Prés,
An abbey not far from here,
That you may enter without fear,   9115
For Charlemagne is their liege lord.
The convent and the abbey pay homage to him."
"My lord," said Huon, "just as you wish."
Worthy Huon chose a messenger, saying:
"My friend, here's what you must do: 9120
Ask for the abbot, and when you find him,
Greet him cordially
In the name of Huon of Bordeaux,
Who is returning from across the Red Sea
And wishes to dine in the abbey at noon.   9125
Tell him to prepare for my arrival
By providing an abundance of food
Without sparing any expense,
For I have thirty packhorses laden with riches."

The messenger replied, "I will relay your message faithfully." 9130
He mounted his horse and rode off,
Never making a single stop
Until he reached Saint-Maurice-des-Prés.
He arrived at the gate, entered the abbey,
And asked for the abbot, who was brought to him at once. 9135
The servant said, "Fair lord, listen to this!
I bring you greetings and affection
From young Huon of the city of Bordeaux.
He is arriving very soon with his knights.
Now prepare for his arrival, 9140
For he has expressed his wish to dine with you."
Hearing this, the abbot rejoiced.
He summoned the ordained monks, saying:
"Go and change into your vestments."
They obeyed his orders, 9145
Changing their clothing and bringing
Their missals, crosses, and reliquaries.
Out of the abbey came the monks and the abbot,
All singing as they went to meet Huon.
When he saw them coming toward him, 9150
The young man dismounted,
And all his knights did the same,
As did Lady Esclarmonde,
Then they all walked toward Saint-Maurice.
There was much rejoicing when the two groups met. 9155
The abbot embraced Huon
And then the noble provost Guiret,
But he did not recognize Geriaume.
The monks turned back toward the abbey
And crossed the threshold joyfully. 9160
The visitors were brought to the best lodgings,
And the abbot received them with great honor.
He had pigs and steers slaughtered in the kitchens below
And entertained Huon most congenially.
Huon went to sit on a bench, 9165

And the fair-featured abbot joined him, saying:
"Huon, in the name of God, tell me:
How are you faring? Are you in good health?"
"My lord," said Huon, "I am well, so help me God,
For I have the mustache and molars of the emir Gaudisse,   9170
As well as his daughter,
Whom I married in Rome.
I will go to France tomorrow at daybreak."
"My lord," said the abbot, "if you wish,
I will send for your brother Gerard."   9175
"Yes indeed," said Huon. "Gladly!"
The abbot called his attendant:
"My friend, go to Bordeaux at once,
And tell Duke Gerard to come quickly
To the abbey at Saint-Maurice-des-Prés   9180
To see his brother, young Huon,
Who has returned from across the sea."
And he replied, "I will relay your message faithfully."
He rode swiftly to Bordeaux
And entered the city at full tilt.   9185
When he arrived at the palace, he climbed the staircase
And found Gerard in the company of his barons.
He took him aside, saying:
"My lord, listen to me:
The abbot of Saint-Maurice has requested   9190
That you come at once to the abbey,
Where you will be able to see your brother."
When Gerard heard this, he nearly lost his mind.
He said to the servant, "My friend, you may go back
And tell my brother that I will come visit him."   9195
And he replied, "My lord, I will relay your message faithfully.
I am going back, but please do not delay."
The messenger returned to the abbey
And relayed Gerard's message to Huon.
Meanwhile, Gerard summoned his lord,   9200
A traitor named Gibouart,

Father of the woman he had married.
"My lord," he said, "come forward, in the name of God,
And counsel me, I beg of you.
Devils have brought back my brother.   9205
He is at Saint-Maurice-des-Prés.
The abbot has just asked me
To go and see my brother,
Who is leaving for France tomorrow at daybreak.
He will recover his land and his country,   9210
And I will be completely dispossessed,
Without a single foot of land to call my own.
What do you advise me to do?"
Gibouart replied, "Do not be dismayed,
For I will counsel you wisely."   9215

77

Gibouart said, "Gerard, be still!
I will advise you, if you wish,
And tell you how to proceed:
Outside the abbey there is a leafy thicket,
Half a league from the main church.   9220
I will bring forty knights
And hide them in the thicket.
You will go and celebrate with your brother,
Bringing only a squire.
In the morning, at daybreak,   9225
Be sure that Huon arises quickly.
He will depart with his knights.
When you are close to the thicket,
Pick a quarrel with your brother.
If he says something to provoke you,   9230
We will emerge from the thicket
And kill all his knights.
You will have Huon thrown into a dungeon
And then inform Charlemagne of the situation."
Gerard replied, "It will be just as you wish."   9235

78

Gibouart said, "Gerard, my brother, listen:
You will go to your brother in the abbey,
Taking only a squire with you.
Ask him how things went on his travels,
Whether he has the mustache and molars;   9240
And if he's brought them with him,
Ask him where they are, where he's keeping them.
If you can, have him rise
Before dawn. Get him moving early,
And we will be hiding, armed, in the thicket.   9245
When you are about to pass by the thicket,
Talk to your brother about something
That will make him angry with you.
When I hear him quarreling with you,
My barons and I will emerge from the thicket   9250
And kill all the pilgrims.[50]
Then you will seize young Huon
And have him thrown into your dungeon.
Next you will steal the mustache and teeth
And go to speak with King Charles   9255
To inform him in private
That you have imprisoned your brother —
Young Huon, who went across the seas.
He came back to your court — you'll say —
Without the mustache   9260
Or the four molars of King Gaudisse.
I know for a fact that Charlemagne hates him,
And if he can take hold of him in Bordeaux,
He could well drag him behind horses and hang him
Without any sort of trial.   9265

50. The men who accompanied Huon to Jerusalem and the Holy Sepulcher were initially termed *chevaliers* ("knights," line 2435) and *barons* (line 2443), but following their successful return are now *pallerins* ("pilgrims") and *palmiers* ("palmers," line 10161).

When he was banished from the kingdom of France,
I saw Huon give over good hostages to affirm
That if, when he returned from across the sea,
He went first to his own home
Before coming to speak with the king,   9270
Charles could drag him behind horses and hang him.
If you agree to do as I have proposed,
Your brother will be destroyed."
Gerard said, "You have given me good advice.
I will carry it out as you have suggested."   9275
Then Gibouart of Viemez turned away,
But he did not depart until after dark.
Meanwhile Gerard set off for the abbey,
Taking only a squire with him.
They rode along and traveled   9280
Until they reached the abbey.
He entered and asked for his brother.
They pointed to him, and Gerard
Entered the room where young Huon was.
As soon as Huon saw him, he arose   9285
And rushed over to embrace him.
Gerard kissed him with the same loyalty
With which Judas betrayed Jesus.
"Dear brother," said Huon, "I am happy to see you!
Holy Mary, where have you been for so long?   9290
And why have you come with so few men?"
Gerard replied, "My lord, this was on purpose.
This is not the time for such display.
You do not know what will happen to you,
My brother, nor how you will regain your lands.   9295
If God grants that you be reconciled
With Charlemagne, who is so bountiful,
Then I will summon the greatest barons
And put on a marvelous feast.
But for now, you must go humbly to Paris."   9300
"My brother," said Huon, "you have spoken wisely."

Then they sat down side by side
And Gerard said, "My lord, as God is my witness,
I am delighted that you have returned.
For God's sake, are you in good health?   9305
Tell me about your wanderings and exploits.
Have you done all that you were ordered to do?"
"My brother," said Huon, "in truth,
I have Emir Gaudisse's mustache
And four molars from his jaw,   9310
And I have brought with me
His excellent daughter Esclarmonde.
I was married to her in the city of Rome
By the noble and holy pope.
And I have thirty pack horses loaded with booty.   9315
Gerard, dear brother, as God is my witness,
If I wanted to tell the whole truth,
It would take quite a long time,
As I have endured many sufferings."
"I believe it well," said Gerard, "in God's name.   9320
But tell me if you will:
Did anyone help you deliver your message?"
"Yes," answered Huon, "a most estimable man
Called Auberon by those who know him.
He is only three feet tall, and I tell you,   9325
Dear brother, that he has magical powers.
He helped me kill the emir,
And then I pulled out his four molars
And cut off his white mustache."
Gerard inquired, "And where do you keep them?"   9330
"I'll tell you," said Huon, "in God's name.
See Geriaume over there? He has them in his side,
Sealed just above his hip,
For that is where Auberon put them."
"Which one is he?" asked mad Gerard.   9335
"That old fellow over there, the one
With the beard as white as flowers in the meadow."

"Where was he born?" asked Gerard.
Huon replied, "I'll tell you:
He's the brother of the noble provost Guiret.   9340
He is called Geriaume by name,
And one could not ask for a more loyal man.
I found him in a wooded bower
Where he had lived for over sixty years
And had endured many hardships.   9345
And you, dear brother, how have you been?
I've heard that you've gotten married."
Gerard said, "You have heard right."
"Dear brother," continued Huon, "tell me:
Who is the woman? And who are her relatives?"   9350
"My lord, I'll tell you the truth:
She is the daughter of Gibouart of Viemez,
A nobleman who holds extensive lands:
All of Sicily, which is a mighty duchy."
"I know him well," said Huon,   9355
"And so help me God, you've made a bad marriage.
You have taken the daughter of a traitor!"
Gerard replied, "My lord, you are very wrong
To call my father-in-law a traitor."
At this point the abbot came up   9360
To Huon and asked him:
"My lord, when would you like to eat?"
Huon replied, "As soon as it is prepared."
"It is ready now," said the abbot.
"Get up and come to table."   9365
Gerard and Huon stood up at once
And went to wash their hands.
Water was brought to them in a large basin.
Huon washed up, and his brother beside him.
Old Geriaume and the provost Guiret,   9370
Along with young Huon's barons,
All sat down at table to dine.
My God! How Gerard stared at Guiret!

He hated him because
He had gone off to seek young Huon.   9375
If Gerard can get him out of the abbey,
He will be the first one to be punished.
While the others ate, Gerard barely touched his food:
He was thinking only of the great evil ahead.
There were multiple courses for the barons,   9380
And all were well served, needless to say.
When they had eaten and drunk their fill,
Servants and young men removed the cloths.
Beds were made up, and they went to rest.
Huon pulled the abbot aside   9385
And spoke to him privately:
"My lord, for God's sake, listen to me:
I have brought great riches here.
Would you please guard them for me
Until the hour I am able to return?   9390
Do not give them to anyone at all
Other than myself, who left them with you.
If I return, you will be amply rewarded."
The abbot said, "They will be kept safe."
At that, they went to rest and sleep.   9395
Valiant Huon slept to one side
In a most beautiful bedchamber,
While Esclarmonde slept in a decorated bed,
For Huon was feeling quite amorous
And had he been beside her, he would have been unable   9400
To resist making love to her,
But he did not wish to violate the sanctity of the abbey.
Huon and Gerard were sleeping side by side,
And Gerard spoke to his brother as you will hear:
"My lord, if it pleases you,   9405
I could wake you up when it's time,
For we must set off early tomorrow."
Huon answered, "As you wish."
No more was said, and they began to rest.

Huon and the other barons slept,   9410
But the traitor Gerard did not,
Because he was anxious about his evil plans.
When he heard the first rooster crow,
Gerard immediately summoned Huon:
"Get up, brother, and hurry!   9415
The rooster crowed a long time ago."
Huon leapt up and called to his men:
"Wake up, my lords, it's time to rise!"
"Heavens," said Geriaume, "is it already morning?
It seems like night fell only a moment ago!   9420
Let us rest a little longer, my lord."
"You are wrong, Geriaume," said Gerard.
"A man who wishes to be about his business
Should never stay in bed."
"Upon my word," said Huon, "that's the truth!   9425
Now get up, by God, because I am very eager
To be able to speak with Charlemagne."
So they all got ready and armed themselves.
The servants went to saddle the horses
And led them forth when they were ready.   9430
The barons mounted without delay.
Meanwhile Esclarmonde had gotten dressed,
And they mounted her upon a mule.
Huon took leave of the abbot,
Who commended them all to Jesus's care.   9435
They were all sad to have arisen so early.
They had the gates unlocked and opened,
Then set off and rode through the fields.

79

Huon and his courtly lady
Arose and left the abbey.   9440
There were fourteen in the company, and she made fifteen.
Wicked Gerard led them forth,

Turning back up the main road to Bordeaux.
Lady Esclarmonde, may God bless her,
Was riding upon a Syrian mule.   9445
She rode along regally,
But kept her head lowered.
When she saw Huon, she said:
"My lord, I am quite upset.
I'm trembling under my fine furs."   9450
"My lady," said Huon, "don't worry."
At this moment her mule stumbled
And came down upon its front knees.
The lady fell off onto the roadway.
When Huon realized this, his blood surged   9455
And he quickly helped her to her feet.
Then he placed her back upon the Syrian mule
And asked her tenderly:
"Are you hurt, my dear sweet friend?"
"My lord, I am a little injured."   9460
"I'm sorry to hear that," said noble Huon.
Geriaume added, "We are fools
To be riding before dawn's light."
Gerard said, "By God, Son of Mary,
I've never seen anyone, by St. Maurice,   9465
Get so frightened over so little!"
Geriaume said, "By my flowing beard,
If anyone were to listen to my opinion,
We would go back to the abbey."
"That's enough, good sir," said Gerard,   9470
"It would be pure folly to return.
Just because a mule stumbled,
You are all acting like cowards!
Let it be. Pluck up your courage
And ride on in the name of Holy Mary."   9475
And this they did, without further delay.
They rode far along the main road
Until they came to the crossroads

That was half a league from the abbey;
Four roads came together there.   9480
Huon called out to his companions:
"Hold your peace, my men,
For we are at the Saint-Maurice crossing stone,
Which was set up by my ancestors.
This road leads to prosperous Bordeaux,   9485
But so help me God I'll not take it,
Because if I turned that way, I would be unfaithful
To my promise to Charlemagne, king of France.
I do not wish to undertake such folly,
For then I would lose my lands.   9490
The road beyond it comes from Romagna,
And the other one to the right
Comes, I believe, from Lombardy,
While this last one comes from rich France.
That is the one I'll take, by God the Son of Mary."   9495
He and his companions took this road,
Accompanied by the false traitor Gerard.
Before they had gone a bowshot's distance,
They reached the leafy bower
Where Gibouart was hiding with his men.   9500
Then the traitor Gerard began his speech:
"Dear brother Huon," he said,
"You are heading toward rich France
In order to reclaim your lands.
I am sure you will get them all back.   9505
I have watched over your lands for you,
And by the One who rules over all,
I have not earned a penny for it,
But have guarded them loyally.
I have become engaged and married   9510
To the daughter of Gibouart of Viemez,[51]

51. For the rhyme, our manuscript *P* has *Gibuart de Saint Gille* and manuscript
M gives *de Sesile*, but in both cases the reference is to the evil traitor Gibouart de
Viemez. We have corrected to avoid confusion.

A man of great esteem and wealth.
You do me wrong to call him a traitor.
If he knew that you are headed
For rich France, he would consider that foolhardy,   9515
Because your lands were the price of my wedding,
Since he believed, by God the Son of Mary,
That you would never come back alive.
Now I no longer have a piece of land
That's worth the price of a rotten apple,   9520
So I beg you to help me,
And I want to know what will be my share
When you return from rich France,
By which I can support myself and my people?"
"My brother," said Huon, "what are you saying?   9525
I have left wealth in the abbey
That even twenty pack horses couldn't carry!
Whatever I have is yours:
I do not have a single penny in my possession
That I would not split with you, dear brother."   9530
Gerard said, "That is not what I require.
I want to have a share of my own
Over which I will have full control."
Hearing this, Huon's blood began to boil,
For it was clear that felony was afoot.   9535
Geriaume said, "Give him what he wants, fair sir."
"Gladly," replied noble Huon, "by St. Gilles.
Gerard, which would please you more:
Bordeaux or Gironville?"
"Leave me whichever you want."   9540
"By God, tell me which you prefer!"
When Gerard — that coward and traitor —
Saw Huon did not wish to argue or quarrel,
But would rather give him whatever he wanted,
He became so upset that his blood began to boil.   9545
Gerard came up to Guiret and said:
"Guiret, you wicked traitor,

You have cost me all my inheritance!
But, by the faith I owe Holy Mary,
You will have your head cut off!"   9550
With these words, he let forth a call to battle.
Gibouart — may God damn him! — heard it
And dug his spurs into his horse.
He burst forth from the thicket,
And he and all his horsemen set upon Huon.   9555

80

Gibouart burst forth from the thicket
With some sixty shields accompanying him.
When Huon saw him, his blood surged.
He called upon God and his power
And would gladly have returned   9560
To the abbey, but the enemy was too swift.
The dastardly cowards ran toward Huon,
Who drew his sharp steel sword
And struck the first enemy who approached.
Neither hauberk nor helmet was worth a dime   9565
For keeping him from being split open to his teeth.
But Huon's defense was worth nothing,
For they were sixty — or even more —
And were well equipped and armed to the teeth.
They fiercely attacked Huon's men   9570
And killed and destroyed a dozen of them.
Seeing this, Huon was sadder than he had ever been:
He realized clearly that his brother had betrayed him.
Evil Gerard and his men did not hesitate:
They seized the first ones who had been slaughtered   9575
And brought them to the banks of the Gironde,
A river with a powerful current,

And threw them in where it flowed the swiftest.
These men would never rescue Huon!
Gibouart approached Huon   9580
And knocked him from his horse.
Gibouart's men ran to where he lay,
Blindfolded him so he could see nothing,
And then bound his wrists together.
Meanwhile Gerard ran to Geriaume,   9585
Knocked him sideways to the ground
And quickly split open his sides,
From which he took the molars and mustache
That had belonged to Gaudisse, the mighty emir.

81

Evil Gerard — may God damn him! —   9590
Had defeated old Geriaume
And opened up his sides.
He removed Emir Gaudisse's molars
And the white mustache that Huon had won
And that King Auberon had sealed in him   9595
The day he had killed the emir.
Geriaume was weeping and made a loud cry.
When the young warrior Huon heard it,
He started shouting to his brother Gerard:
"My lord, for the sake of God in majesty,   9600
I urge you not to kill him!"
Gerard replied, "I'll not hurt him further."
Then Gerard bound his wrists together
And blindfolded Geriaume's eyes.
Lady Esclarmonde was lamenting loudly,   9605
And Huon begged Gerard for friendship's sake
Not to do any harm to his wife.
The traitor said, "That's enough!"
He seized hold of the fair-faced lady,
Blindfolded her, bound her wrists together,   9610

And then had all three placed upon three horses.
They all set off without delay
And rode in the direction of Bordeaux.
How painful it was to see Huon, Geriaume,
And Esclarmonde led toward Bordeaux.   9615
Oh God! How the lady wept for Huon:
"My lord, what a misfortune for your men!
When we were in my kingdom, you told me
That, when you reached the city of Bordeaux,
You would give me a crown to wear.   9620
But now, alas, we are in such a miserable way!
What an evil brother you have found!
The French are evil, by God!
There is much more loyalty among Saracens."
"My lady," Huon said, "as God is my Savior,   9625
My brother has vilified and shamed me,
And may God make him pay for this cruelty!
I feel more sorrow for you than for myself."
While they were conversing in this manner,
They entered Bordeaux before sunrise   9630
And did not know just where they had been brought.
Once the barons were within the city,
Gerard hurried them along
Until they entered the castle.
This way, the good bourgeois of the city   9635
Did not realize how miserably
He and his men were treating Huon.
Had they known, you can be sure,
They would rather have been dragged by horses and killed
Than to have allowed Huon to be handled in this vile manner.   9640
But the traitor had acted so stealthily
That no one alive knew of it,
Except those whom he had brought with him.
The despicable traitors managed to sneak
Into the castle without being detected.   9645
There they dismounted and removed their armor.

They seized Huon and valiant Geriaume
And the beautiful Esclarmonde.
They threw all three into the dungeon,
But first they unbound all their wrists   9650
And removed the blindfolds from their eyes.
Now they were in the deadly dungeon,
Where there was no sun nor other light,
And Gibouart — may God destroy him! —
Had a cousin of his guard the dungeon.   9655
He ordered him on pain of being blinded
To give them only a single barley loaf to eat
And two portions of water to drink
Between morning and nightfall — nothing more.
His cousin swore that unless he were dragged behind horses   9660
He would not give them any more than had been ordered.
The next morning at daybreak,
The proven traitor Gerard mounted his horse
Along with his lord, Gibouart of Viemez,
And a great number of their barons.   9665
They spurred their horses out of the city
And rode toward the abbey.
They rode so long and hard
That they arrived before the noon meal.
They entered and found the abbot;   9670
As soon as he saw him, Gerard spoke:
"My lord," he said, "listen to me:
Huon has made me return here
To fetch the goods he left in your care
And bring them to him.   9675
When he reaches the great city of Paris,
He intends to share them generously
With his own barons and those at court."
"Gerard," said the abbot, "stop at once,
Because I swear on my boots and large shoes   9680
That you will not carry off a single penny,
Since your brother made it very clear to me

Not to trust anyone at all."
"Scoundrel, you're lying!" said Gerard.
"You intend to keep it all for yourself.   9685
I'll take it in spite of you,
And indeed, you'll pay dearly for this!"
He stepped forward and seized the abbot
By his hair and began pulling it.
Gibouart ran up, and the two of them   9690
Managed to throw the abbot to the ground
And give him such dreadful blows
That his heart failed within his breast.
After killing him, they abandoned him.
All the monks fled,   9695
Pursued by the evil and haughty Gerard
And by Gibouart with a drawn sword.
When they saw him, the monks exclaimed:
"Have mercy, Gerard, for God's sake!
We will give you everything in our treasury."   9700
Gerard responded, "Now you are talking sense.
Get it quickly and bring it to me at once!"
They replied, "As you wish."
They led him to where the great treasure was hidden.
Gerard had it packed up at once,   9705
Not leaving behind so much as a glove:
Everything was brought before him.
They did not leave a cross or candelabra,
Not a reliquary or gilded crucifix.
They brought forth all the chalices,   9710
Leaving only two behind for the abbey.
"That's enough for them," Gerard said.
The traitor had the large drinking vessels
And the golden goblets
And all the tubs for washing carried off.   9715
Choir robes, chasubles, altar cloths —
There was enough to load up fifteen packhorses.
There was a traitor's son living in the abbey.

Gibouart of Viemez had him made a monk
And then immediately named him the new abbot.　9720
Then they departed and rode off,
Taking the new abbot with them.
They headed straight for Bordeaux
And did not stop for anything
Before they entered the town.　9725
The good bourgeois stared at them,
And everyone in the city
Wondered where they had found such wealth.
They rode on
Until they reached the splendid palace.　9730
They dismounted from their powerful horses,
And Gerard had the treasure unloaded.
Five of the pack horses were singled out
And quickly unloaded in his treasury,
While the other ten were sent immediately　9735
Straight to Paris along the cobble-stoned road.
They sat down to eat,
But the thieves did not tarry long at table.
After eating, they arose at once
And found their horses saddled and ready.　9740
Gerard — may God damn him! — mounted,
As did Gibouart and the new abbot.
They were accompanied by two squires and a monk.
The six of them rode along.
I'll not tell you about their days,　9745
But they rode so long and hard
That they reached Paris one evening at sundown.
That night they went to their lodging,
And at dawn the next morning,
They quickly dressed and prepared themselves.　9750
They came to court and found their king.
Gerard had the pack horses led forward
Directly into the palace.
He gave two to the queen

And presented three to Charlemagne.　　　　　9755
All the barons at the king's court
Were given beautiful jewels,
Or gold cups, or gilded goblets,
Or silk cloths, or materials from across the seas.
The servants were given fine mantles,　　　　　9760
And the serving boys received ermine.
He gave away so much that everyone praised him.
Only Duke Naimes refused to accept anything,
Because he suspected that it was ill-gotten gain.
Charlemagne, however, had his gifts carried off,　　　　　9765
But did not want to remove a single penny
Until after he had spoken with Gerard.
Charlemagne invited Gerard to come sit with him,
Along with Gibouart and the abbot.
Charles even summoned the monk　　　　　9770
To the high table, since one customarily
Honors a person bearing gifts.
"Gerard," said Charles, "tell me what you want from me."
Gerard said, "My lord, I will tell you at once:
You must know — may God have mercy on me! —　　　　　9775
That I have had you sent and given as much
As I have, both to you and your barons,
Because I must speak with you.
I am in such need as one's never known.
I will tell you, though it will make you sad at heart,　　　　　9780
And I would rather be across the sea
Than have to tell you this in your palace.
It is difficult to relate, but worse to hide.
I tell you this out of holy charity,
For I know that I will be blamed,　　　　　9785
But I prefer to preserve my honor
Than to worry about what men might say."
"You are right," said Charlemagne, "in God's name."

82

Gerard said, "My lord, listen to my words:
You knighted me, as everyone knows,   9790
And strapped on my golden spurs.
What more can I say? I am your liege man
And seek only to serve you well.
I am well aware, may God have mercy on my soul,
That what I am about to tell you   9795
Will grieve the peers of your household,
And my heart already trembles because of it."
"Gerard," said Naimes, "you talk too much:
Get on with it! Shorten your speech!
From what I hear, no good can come of this."   9800
"Listen now," Gerard said to Charlemagne,
"The other day I was in my house in Bordeaux —
I was not there like a rogue,
For I had a hundred knightly barons with me.
My gates were opened wide to all.   9805
As I was looking out at my drawbridge,
I saw my brother Huon approaching.
He was carrying a pilgrim's staff and purse,
And with him was a fair-faced lady.
Also with him was an elderly man,   9810
Whose name, I believe, is Geriaume."
Hearing this, Naimes furrowed his brow.
"My God!" said the duke, "where has the old man been?
I remember seeing him at the Châlons tournament
Where he killed Count Salemon.   9815
He and I used to be close friends."
Gerard continued, "My lord, hear all I have to say.
I was shocked, of course, to see Huon,
But nonetheless — may my soul be pardoned for it —
I stood up when I saw the baron,   9820
As did all the peers of my household.
I led him up to my palace

And fed him abundantly.
After he had eaten, I spoke to him
And asked him where he was coming from.　　　　　9825
When I asked him about the Temple of Solomon,
He was incapable of giving an answer.
I asked him, Emperor Charlemagne,
If he had the molars and mustache
Of King Gaudisse, who was so wicked.　　　　　9830
Again, he was unable to respond.
When I saw this, my heart trembled,
And I did not know what to do.
I am loyal to you, Emperor Charlemagne,
And I was afraid of doing you wrong.　　　　　9835
I did not wish to be accused of treason,
So I threw my brother into my dungeon,
Along with his wife and his companion.
I tell you all this to unburden my conscience.
Now do with them as you will."　　　　　9840
When the noble barons heard this,
There was not a one who did not weep for Huon.
They all cursed the traitor Gerard.
His companions were saying to one another:
"Gerard is responsible for this treachery!"　　　　　9845
But the emperor Charles rose to his feet.
In his hand he held an olive branch,
And he spoke forcibly in these words:
"Listen to me, Frenchmen and Burgundians:
Today I demand that those who stood hostage for Huon　　　　　9850
Turn over to me this wicked traitor,
Or else, by the faith I owe St. Simon,
I will have them hanged with no respite."
Charles sat back down after speaking
And summoned the valiant Duke Naimes:　　　　　9855
"Naimes," he said, "what do you say about Huon?"
"My lord, for God and his holy name,
I believe — why hide it from you? —

That Gerard has acted with mortal treason."
Gerard said, "Naimes, you may say whatever you want,   9860
But by St. Peter whom we venerate in Nero's Meadow,[52]
I will provide loyal witnesses to all I've said:
My lord, the valiant baron Gibouart,
This abbot who is so noble,
And also his companion, the monk."   9865
The three replied, "Everything he says is true."
"By God," said Naimes, "you are all scoundrels!"

83

"Naimes," said Charles, "what advice do you give me
Concerning these two brothers you've heard about?"
"My lord, I've never before heard such a thing: 9870
This traitor throws his brother into his dungeon
And then comes to tell you about it!
By the Lord who suffered upon the cross,
If I had a blood brother
Who had been banished from France   9875
And then returned one day to my house,
I would have been very wicked indeed
If I had thrown him into my prison
And then come to your court to accuse him.
I would not have done it for all your wealth,   9880
For I would have thought, as God is my Savior,
That a hundred devils would carry me away.
Instead, I would have fed him generously
For two or three days and then let him leave.

52. Nero's Meadow (or Gardens) refers to the area, now located within the Vatican, where the apostle Peter was venerated by medieval pilgrims. He was crucified (c. 64 CE) by order of the Roman emperor Nero in the Circus of Nero, at a spot later marked by an obelisk, and buried nearby on Vatican Hill. The original St. Peter's Basilica, begun by the Emperor Constantine in the fourth century, was built over the supposed original tomb and was a major pilgrimage site throughout the Middle Ages. It is also mentioned at line 10392.

And if he had wanted to take some of my goods, 9885
I would have given him everything he wished.
But in this man there is little loyalty
And I would have a hard time trusting him
When he has behaved so badly toward his brother.
I am quite certain, as God is my witness, 9890
That Gerard has behaved treasonously,
And I tell you in perfect loyalty
That this man should be hanged and dragged by horses,
Along with Gibouart and the abbot
And the monk he brought with him. 9895
I will swear on relics, so help me God,
That all four have borne false witness."
When Gerard heard this, his blood boiled.
He was wishing now — and it is the truth —
That he had never gotten mixed up in all this. 9900
He was repentant, but he could not go backwards.
He repeatedly cursed Gibouart de Viemez,
Who had suggested this course of action.
He said to Naimes, "Sir, you are greatly mistaken.
I don't know why you hate me so much." 9905
"Upon my word," said Naimes, "it's because of your wickedness!
A while back you wanted to be one of our peers.
God! What advice you would have given us!
To tell the truth, I'd rather have one of my feet cut off."
"You're wasting your breath," said valiant Charlemagne. 9910
"You must sing me a different tune."
Then he addressed all of Huon's hostages:
"My lords, keep your promises to me
And turn over the young warrior Huon.
If you don't do this, as God is my Savior, 9915
I'll have you all hanged and dragged by horses."
"My lord," they pleaded, "have mercy on us!
For the love of God, let us be given a fair trial."
"Most willingly," he said, "in God's name.
Naimes, what counsel do you give me?" 9920

"Sire," he replied, "you will know it at once.
I will tell you how you must act:
You will take your powerful barons,
All the noble men that you can assemble,
To Bordeaux, if you please,   9925
And release Huon from the dungeon.
Then you can listen to what he has to say.
If he speaks the truth,
Have pity on him, for the love of God."
"Truly you have spoken well," said Charles.   9930
"I will do it since you have suggested it."
Then Charles had all his barons prepare themselves.
He sent for as many as one hundred forty.
He also brought along his eleven peers,
With bright-faced Huon making twelve.   9935

84

The king made his preparations:
He had over one hundred men saddle up
And did not forget the eleven peers.
Then he had all ten knights
Who stood hostage for brave Huon arrested   9940
And thrown into his prison,
But Duke Naimes stood up as guarantor for them
And had them ride along with the king.
Then they all set off along the highway.
May the Lord God help Huon today   9945
Because, if He does not, Huon is a dead man!
The king rode so long and hard
That they saw the walls and church towers of Bordeaux.
As they were nearing the city,
Gerard called out to proud Charlemagne: 9950
"My lord, please give me leave,
And let me ride ahead
So that I can prepare your welcome."

"No Gerard," said Charles, "you certainly may not!"
Hearing this, Naimes was delighted and overjoyed.   9955
He said to Charles, "As God is my helper,
That answer is worthy of a true warrior.
Blessed be the heart that inspired such a reply."
With these words, they spurred on their horses,
And everyone rode so long and hard   9960
That they soon were within the walls of Bordeaux.
They did not pull up until they reached the palace,
Where they dismounted before the cut-stone steps.
The good bourgeois wondered
Why the emperor Charlemagne had come there.   9965
Charles went up into the main hall
And sat down upon the pure golden throne
With all his barons surrounding him.
Gerard had a meal hastily prepared
And the large tables set up.   9970
Water was brought forth in large golden basins.
The king washed up and then sat down to eat.
Beside him was bold-faced Naimes,
While the knights sat at other tables.
The servants bustled about between the rows   9975
As one person called for bread and another aged wine.
Huon, in the dungeon, heard the noise overhead
And quickly summoned the jailer:
"My friend, as God is your helper,
Who are those people I hear up there?"   9980
The jailer, who was cold and cruel, said:
"It's Charlemagne, ruler of all France,
Who's come with his men to judge you.
You'll be hanged before nightfall."
"May God damn you," said Huon,   9985
"For telling me such bad news!"

85

Up in the palace Charles was seated at table,
With bearded Naimes beside him.
While the rest were eating, Naimes began to weep,
Then leapt up from the table,   9990
Bumping against it so hard
That he made the goblets spill.
"Naimes," said Charles, "for God's sake, what's the matter?
You are inconsiderate to spill my wine."
"No, I'm right to do so, by God,   9995
Because I'm so upset and angry
That you're behaving so stupidly!
For God's sake, what are you thinking?
Have you come to Bordeaux
Just to drink wine and claret?   10000
Don't you have enough of that in France?
You must realize, emperor,
That you are not about to ask us
To swear to some trifling thing,
But rather, it is to pass judgment   10005
On one of our twelve peers, so help me God.
When we have stuffed ourselves with food
And drunk enough to be inebriated,
How can we decide upon a man's death?
By the Lord who suffered on the cross,   10010
Any man here in this building
Who drinks more wine and claret today
Will lose my friendship from this day forward."
The king said, "I will do as you suggest."
Then he shouted, "Remove the tablecloths!"   10015
The servants and young men took down the tables.
The king ordered them to bring forth Huon,
And those he had ordered did so:
They took Huon out of the dungeon
And immediately brought him up to the palace,   10020

Along with his wife and valiant Geriaume,
All of them with shackles on their feet.
As soon as Huon saw valiant Charlemagne,
The blood rose up from his feet to his head.
The ten men who stood hostage   10025
For valiant Huon rose to their feet.
The hostages for young Huon
Approached Charles, the powerful crowned king.
As soon as they saw him, they called out:
"Sire, hear what we have to say: 10030
There you see the young warrior Huon.
Have we not kept our word to you?"
"Yes," said Charles, "by holy charity,
Since I see him, you have kept your word.
I'm quite certain he cannot escape from here."   10035
Huon passed in front of the king
And then bowed low before him.
"Sire," said Naimes, "now listen for God's sake
And hear what he has to tell you."
"Upon my word," said Charles, "I'll not refuse to do so."   10040
Thereupon Huon cried out for mercy:
"Sire, for God's sake, listen to me:
Before God and your highness
And before the barons I see assembled here,
I wish to speak out against the traitor standing there.   10045
I mean Gerard, may God destroy him.
He would be my brother if he were loyal,
But he is false and full of wickedness.
Since the day God was born
And Cain, who was so deranged,   10050
Killed his blood brother Abel,
No one has ever heard tell
Of a brother so evil and treasonous."
The barons heard this and wept for pity.
From every side they looked at Huon   10055
And said among themselves:

"This man has not been courting the ladies.
He is so changed and different:
We knew him as a handsome young man,
But now he is so emaciated and discolored.   10060
What has become of his great beauty?"
Huon spoke once more to Charlemagne:
"Sire, if you please, listen to me.
So help me God, I'll speak the truth.
Indeed, I crossed over the Red Sea   10065
To King Gaudisse, as I was ordered to do,
And I delivered your message, so help me God,
Every word of it, leaving nothing out.
He showed no respect at all for you,
So help me God, and became quite haughty   10070
When I asked for his white mustache
And the four molars from his mouth.
I was imprisoned in his dungeon
But rescued by the fairy Auberon,
A diminutive king who was born in Monmur.   10075
He helped me kill the emir.
I pulled out his four molars
And cut off his white mustache
With Auberon at my side all the while.
Once I had the mustache and the molars,   10080
I didn't know where to put them.
I asked him out of friendship
To put them somewhere for me
Where I would not lose them or remove them.
He immediately put them into Geriaume's side   10085
And used his magic to enclose them
Above his hip, according to God's will.
You've never heard tell of such a man!
Then I returned to this kingdom
And brought with me the emir's daughter,   10090
Esclarmonde, who is so beautiful.
There she is, beside those pillars.

Sire, if I wished to tell all of the adventures —
How I crossed the sea and how I returned —
It would take a long while to relate,   10095
But this is not the place for that.
As God is my Savior, what should I say?
I endured many hardships.
I came back first to the city of Rome,
Where I had Esclarmonde raised up and baptized   10100
And then took her to be my wife.
The pope, who is so noble and valiant,
Performed the ceremony, so help me God.
If you do not believe, noble king, everything I've said,
Send to the pope in Rome   10105
To determine whether I am telling the truth.
If he does not confirm what I've told you,
Sire, you may have me hanged.
I will not say a single word in this palace
That I cannot prove to be true.   10110
There is still more to be told:
When I returned from across the sea,
I had with me a large amount of silver and gold.
I was accompanied by the pilgrims
You allowed to go with me when I left,   10115
Because they never wished to leave me.
There were fourteen of them, so help me God,
Who all returned with me.
I did not want to delay for a day or night,
So eager was I to speak with you.   10120
I rode long and hard
Until I came to Saint-Maurice-des-Prés,
For I did not at all wish to enter Bordeaux.
I reached the abbey by noon.
The noble abbot sent for my brother —   10125
For he felt that he would want to honor me —
And he came, the worthless traitor,
Bringing only a squire with himself.

I could tell by that that he was planning trouble."
"Upon my word," said Naimes, "you are telling the truth.   10130
This showed how little he cared for you:
He should have brought many men with him."
"My lord," said Huon, "you are speaking the truth.
So help me God, the King of majesty,
Gerard did me the greatest wickedness: 10135
He questioned me carefully about all I had done
And inquired, as if he were my friend,
Whether I had spoken to Gaudisse
And given him your message,
And if I had the four molars   10140
And the emir's white mustache.
I told him I had brought them with me.
Then the proven traitor asked
Where I had put and enclosed them,
And how I safeguarded them.   10145
I told him everything, without holding anything back,
Because, sire, I could not keep anything from him.
I did not at all suspect his great wickedness.
He exhorted and befuddled me so much
That he persuaded me to arise before midnight   10150
And set off from the abbey with him.
When I had passed the crossroads,
Where the various highways diverge,
And I was about to take the road toward France,
He began to quarrel with me.   10155
Gibouart of Viemez was hiding
In the leafy woods nearby
Along with sixty mounted men.
Before I realized it, I saw all the armed men
Attacking me from every direction.   10160
They killed and beheaded the twelve pilgrims,
And I saw them tossed into the Gironde.
Then they forced me off my horse,
Blindfolded both my eyes,

And tied my two hands behind my back.   10165
They did the same thing to my wife.
Gerard seized bearded Geriaume
And sliced open his sides with his steel sword,
There where Auberon had sealed in
The emir's mustache and four molars.   10170
The deep wound, indeed, is still visible."
At that moment bearded Geriaume stood up
And showed the wound to the assembled Frenchmen.
Huon said, "Sire, as God is my Savior,
He then had us mount up on three horses,   10175
With our hands tied and eyes blindfolded.
He led us here to this city of Bordeaux
And threw us into his prison.
He stole everything I had from me.
I was brought here against my will, I assure you,   10180
And if he says that I'm lying,
Have both him and Gibouart of Viemez
Put on their armor and take up their weapons.
I will enter the jousting field against them both.
If I cannot defeat them both   10185
And force them to admit their guilt before nightfall,
Then you may hang me from the gibbet.
But if I win, then return my lands to me
And let me enjoy my inheritance in peace."
"By God," declared Naimes, "Huon has said enough."   10190
Gerard said, "Sire, he has had his say,
But I never committed such great wickedness,
Nor, by the faith I owe to God,
Do I wish to do combat against my brother.
Let the king judge as he will."   10195
"Oh God!" said Naimes, "listen to the traitor!
How well he covers up his crimes!"
"Huon," said Charles, "let this be.
I don't know how you did it,
But I do want to see the four molars   10200

And the white beard of the emir Gaudisse."
"My lord," replied Huon, "have mercy on me for the love of God!
They have stolen them all and taken them away."
"I have one more thing to say," continued Charles.
"When you left the kingdom of France,   10205
I said that I would cut off your limbs
When you came back from across the Red Sea,
If you should return to your own lands
Before you came to speak first with me.
You offered me good hostages to assure this.   10210
They have acted accordingly, and I released them
Because you are here and cannot escape.
I am free to have you hanged and dragged by horses
Without further judgment by anyone
Because I warned you when you left.   10215
So now, upon the faith I owe the Lord God,
Before sunset I will have you dragged by horses,
Since I have found you here in your own house."
"Sire, have mercy on me for the love of God.
I did not come of my own accord. I was brought here   10220
In spite of myself. I entered here unwillingly.
For God in majesty, treat me fairly!
Please let me be tried before the court."
"I swear," said Naimes, "you have condemned him to death."
The duke addressed valiant Charlemagne: 10225
"Sire, for the love of God in majesty,
Please take pity on young Huon
And do not give him the maximum penalty.
Do not cause the poor young man to suffer any more,
For it would be a sin and great wickedness."   10230
"Naimes," said Charles, "I do not care to grieve him.
Had I wanted to be cruel, you know
That he would already have been dragged to death.
But since he is beloved and one of your peers,
I agree to submit him to judgment."   10235
All the peers present there rejoiced greatly

When they heard the king speak in this manner.
Huon sat down near a pillar
With his wife and valiant Geriaume.
Then the king spoke to all the peers: 10240
"My lords, listen now and come forward
To judge this poor unhappy youth.
I conjoin you on your word of honor
And according to your loyalty toward me
To judge rightly, my lords.   10245
Do not judge Huon harshly
On account of the love you have for me,
But do not be false to me
Out of your desire to free Huon.
I wash my hands of this decision here and before God,   10250
And I charge you peers with it in the presence of all the barons."
When the peers heard Charles speak these words
And place the burden of judgment upon them,
They retired in sadness to a nearby room.
They sat down on benches around the room   10255
And stared for quite some time at one another.
No one said anything for a long while.
Finally, Naimes spoke, "My lords, listen to me:
The king has made us swear to judge honestly.
Let us be careful not to speak falsely,   10260
Because any evil would be blamed on us."
Then a very handsome knight,
Whose name was Gautier, stood up.
He was a relative of Ganelon and Hardré,[53]
But was one of the peers in spite of this,   10265
Because he was heir to the appropriate lands.
It was his right to speak before them.
"My lords," he said, "be silent and listen to me.
I say in all loyalty
That Huon should be hanged and dragged by horses,   10270

53. Traitors were often linked by family ties in the *chansons de geste*. Ganelon betrayed Roland, and a number of epic traitors are named Hardré.

Because the king has found him in Bordeaux.
It is his right, and there is no sin in doing so.
If I speak the truth, and if you agree,
Let Gerard be heir to all the lands
Because I would like him to be one of our peers."   10275
Next Henry of Saint-Omer spoke
And said to Gautier, "Go sit down!
Your word must not carry the day."

86

Henry said, "Noble knights,
So help me God, who judges all things,   10280
I declare loyally and without deceit
That Huon should recover his land and his fief,
For he faithfully accomplished his mission,
And the noble warrior has a credible witness —
The pope, a most praiseworthy man.   10285
But Gerard betrayed and tricked Huon
Because he coveted his brother's land.
Here is the judgment I propose, so help me God,
If you agree to it:
Huon should recover his land and his fief,   10290
And let Gerard be dragged by horses,
For he betrayed his brother out of malice."
Henry fell silent and sat down on the bench.
The count of Flanders then stood up
And spoke as befitting a worthy warrior.   10295

87

Baldwin of Flanders rose to his feet
And said to Henry, "Go and sit down,
For we will do none of what you proposed.
By God, I will tell you
The best way to proceed, as I see it.   10300

My lords, by God in heaven,
As you can see, this world isn't worth two pennies.
No longer can one find a loyal friend.
The case of these two brothers makes it quite clear,
And their dispute is indeed deplorable. 10305
We must do the right thing, by God in heaven:
Let us go together to the king of Saint-Denis
And beseech him, by God in heaven,
To have pity on both brothers:
Let him return to Huon his country and his land 10310
And grant a different land to Gerard.
Let them behave as brothers of the same flesh.
This is the result we must strive for."
Then the noble count sat down.

88

The next to speak was the old count of Châlons. 10315
He said to Count Baldwin, "You are a very honorable man,
And you have spoken eloquently,
But I am certain, upon my soul's salvation,
That the emperor Charlemagne would never hear of it.
All your fine words are completely worthless. 10320
But if you agree, my lords,
Let us put our faith in Duke Naimes
And follow his advice to the letter."
The others replied, "Blessed be God!"
Thus the barons reached an agreement. 10325
They addressed the duke with great courtesy, saying:
"Ah, noble duke, help us conclude our deliberations!"
Naimes heard them but said nothing.

89

All eleven peers were assembled in the council,
And Huon was outside next to a pillar. 10330

God! How the Frenchmen stared at the young man!
Lady Esclarmonde wept quietly.
"Huon," she said, "how dreadful that you are held
In such poor esteem in your own city.
No one listens to you at all.   10335
Valiant Charlemagne refuses to believe
That you went to Babylon,
And yet you were there, upon my salvation!
I saw you kill my father,
Pull four teeth out of his mouth,   10340
And cut off his white mustache.
It will be a great pity, my lord, if you die like this,
For you are a faithful and loyal man.
In this place, however, as far as I have heard,
There is not a single virtuous man.   10345
Even the king, who reigns over them,
Is corrupt and deceitful from what I have seen,
For he has treated you most disloyally.
But if God permits such a great injustice,
Allowing you to be hanged and dragged by horses,   10350
Then I declare that Mohammed is certainly more worthy.
Be assured that if you die,
I will never invoke your God,
But rather I will renounce holy Christianity."
Hearing this, the French wept with pity.   10355
"My lady," said Huon, "do not lament,
For you don't know what God has in mind."
Now I shall tell you about bearded Naimes.
He assembled his companions, saying:
"My lords, listen to me.   10360
May God save me, I am so filled with sorrow
When I think about these two brothers
That I cannot find a good solution.
What do you say, by God in majesty?
Tell me again what you advise."   10365
And they replied, "Noble and worthy duke,

If you cannot find any counsel to give us,
We certainly have no advice to offer you!"
"My lords," said Naimes, "why beat around the bush?
You will now hear the verdict: 10370
This court has sentenced Huon to be dragged by horses."
Hearing this, the barons were filled with sorrow.
"My lords," said Naimes, "I can offer you this:
I will find a way of preventing Huon
From being judged today in this court.   10375
You must all go along with everything I say."
"My lord," they replied, "may Jesus save you!"

90

The eleven peers, all worthy and renowned men,
Agreed to support Naimes's wishes.
They all left the room,   10380
And the squires and valets fell silent.
Even the highest ranking men did not utter a word:
All were praying for the unfortunate young Huon,
Who shed many tears from his beautiful eyes.
Both the lovely Lady Esclarmonde   10385
And Geriaume grieved bitterly,
For they greatly feared the emperor Charles.
God! How Huon watched Naimes,
Knowing that he would be the one to speak.
The noble young man dreaded the verdict.   10390
"True God," he said, "you who suffered the passion,
Sent St. Peter to Nero's Meadow,
And converted his companion St. Paul,
As truly as you were both God and man,
Help me today in my hour of need.   10395
As truly as we are blameless,
Release me today from this prison."
Then Duke Naimes spoke to Charles, saying:
"Noble king, do you wish to hear our opinion?"

"Yes," said Charles, "by St. Simon."　　　　　　　　　　　10400
"Rightful emperor," said Duke Naimes,
"Think carefully, in the name of God:
In what land or region
Should we judge a peer of the realm?"
"Naimes," replied Charles, "you are a very virtuous man,　　10405
But everything you've said is designed to acquit Huon.
By the One who suffered the passion,
None of this will help him one bit!"

91

"Sire," said Naimes, "in the name of God, you are wrong!
Consider, for God in majesty,　　　　　　　　　　　　　10410
What is the proper place to assemble your barons
When a peer of the realm must be judged?
I will tell you, in case you do not know:
One is the city of Saint-Omer,
Another the city of Orleans,　　　　　　　　　　　　　10415
And the third is Paris, I tell you truly.
Noble and valiant emperor,
If you really wish to put Huon on trial,
Have him brought to one of these three places,
For no man born of a woman　　　　　　　　　　　　　10420
Will consent to judge him in this palace."
Hearing this, the king grew very angry.
"Naimes," he said, "such loyalty!
You are saying this to acquit Huon.
I intended to have him judged　　　　　　　　　　　　　10425
In such a way that no one could blame me,
But since you refuse to tell the truth,
By God, you will never serve as his judge,
For by the mustache that flows beneath my nose,
I will eat but one single meal　　　　　　　　　　　　　10430
Before Huon is hanged and dragged by horses."
Then he shouted, "Prepare the table!"

When the filthy traitor Gerard heard all this,
His heart was full of joy,
But he dared not show it in the presence of the French.   10435
God, how greatly Huon despaired
And how tenderly Esclarmonde wept!
"My lord," she said, "I can plainly see that you are going to die.
If I had a sharp knife,
I would stab myself in the heart, so help me God!"   10440
Hearing this, the barons wept with pity,
For many of them were saddened on account of the lady.
Old Geriaume lamented bitterly, saying:
"Alas, I regret the day I was born!
I spent my youth in misery,   10445
And now I will die a wretched death."
Then all three of them lamented piteously.
They believed the end was near
Because Charles had sworn so vigorously,
But in the end, he would break those promises,   10450
As you will hear, before this evening,
If God protects the fairy Auberon,
Who was in the woods with his knights.
That noble king was seated for a meal
When tears began to fall from his beautiful eyes.   10455
His men asked, "Sire, what is wrong?"
Auberon replied, "My lords, I will tell you:
I am remembering a poor unfortunate man —
Huon, for whom I had such great affection.
He has endured great hardships.   10460
Now he has returned from the land across the sea
And has legally taken a wife,
Whom he married in the marvelous city of Rome.
He made his solemn confession to the pope
And then returned to the kingdom of France,   10465
But his wicked brother has betrayed him,
And thus poor Huon is in such a bad way
That he has never been in such mortal danger.

He is in Bordeaux in the splendid palace
With his feet bound in sturdy shackles,   10470
And Charlemagne is seated for a meal,
Having sworn upon his mustache
That after he has finished eating
And left the table,
Huon will be hanged and dragged by horses.   10475
But by the One who suffered on the cross,
That white mustache will prove to be a liar,
For I will help the young man.
I desire that my table be placed in his court
Next to the one where Charles is to dine,   10480
And I want it to be a good two feet taller than his.
Let my golden goblet be placed on the table,
Along with my ivory horn and gilded hauberk.
I will also require a hundred thousand armed men,
Or perhaps more, if I need them."   10485
His wishes were answered at once:
The table appeared in the splendid palace
Next to the one where Charles was dining,
And it was a good two feet taller
Than the one where Charles was sitting.   10490
The horn and the gilded hauberk were there,
Along with the goblet of pure gold.
Charles saw this display and showed it to Naimes:
"Naimes," he said, "for the love of God, look at that!
I believe we have been enchanted!"   10495
The barons were quite amazed
By the table, which they observed intently.
Geriaume raised his head
And saw the hauberk, the golden goblet,
And the ivory horn. He recognized all of them.   10500
He said to Huon, "You need not worry,
For there I see your fine gilded hauberk,
Your ivory horn, and your golden goblet.
I am certain that you will be rescued."

Hearing this, Huon greatly rejoiced.	10505
"Praise be to God!" he exclaimed.	
"My noble lord has not forgotten me!"	
At that moment, the fairy Auberon	
Entered the city with his barons.	
He called out to them, saying:	10510
"My lords, listen to me:	
I order you to guard the gates carefully	
To prevent any man alive from leaving."	
And they replied, "Just as you wish."	
At every gate in the fine city	10515
There were ten thousand armed men.	
They filled the streets on all sides.	
Auberon rode toward the palace.	
He left twenty thousand men at the entrance,	
Ordering them, on pain of death,	10520
Not to let a single man escape.	
He then went up to the palace,	
Bringing many of his barons with him.	
He was dressed in a silken garment	
Fastened on the side with thirty laces.	10525
He was as beautiful as the sun in summer.	
He passed by the king fiercely,	
Bumping him so hard on the shoulder	
That Charles's hat tumbled off his head.	
"My God, this dwarf is quite hunchbacked!	10530
Holy Mary, how beautiful he is!"	
Said the feared King Charles.	
Auberon passed by him	
And approached Huon, bidding him to stand up.	
He had all the fetters and shackles removed	10535
From Huon, his wife, and valiant Geriaume,	
Thus liberating all three on the spot.	
He then had them seated beside him at the table.	
Auberon picked up his fine golden goblet	
And made the sign of the cross over it.	10540

The goblet filled with clear red wine.
He gave the goblet to the lady,
Who drank from it and then passed it to Huon,
Who gave it to bearded Geriaume.
All three drank heartily.   10545
Auberon said to Huon:
"My friend, get up quickly!
Take this fine golden goblet
And bring it to valiant Charlemagne.
Let him drink from it as a sign of peace between you."   10550
"Sire," said Huon, "just as you command."
He rose, picked up the goblet,
Went up to Charles, and gave it to him.
Charles accepted it, not daring to refuse,
But as soon as he touched the goblet, the wine disappeared.   10555
"Lowly vassal," said Charles, "you have cast a spell over me!"
Auberon replied, "It is rather your evildoing,
For the goblet is endowed with magical powers.
No one may drink from it except a virtuous man:
Someone pure, upright, and free from mortal sin.   10560
I happen to know a serious sin you committed
A very long time ago,
Which you have never confessed to a priest.[54]
Were it not for the fear of humiliating you,
I would reveal it here before all your barons."   10565
Hearing this, the king was filled with horror.
Huon took back the golden goblet,

54. The idea of a secret sin that Charlemagne never dared confess is first attested in the ninth-century Latin legend of St. Gilles [Aegidius]. In the thirteenth-century Icelandic translation of the *Karlamagnus-Saga*, it is said that he committed incest with his sister Gille (not to be confused with St. Gilles). In French tradition, represented by the fourteenth-century *chanson de geste Tristan de Nanteuil* and the prose *Berte aux grands pieds*, the child born of this incest was Roland. In Germanic tradition, the sin was necrophilia (or even sodomy), stemming from his obsession with his dead wife. See Gaston Paris, *Histoire poétique de Charlemagne* (Paris: Bouillon, 1905); and Suzanne Hafner, "Charlemagne's Unspeakable Sin," *Modern Language Studies* 32 (2002): 1–14.

And the wine returned as soon as he touched it.
He brought the goblet to bearded Duke Naimes,
Who took it and drank heartily.   10570
However, no other baron in the entire court
Could touch the goblet
Without all the wine disappearing at once.
Huon returned to Auberon
And sat down beside him under the gaze of the barons.   10575
Auberon asked Naimes to stand up
And had him sit beside him.
The diminutive king called out to Charles:
"Rightful emperor," said valiant Auberon,
"Now listen to me, in the name of God!   10580
Behold Huon, whom you have disinherited.
Depriving him of his land was most unjust,
For he is a virtuous and loyal man.
King, I tell you truly
That he delivered your message across the sea   10585
To King Gaudisse, as you commanded.
I helped him kill the emir,
By throwing him at Huon's feet.
He pulled out the emir's four molars,
And I saw him cut off his white mustache,   10590
Then he placed all these items in Geriaume's side,
Concealing them just above the hip.
I do not wish to tell you the whole story right now,
But I swear to you upon my honor
That I witnessed the truth of these events.   10595
I can attest to the truth of
Everything I have told and described to you.
Gerard, there, is the evil traitor
Who betrayed his brother out of pure malice,
Just as you are about to hear."   10600
Auberon said, "Gerard, come forward."
And Gerard came forward, not daring to refuse.
He began to tremble just like

A leaf blown by the summer wind.
Auberon said, "Gerard, listen to me: 10605
I entreat you, by God in majesty
And by the power that Jesus gave me,
To tell the truth
And to admit your great evildoing.
I am certain that you will not lie about it."   10610
When Gerard heard this, his blood began to boil.
Now he could neither lie nor retreat.
He said, "Sire, what's the point of hiding it?
I went to see and visit my brother
At the abbey of Saint-Maurice-des-Prés.   10615
My lord Gibouart of Viemez
Hid in a thicket, clad in his hauberk
And accompanied by members of his powerful family.
We were laying a trap for young Huon.
What can I say? May God save me,   10620
I made sure my brother left the abbey.
This was before midnight.
When we came to the leafy thicket,
I began to pick a quarrel with him.
When my lord heard us speaking,   10625
He burst out of the thicket with sixty men-at-arms,
Who butchered all of Huon's men.
We tossed twelve of them into the Gironde,
And then we captured young Huon
Along with his wife and valiant Geriaume.   10630
We brought them here,
Blindfolded and hands bound.
It was I who cut open Geriaume's side,
And I who pulled out Gaudisse's mustache and molars.
I can fetch them if you like."   10635
Auberon said, "You won't escape from me!
I will have these items when I please, by God!"
Gerard replied, "Sire, in the name of holy charity,
I know very well that I cannot escape.

That is why I am telling you the absolute truth.　　10640
I had my brother thrown into prison
And then accused him before Charles,
For I truly believed, by God in majesty,
That he would be hanged and dragged by horses,
And his entire inheritance would come to me.　　10645
But it was Gibouart of Viemez who made me
Commit this treasonous and evil act.
If it weren't for him, I never would have thought of it."
Auberon said, "May God save me!
The two of you will hang for it."　　10650
"By God," said Charles, "he will not get away with this!"
"Sire," said Naimes, "now you realize
How sinful it is to harm a virtuous man."
The assembled barons all made the sign of the cross,
Wondering how Gerard could have committed such a sin.　　10655
Auberon said, "Gerard, listen to me:
Where are the mustache and the molars?"
Gerard replied, "Sire, they are well hidden away.
I will fetch them and give them to you at once."
"I can have them when I please," said valiant Auberon.　　10660
"In the name of God, I wish for them
To be brought and placed on this table."
Just as he commanded, the items appeared.
The French were astounded at the sight.
And Huon said to Auberon:　　10665
"Sire, I beg you, if you please,
Forgive Gerard for his evildoing,
And let the two of us be reconciled.
From this day forward, we will be true brothers."
Hearing this, the French wept with pity.　　10670
Auberon said, "May God save me!
All the gold in the world could not redeem him.
I wish them taken to the middle of that meadow,
And I wish Gerard to be hanged from the gallows
Along with his lord Gibouart of Viemez.　　10675

And I wish the abbot there as well,
Because he gave false testimony.
I also wish that the gallows
Be higher than the flight of an arrow."
All of this happened immediately, just as he had wished: 10680
The three men were suspended and hung from the gallows.
Thus did they pay for their evil deeds.
"By my faith," said Charles, "this man is God!
If he wished it, we would all be dead."
Auberon said, "I will not harm you.   10685
Upon my honor, noble and valiant emperor,
I am not God. I am a man of flesh and blood.
My name is Auberon,
And I was born in Monmur.
I was raised by Julius Caesar,   10690
Who had so many roads planned and built.
The beautiful Morgan la Fée
Was my mother, so help me God.
She carried me in her womb for nine full months.
When I was born, there was great rejoicing: 10695
All the great lords of the realm were summoned,
And my father, Julius, had a great feast prepared.
The noble barons were richly attired.
Fairies came to visit my mother.
One of them, who was most displeased,   10700
Gave me the gift you see before you,
Namely, that I would be a small hunchbacked dwarf.
And that is what I am, to my great chagrin.
I have not grown a bit since I was three years old.
When the fairy saw how I had turned out,   10705
She decided to modify her wish
And gave me another gift, as you can see:
Namely, that I would be the most beautiful man
Who ever existed, after God.
And as you can see, her wish came true: 10710
I am as beautiful as the sun in summer.

Another fairy gave me an even better gift,
But I do not wish to tell everything
That the fairies said and gave to me.
Rightful emperor," continued valiant Auberon,   10715
"So help me God, the King of majesty,
I greatly prize righteousness, faithfulness, and loyalty:
This is why I value Huon so much.
I have put him to the test, and he is a virtuous man."
He then said to Huon: 10720
"My friend, get up at once.
Take the mustache and the molars,
And bring them to valiant Charlemagne:
He will return your lands and your possessions."
"Sire," said Huon, "gladly and willingly."   10725
Huon arose and went to Charlemagne.
"Sire," he said, "accept this mustache
And the four teeth of the emir Gaudisse."
Charlemagne took them and said to Huon:
"Huon, you have paid your debt.   10730
I hereby return your entire inheritance
And forgive any rancor or evildoing on your part."
"Sire," said Huon, "may God reward you!"
Charles arose and embraced Huon.
Peace was concluded, God be praised!   10735
Thus Huon recovered his entire inheritance,
Which delighted the powerful barons,
Especially bearded Naimes.
The court disbanded without delay.
King Auberon said to Huon: 10740
"My friend, now listen to me:
I command you, in the name of our friendship,
To come to Monmur in three years' time.
You will then receive my entire kingdom
With all the privileges accompanying it: 10745
You will wear a golden crown upon your head.
You will turn over your lands to Geriaume,

For he has earned them, so help me God:
He has served you willingly and without deceit
And suffered many hardships on your account.   10750
He is a man of great virtue and loyalty.
May God save me, he is most deserving."
"Sire," said Huon, "I couldn't agree more.
I will give him my inheritance, since you wish it."
Auberon said, "My friend, now listen to me: 10755
I no longer wish to live in this world.
I must make my way to heaven,
For our Lord has called me there.
My seat by his side has been prepared.
I no longer wish to remain in the land of the fairies.   10760
Huon, fair friend, for God in majesty,
Do not forget what I am about to say:
I forbid you, on pain of death,
To have any further conflict with the king.
He is your lord, and you must be faithful to him."   10765
"Sire," said Huon, "I will honor your wishes."
King Auberon took his leave.
He spoke to valiant Charlemagne before his departure,
Commending young Huon to him.
He kissed Huon and then departed,   10770
Returning to his city of Monmur
In the company of all his powerful barons.
King Charles returned to Paris,
And Huon remained in Bordeaux.
Thus the young man was reconciled with Charles,   10775
And Gerard was hung from the gallows,
Along with Gibouart and the abbot.
Huon then went to the abbey
And made reparation for the losses they had sustained.
In addition, he granted them   10780
Rich and fertile lands near the abbey,
And a virtuous man from within its walls
Was chosen to be the new abbot.

Huon returned to the city of Bordeaux,
Where the bourgeois as well as the noble lords   10785
From across the land greatly rejoiced,
Delighted that Huon had recovered his inheritance.
The beautiful Lady Esclarmonde
And Geriaume were equally joyful.
I have nothing else to tell you about young Huon,   10790
Nor about Auberon, the little fairy king.
Indeed, it is time to end our song.
Let us all pray to God, the King of majesty,
That He might grant honor and bounty
To all those who sustain us for love of him.   10795
May the King of heaven, in his holy mercy,
Grant us his grace, if it pleases him.

AMEN.

APPENDIX[1]

JONGLEUR'S INTERVENTIONS

43

Worthy lords, as you can see,
It is nearly evening, and I am very tired.
Thus I pray all of you, out of esteem for me
And for Auberon and the valiant Huon,
To return tomorrow after dinner;   4980
Let us go and have a drink, for I have been wanting one.
Truly, I cannot hide my feelings;
I must say what I have been thinking:
I am filled with joy when I see evening approaching,
For I wish to take my leave.   4985
Come back tomorrow after dinner,
And I beg each of you to bring me,
Tucked in your shirt-tail, a *maille*,[2]
For these *poitevines*[3] are of little value.
Whoever established them was as miserly and greedy,   4990
As was anyone who ever gave them to a courtly minstrel.
[...]

52

Quiet down now, if you please, and listen: 5510
I shall tell you a song if you wish.
By the saints created by God,
I have told and finished my song,

1.   Based on ms. *M*, Bibliothèque Municipale de Tours 936, from Ruelle, *Huon de Bordeaux*.
2.   Small copper coin.
3.   Coin of the Poitou region, of lesser value than the *maille*.

Unless you give me some money.
Know this — may God grant me health —   5515
I will soon conclude my song for you.
I excommunicate — by my authority
And by Auberon's magical powers —
All those who do not open their purses to give to my wife.

MAJOR CHARACTERS

AMAURY: Traitor who accuses HUON of treason against CHARLEMAGNE; killed in a judicial combat by Huon.

AGRAPART: Brother of ARROGANT, who accuses GAUDISSE of killing his brother; defeated in single combat by HUON at Gaudisse's court.

ARROGANT: Giant who inhabits the castle of Dunostre, defeated and slain by HUON.

AUBERON: Dwarf fairy king, son of Julius Caesar and Morgan la Fée, who uses his magical powers to assist HUON in his "impossible" quest.

CHARLEMAGNE: Or Charles the Great, king of the Franks and the Lombards, and emperor of the Romans; HUON's liege lord, who banishes him for killing his son CHARLOT and sends him on his quest across the seas.

CHARLOT: Unworthy son of the emperor CHARLEMAGNE, killed by HUON after treacherously ambushing the hero.

DUDON: Evil uncle of HUON who now resides at Tormont in the Holy Land; killed by Huon after betraying him.

ESCLARMONDE: Daughter of GAUDISSE who falls in love with HUON and helps him accomplish his mission.

GALAFRE: King of Aufalerne; he rescues and weds ESCLARMONDE, but the marriage is never consummated.

GARIN OF SAINT-OMER: Cousin of HUON and mariner living in Brindisi. He facilitates Huon's journey and accompanies him to the Orient; he dies outside the walls of Aufalerne.

GAUDISSE: Emir of Babylon, father of ESCLARMONDE; he imprisons HUON, who is eventually released to fight against AGRAPART. Huon slays Gaudisse after he refuses to convert to Christianity.

GERARD: Younger brother of HUON.

GERIAUME OF GIRONVILLE: Penitent living in the Holy Land who accompanies HUON on his quest as far as the Red Sea, then again later proves a faithful companion to Huon.

GIBOUART: Traitor and father-in-law of GERARD. Together they ambush HUON, imprison him, along with ESCLARMONDE and GERIAUME, and falsely accuse him before CHARLEMAGNE.

HUON OF BORDEAUX: Son and heir apparent of Seguin of Bordeaux; exiled by CHARLEMAGNE to Babylon (Cairo) on an apparently impossible quest for having killed CHARLOT.

INSTRUMENT: Aptly named minstrel who accompanies HUON when he is seeking to return to France after completing his mission.

LIETRIS: Cousin of HUON and abbot of Cluny.

MALABRON: Sea creature who, like AUBERON, possesses magical powers that aid HUON in his quest, notably by transporting him across the Red Sea.

NAIMES: Wise counselor and peer at CHARLEMAGNE's court.

YVORIN: Emir of Monbrant, brother of GAUDISSE, overlord of GALAFRE, and uncle of ESCLARMONDE. HUON helps him defeat Galafre.

GLOSSARY OF MEDIEVAL TERMS

BASINET: Close-fitting, iron head-covering that was worn under the helmet (5214).

BOSS: Circular prominence in the center of a shield, designed to deflect weapons (1823, 6750, 8033, 8384).

BUCKLER: Small round shield (8028, 8365).

CLAVAIN: Piece of armor designed to protect the neck, worn between the hauberk and helmet (5023).

COIF: Hood attached to a hauberk [q.v.] (910 *et passim*).

EMIR: High-ranking, independent Muslim leader, also referred to in our text as a king (2389 *et passim*).

FAUSSART: Long-bladed sword wielded with two hands (5934, 5937).

FIEF, FIEFDOM: Landed estate held by a vassal under another noble or the king (96 *et passim*).

GAMBESON: Coat made of leather or cloth, stuffed with padding and quilted, used as armor or under the hauberk for extra protection (5021).

GONFANON: Banner or cognizance, usually long and tapered, affixed to a standard or weapon to identify a knight (702, 1775).

HAUBERK: Coat of mail woven from round interlocking links, usually weighing sixty pounds or so and extending to mid-thigh. It had short sleeves and a hood or COIF, also of chain mail, that is pulled over the head (184 *et passim*).

HILT: Handle of a sword, dagger, or similar weapon (701, 5010, 6125, 6714, 6947).

MACE: Heavy medieval war club, usually with a spiked metal head, used against armored enemies (4607, 4765, 4825, 4849, 5318).

MANTLE: Loose, usually sleeveless garment worn over other clothing; a cloak or cape (444 *et passim*).

MONJOIE: War cry of Charlemagne in Old French *chansons de geste*, but also used by others as a remembrance and/or evocation of the great emperor (4408, 8476).

PALFREY: Saddle horse (138 *et passim*, cf. note to 1481).

Peer: Any of the twelve nobles of Charlemagne's entourage; more generally, any male noble (59 *et passim*).

Pommel: Knob on the hilt of a sword or dagger (1514, 1631, 5796).

Postern: Small rear gate to a castle (8970, 8972).

Provost: Chief magistrate in charge of a city or other geographical entity (560 *et passim*).

Seneschal: Steward having general charge of the household of a medieval noble (4111, 7888).

Ventail: Collar of a hauberk to protect the neck (8377).

SELECT BIBLIOGRAPHY

PRIMARY SOURCES

Aspremont: Chanson de geste du XIIe siècle. Edited and translated by François Suard. Paris: Champion, 2008.

Aye d'Avignon, chanson de geste anonyme. Edited by S. J. Borg. Geneva: Droz, 1967.

La Chanson de Roland / The Song of Roland: The French Corpus. Edited by Joseph J. Duggan, Karen Akiyama, et al. 3 vols. Turnhout: Brepols, 2005.

La Chevalerie d'Ogier de Danemarche. Edited by Mario Eusebi. Milan: Istituto Editoriale Cisalpino, 1963.

Esclarmonde, Clarisse et Florent, Yde et Olive: Drei Fortsetzungen der "Chanson von Huon de Bordeaux." Edited by Max Schweigel. Ausgaben und Aufhandlungen aus dem Gebiete der romanischen Philologie 83. Marburg: Elwert'sche Verlagsbuchhandlung, 1889.

"Esclarmonde, Clarisse et Florent, Yde et Olive I, Croissant, Yde et Olive II, Huon et les géants: Sequels to 'Huon de Bordeaux': An Edition." Edited by Barbara A. Brewka. PhD diss., Vanderbilt University, 1977. ProQuest Dissertations & Theses Global (302859852).

Huon de Bordeaux. Edited by Pierre Ruelle. Brussels: Presses Universitaires de Bruxelles, 1960.

Huon de Bordeaux: Chanson de geste du XIIIe siècle, publiée d'après le ms. Paris BNF fr. 22555. Edited and translated by William W. Kibler and François Suard. Paris: Champion, 2003.

Le Huon de Bordeaux en prose du XVème siècle. Edited by Michel J. Raby. New York: Peter Lang, 1998.

Lion de Bourges, poème épique du XIVe siècle. Edited by William W. Kibler, Jean-Louis G. Picherit, and Thelma S. Fenster. 2 vols. Geneva: Droz, 1980.

Norton, Andre. *Huon of the Horn.* New York: Harcourt Brace, 1951.

The Song of Roland. Translated by Glyn Burgess. London: Penguin, 1990.

Sinclair, Keith V. "Un nouveau manuscrit de la version décasyllabique de *Huon de Bordeaux.*" *Le Moyen Âge* 85 (1979): 445–64.

Vivien de Monbranc. Edited by Wolfgang van Emden. Geneva: Droz, 1987.

Yde and Olive. Edited and translated by Mounawar Abbouchi. *Medieval Feminist Forum 52.4 (2018), Subsidia* 8, Medieval Texts in Translation 5 (2018). DOI 10.17077/1536-8742.2152.

Secondary Literature

Berthelot, Anne. "L'Autre Monde féerique comme distorsion de l'Orient dans *Maugis d'Aigremont, Huon de Bordeaux* et *Le Roman d'Auberon.*" In *L'Épopée Romane, I-II*, edited by Gabriel Bianciotto et al., 647–53. Poitiers: Centre d'Études Supérieures de Civilisation Médiévale, Université de Poitiers, 2002.

—. "*Huon de Bordeaux* ou l'irruption de la féerie dans la geste." In *L'Épopée romane au moyen âge et aux temps modernes*, Actes du XIVe Congrès International de la Société Rencesvals, edited by Salvatore Luongo, 2:829–42. Naples: Fridericiana Editrice Universitaria, 2001.

Calin, William. *The Epic Quest: Studies in Four Old French Chansons de Geste.* Baltimore, MD: Johns Hopkins University Press, 1966.

—. *A Muse for Heroes : Nine Centuries of the Epic in France.* Toronto: University of Toronto Press, 1983.

Cazanave, Caroline. *D'Esclarmonde à Croissant: "Huon de Bordeaux," l'épique médiéval et l'esprit de suite.* Besançon: Presses Universitaires de Franche-Comté, 2007.

—. "*Huon de Bordeaux* à la sauce enfantine." In *Grands textes du moyen âge à l'usage des petits*, edited by Caroline Cazanave and Yvon Houssais, 123–61. Besançon: Presses Universitaires de Franche-Comté, 2010.

—. "*Huon de Bordeaux* au théâtre: Les temps modernes." In *Études médiévales*, edited by Danielle Buschinger, 71–102. Amiens: Presses du Centre d'études médiévales, Université de Picardie–Jules Verne, 1999.

Daniel, Norman. *Heroes and Saracens: An Interpretation of the Chansons de Geste.* Edinburgh: University of Edinburgh Press, 1984.

de Weever, Jacqueline. *Sheba's Daughters: Whitening and Demonizing the Saracen Woman in Medieval French Epic.* New York: Garland, 1998.

Hafner, Suzanne. "Charlemagne's Unspeakable Sin." *Modern Language Studies* 32 (2002): 1–14.

Harf-Lancner, Laurence. *Les Fées au Moyen Age: Morgane et Mélusine: la naissance des fées.* Paris: Champion, 1984.

Jones, Catherine M. *An Introduction to the Chansons de Geste.* Gainesville: University Press of Florida, 2014.

—. "'Je ne soz queil homme j'oz ocis': Ignorance et innocence dans *Huon de Bordeaux* et *Garin le Lorrain*." In *La faute dans l'épopée médiévale: ambiguïté du jugement,* edited by Bernard Ribémont, 123–36. Rennes: Presses Universitaires de Rennes, 2012.

—. "Roland versus Oliver," *Approaches to Teaching the* Song of Roland, edited by William W. Kibler and Leslie Zarker Morgan, 201–06. New York: Modern Language Association of America, 2006.

Kay, Sarah. *The Chansons de Geste in the Age of Romance: Political Fictions.* Oxford: Clarendon Press, 1995.

Kibler, William W. "La chanson d'aventures." *Essor et fortune de la chanson de geste dans l'Europe et l'Orient latin,* Actes du IXe congrès international de la Société Rencesvals, edited by Alberto Limentani, 2:509–15. Modena: Mucchi, 1984.

—. "Huon de Bordeaux in Its Manuscripts." In *De Sens Rassis: Essays in Honor of Rupert T. Pickens,* edited by Keith Busby et al., 325–37. Amsterdam: Rodopi, 2005.

—. "Three Old French Magicians: Maugis, Basin, and Auberon." In *Romance Epic: Essays on a Medieval Literary Genre,* Studies in Medieval Culture, 24, edited by Hans-Erich Keller, 173–87. Kalamazoo: Medieval Institute Publications, 1987.

Paris, Gaston. *Histoire poétique de Charlemagne.* Paris: Bouillon, 1905.

Plouzeau, May. "Vert heaume: Approches d'un syntagme." In *Les Couleurs Au Moyen Age,* 589–650. Aix-en-Provence: Centre Universitaire d'etudes et de recherches médiévales d'Aix, Université de Provence, 1988.

BIBLIOGRAPHY

Ramey, Lynn Tarte. *Christian, Saracen and Genre in Medieval French Literature.* New York: Routledge, 2001.

Rossi, Marguerite. *Huon de Bordeaux et l'évolution du genre épique au XIIIe siècle.* Paris: Champion, 1975.

—. "Sur quelques aspects littéraires de la version en alexandrins de *Huon de Bordeaux* (B.N. 1451)." In *Mélanges de langue et de littérature médiévales offerts à Alice Planche*, Annales de la Faculté des Lettres et Sciences Humaines de Nice 48, edited by Maurice Accarie and Ambroise Queffélec, 2: 429–37. Paris: Les Belles Lettres, 1984.

Rychner, Jean. *La chanson de geste. Essai sur l'art épique des jongleurs.* Société de publications romanes et françaises 53. Geneva: Droz,; Lille: Giard, 1955.

Subrenat, Jean. "D'étranges machines étrangères dans le cycle de Huon de Bordeaux: Les automates, gardiens de Dunostre." In *De l'étranger à l'étrange ou la conjointure de la merveille*, 463–80. Aix-en-Provence: Presses Universitaires de Provence, 1988.

—. "Merveilleux chrétien et merveilleux païen dans le prologue d'*Huon de Bordeaux*." *Société Rencesvals, Proceedings of the Fifth Conference (Oxford, 1970)*, edited by Geoffrey Robertson-Mellor, 177–87. Salford: University of Salford, 1977.

Sunderland, Luke. "Genre, Ideology and Utopia in *Huon de Bordeaux.*" *Medium Ævum* 81 (2012): 289–302.

—. *Rebel Barons: Resisting Royal Power in Medieval Culture.* Oxford: Oxford University Press, 2017.

Taylor, Andrew. "Was There a *Song of Roland*?" *Speculum* 76 (2001): 28–65.

REFERENCE TOOLS

Bulletin bibliographique de la Société Rencesvals pour l'étude des épopées romanes. Paris: Nizet, 1958–.

Godefroy, Frédéric. *Dictionnaire de l'ancienne langue française et de tous ses dialectes du IXe au XVe siècle.* 10 vols. Paris: Librairie des Sciences et des Arts, 1937–38.

Greimas, Algirdas Julien. *Dictionnaire de l'ancien français: Le Moyen Âge.* Paris: Larousse, 1992.

Hindley, Alan, Frederick W. Langley, and Brian J. Levy. *Old French-English Dictionary*. Cambridge: Cambridge University Press, 2000.

Holmes, Urban T., Jr. *Daily Living in the Twelfth Century, Based on the Observations of Alexander Neckam in London and Paris*. Madison: University of Wisconsin Press, 1952.

Kibler, William W. *An Introduction to Old French*. New York: Modern Language Association of America, 1984.

Moisan, André. *Répertoire des noms propres de personnes et de lieux cités dans les chansons de geste françaises et dans les œuvres étrangères dérivées*. 5 vols. Geneva: Droz, 1986.

Robert, Paul, et al. *Le Petit Robert 1: Dictionnaire alphabétique et analogique de la langue française*. Paris: Le Robert, 1985.

Suard, François. *Guide de la chanson de geste et de sa postérité littéraire (XIe–XVe siècle)*. Paris: Champion, 2011.

Sunnucks, Anne, and Max Euwe. *The Encyclopaedia of Chess*. New York: St. Martin's Press, 1970.

THIS BOOK WAS COMPLETED
ON 1ST DECEMBER 2020
AT ITALICA PRESS,
BRISTOL. IT WAS
TYPESET
IN GARAMOND
AND CHARLEMAGNE.